The Gospel of Garab Dorje

The Highest, Secret Teachings of Tibetan Buddhism

Yeshe Donden

(Roger Calverley)

P O Box 325
Twin Lakes, WI 53181 USA

©2022 Roger Calverley

ALL RIGHTS RESERVED. No part of this book may be reproduced in any form or by any electronic or mechanical means including information storage and retrieval systems without permission in writing from the publisher, except by a reviewer who may quote brief passages in a review.

First Edition 2022

ISBN: 978-1-6086-9277-4

Library of Congress Number: 2021949972

Published by:

Lotus Press

P.O. Box 325
Twin Lakes, WI 53181 USA
800-824-6396 (toll free order phone)
262-889-8561 (office phone)
262-889-2461 (office fax)
www.lotuspress.com (website)
lotuspress@lotuspress.com

Printed In USA

TABLE OF CONTENTS

DEDICATION

I would like to dedicate **The Gospel of Garab Dorje** to Lama Lhanang Rinpoche, whose solicitude, Wisdom and affection have been a tremendous support on the path and whose teachings, empowerments and counsel have been and remain invaluable. My heart's gratitude will always be extended to Lama Lhanang Rinpoche as a model of tireless self-giving and boundless compassion in action, changing my life and the lives of countless others for the better.

ACKNOWLEDGMENTS

I would like to thank the Dalai Lama, Lama Ayang Rinpoche, Lama Lhanang Rinpoche, Lama Khenchen Tsewang Gyatso Rinpoche, Lama Sonam Rinpoche, Lama Lena and Namgyal Rinpoche without whose teachings, empowerments and personal guidance this work would not have been possible. I would also like to thank Jim Valby, Christopher Wilkinson and other translators whose work has been indispensable and for their kindness in helping resolve various questions. Lastly, my undying devotion and veneration goes to Garab Dorje and Longchenpa who have been guiding lights and sources of boundless inspiration in the inner world.

PREFACE

"The primarily pure awareness of all sentient beings is inherently pure. It needs no refinement, knows no enlightenment and cannot be an object of intellectual understanding. For it, there is no arising or cessation, no worlds or events, no improvements or losses. It is the sky-like singularity of the Bodhichitta itself."

Well, there you have it. Full Stop! and Slam Dunk! But if you need, or want, more there is plenty of it in Yeshe Donden's truly masterful compilation of the highest and best teachings of Garab Dorje and his direct disciples and those who subsequently carried on the work of transmitting this pinnacle of all nondual teachings called Ati Yoga.

There are 10 books in The Gospel of Garab Dorje, and each one of them a priceless gem.

Having read many books, too numerous to count, in the Vajrayana, Shaiva Tantra, and other non-dual traditions, both East and West, I can say without the slightest hesitation that this book is simply the best, bar none.

I only hope that it receives the recognition and appreciation it so clearly deserves.

As Garab Dorje reminds us in 10 Points, which constitute the essence of the Ati Yoga teachings, "There is no path one has to tread."

However, if there was a path that one had to tread, this path would certainly be it.

Rigzin Dorje (Gary Falk)

Woodstock NY
Oct. 28, 2021

INTRODUCTION

In the Nyingma School of Tibetan Buddhism, the Great Perfection is considered the most profound and direct path to enlightenment. The teachings of this tradition present a spiritual shortcut—a radically direct approach that cuts through confusion and lays bare the mind's true nature of luminous purity.

In the history of the Indian subcontinent, there have been many spiritual luminaries, and one of the most remarkable of these, although not widely known, was Garab Dorje. He was apparently born enlightened and would be considered by current Hindu standards to have been an avatar. He lived long enough to pass on his realization and his Wisdom to a number of disciples who also attained enlightenment and even the rainbow body experience within one lifetime.

Garab Dorje was still alive when Manjushrimitra approached him at some point in the second half of the seventh century. Manjushrimitra was a Brahmin scholar from Nalanda university, who had travelled north to Oddiyana to debate Garab Dorje, and ended by becoming his principal devotee.

If we want to understand the pure, original Ati Yoga teachings which Garab Dorje passed on to Manjushrimitra, who then transmitted them to Sri Simha, our best source is Vairochana. Vairochana's challenge was to translate the utterances of Garab Dorje from Sanskrit into a form of Tibetan that would be comprehensible for his Tibetan contemporaries. John Myrdhin Reynolds described the situation as follows:

> In the early days, the masters relied less on written texts than on memory. Often their texts were merely mnemonic devices. Only at a later time were these root texts, composed in a highly terse and elliptical language, written down and explicated by commentaries authored by monk-scholars resident in monasteries supported by royal patronage. (The Golden Letters, pg. 203)

There was a time when the Ati Yoga Wisdom existed only in the minds and hearts of realizers like Garab Dorje, in the area where they lived in northwestern India. There came a time when Garab Dorje began to teach his followers and to write down his teachings in the form of Tantras. These were transmitted to Manjushrimitra (who organized and preserved them), and passed by him to Sri Simha. They were then transmitted to Vairochana, with the appropriate empowerments and private coaching. He and another Tibetan named Vimalamitra translated a number of Garab Dorje's works into the Tibetan language. At one point, Padmasambhava became involved in this project too. The Nyingma yogis of Tibet became the keepers and custodians of this Wisdom.

If these traditional accounts are to be believed, at some point in the last half of the eighth century, Vairochana travelled from Tibet to Northern India, received the Ati Yoga tantras and transmissions directly from Sri Simha, and wrote everything down using goat's milk as a kind of invisible ink. He brought these teachings back to Tibet, where he worked in concert with Vimalamitra and Padmasambhava, to produce a set of authentic translations which would thereafter act as source texts for Ati Yoga in Tibet.

These pure, original teachings of Ati Yoga, often integrated into pre-existing tantric practices of Tibetan Vajrayana Buddhism, became the secret, highest Wisdom of Tibetan Buddhism, where it was known as Dzogchen (Great Perfection). Gradual rather than sudden awakening was the prevailing view among tantric yogis and Buddhists in Tibet at that time. Activities such as chanting, visualization, deity yoga and various rituals were required preliminaries before the secret and sacred Ati Yoga Tantras could be studied and practiced. These Ati Yoga Tantras were not widely taught, but reserved for students of the highest aptitude.

Upon his return to Tibet, the difficulty facing Vairochana was how to to translate the teachings of Garab Dorje from a foreign language like Sanskrit into words that would be meaningful to his Tibetan contemporaries. He had to develop a new vocabulary, and a new way of writing. The challenge facing a modern translator of Vairochana's writings from his archaic Tibetan into modern English is to remain faithful to the intent and meaning of the ancient Tibetan texts while rendering the material comprehensible to the minds of contemporary readers from the west.

A handful of scholars have come to believe that Dzogchen, Chan and Mahayoga evolved together within the borders of Tibet. They cite as evidence the similarities between the three, and the fact that Dzogchen tantras appear to be written in the native rhythms of the Tibetan language rather than translated from Sanskrit. And there is the fact also that no original Ati Yoga texts have been found in India, written in Sanskrit.

On the other hand, we have attestations from Bu-ston and his two teachers, Rig-ral and sMra-ba Nyi-ma'i mtshan-can that the Sanskrit originals of Garab Dorje's Tantras were still to be seen in the Samye monastery as late as the eleventh century. We know that Muslim invasions and the burning of the Buddhist libraries at Nalanda and elsewhere in the eighth century account for the surprising absence of original Tantra texts in India.

For skeptical scholars, Garab Dorje is a legend rather than a historical figure. They believe that the connection of Ati Yoga Tantras with India was a retrospective attribution designed to lend spiritual authority to writings of Tibetan provenance. While there is no doubt that the Space and Upadesha sections of the Ati Yoga teachings have Vajrayana methods and perspectives, the Semde tantras are decidedly anti-Vajrayana in their rejection of virtually all aspects of the contemporary tantric view and practice. They are highly critical of cause-and-effect thinking, graduated paths, striving, accepting and rejecting, the eight lower yanas and they go against the grain of tantric Buddhism in Tibet in the eighth and ninth centuries.

Both the "Space" (Longde) and Upadesha (Secret Instruction) Dzogchen source texts that have come down to us appear to have been composed from the eleventh to the fourteenth centuries in Tibet, whereas Vairochana's early translations of Semde texts originated in the eighth or early ninth centuries and are claimed to have their origin in India. Semde and Longde texts are transmitted whereas the Upadesha texts are rediscovered (termas). A number of "Space" section tantras are attributed to Vairochana both in pure, original Ati Yoga traditions and in the more "tantric" forms of Dzogchen. The Upadesha teachings come from Vimalamitra and Padmasambhava and are "tantric" in form.

It is very easy to read Ati Yoga source texts translated into English and feel completely lost. "What's he saying?" one asks. In Vairochana's translations of Garab Dorje's words (from Sanskrit) there are many references, assumed understandings and turns of phrase which, although perhaps meaningful to the scholarly mind of an eighth century Tibetan monk, prove puzzling to a modern reader educated in North America or Europe in the twenty-first century. Translators face a huge challenge in trying to bridge this gulf.

The pith Wisdom of Ati Yoga shines out clearly if the reader has a sound understanding of emptiness (anatta) and an experiential introduction to the Nature of Mind, plus a few years or decades of meditation of the right kind as well as the advice of a seasoned mentor. Clear insight into the "mind only" doctrine and full implications of impermanence are also extremely helpful if one wishes to understand these writings.

It helps to bear in mind that the Semde texts are rooted in direct experience of both their composers and translators. They point to pristine awareness as an authentic insight and realization, not merely a rather abstruse spiritual philosophy. They teach that sincere and apt students of truth can have direct access to this Reality, not merely discursively but immediately in direct, lived experience. Right understanding of the pure, original Ati Yoga teachings comes only AFTER one has achieved a certain familiarity with its topics in personal experience. A merely intellectual grasp based in words and ideas is not enough.

The original Ati Yoga teachings are written in such a way as to evoke this direct experience of pristine awareness and Presence. Moving the reader toward a direct, personal (or transpersonal) experience is, in fact, the primary intent of the teachings. They are not primarily concerned with informing the intellect about doctrines and philosophies that could be elaborated in theory and debated in public. Their intent is to awaken insight, and their intended readership is the select few who, because of their dedication, aptitude and prior preparation are ready. In this case, the word "ready" means that they have decided that the rest of life will be about one thing: realization in this life, as Garab Dorje indicated in his second precept.

Most westerners get to know something about Dzogchen from the traditions of practice and study which began to come to the west at about the same time that the Dalai Lama made his escape from the communist Chinese. In Tibet, Dzogchen was typically taught only to a few apt students and then only after they had spent many years of active striving in Vajrayana. Nor was Dzogchen instruction an option unless several years of practicing Ngondro "preliminaries" had been completed.

In my personal experience, completion of the Ngondro and a decade of Vajrayana preliminary practice do provide a helpful background for understanding how precious the Ati Yoga material really is. But I have come to see also that the Ati Yoga of the early masters, as found in the Semde texts, is a complete path that stands on its own and needs no addons from the views and methods of Vajrayana.

Although the Ati Yoga Semde texts give little importance to Guru Yoga, it is the central pillar of Vajrayana and Nyingma Tibetan Buddhism. We do find passages in the eighteen primary tantras that mention the importance of love, and virtues such as devotion, and there is no doubt that love and devotion have their place when right relation to a master has awakened naturally in the heart of a devotee. Nor can there be any doubt that the master-disciple relationship was at the heart of all yoga practice in ancient Tibet.

In the pages which follow, I summarize the pure, original Ati Yoga Wisdom of Garab Dorje as found in texts such as The Magic Key, The Force of Wisdom Tantra, The Spaciousness of Vajrasattva, the Three Precepts, Kunje Gyalpo and others. I have drawn from English translations currently available by writers such as Christopher Wilkinson, Jim Valby, Namkhai Norbu, Clemente, Neumaier, Dargyay and others. I have focused on the Semde Tantras in particular and rendered chosen texts in a style similar to "pith instructions", writing with the directness of spoken rather than literary language with the goal of conveying the meaning and intent of the original as clearly as possible.

As mentioned, the early Ati Yoga texts embody Garab Dorje's Wisdom as imparted to Manjushrimitra, thence to Sri Simha and from him to Vairochana, who translated the texts from Sanskrit into Tibetan. This is the origin story that the Tibetans have always believed, which all their documents rely on, and which, although new research may raise questions, remains firmly and widely in place at this time. The material presented here is based in the firm conviction that Garab Dorje, Manjushrimitra, Sri Simha and Vairochana were real historical figures who by working together brought Ati Yoga into the world and blessed the Buddhists of Tibet with their highest teachings. It was this faith which informed the practice of many hundreds of individuals who attained the rainbow body for over a thousand years.

One or two researchers assert that because the Semde texts were written in the natural rhythms of the Tibetan language they could not have been translations. But this does not disprove the Nyingma traditions about the origins of the texts in India. One has only to read Pope's rendition of Homer ("The Iliad of Homer Translated by Alexander Pope") to see that ancient classical Greek can be rendered and even versified in the English language couplets of Enlightenment England. We have any number of Sanskrit texts rendered in modern English, with never a nod to the original rhythms of the Sanskrit language. Any ancient language can be "rendered" (not exactly translated) in any modern language, and so it is possible that, just as stated, while working out a new vocabulary for Sanskrit spiritual terms, Vairochana, and Vimalamitra (principally) "rendered" the material they received from Sri Simha into readable Tibetan of that time period (eighth century). They made it read like indigenous Tibetan, not rhythmically tortured translations striving to be true to the original Sanskrit rhythms and tropes.

Bear in mind that although such texts are called "tantras", the material in them is not necessarily "tantric" in the Vajrayana sense. As regards the Ati Yoga tantras which are the topic of this book, there was clear and consistent rejection of cause and effect, striving for achievement, active practices and rituals, mantra repetition, accepting and receiving, the idea of gradual progress and other vital features of tantric Buddhism.

Vairochana's training manual, based on his early five translations, and known as The Sun Of My Heart, is one of the works included under this cover (selectively), so a modern reader can have a very good idea of what he as a master of Ati Yoga emphasized in training his own students.

When we read Vairochana's writings (and his translations of the words of Garab Dorje), it is clear that certain key themes are repeatedly hammered home. These are the foundational principles which Garab Dorje (and all who received his transmission, whether directly or through the lineage) understood as fundamental to the path. The teachings may be, and often were, expressed as succinct but memorable points that go directly to the essence of view and practice. This style is known as "pith teachings". I make use of it frequently to cast Garab Dorje's Wisdom in the manner which a master would have used with a small circle of his sincere students. This is how he might have spoken to his immediate band of disciples, in person, face to face, with no literary elaborations or abstruse turns of phrase of the kind which we find in the written tantras of that period. This style of communication is quite different from the written style of the Ati Yoga tantras which are, as John Myrdden pointed out "terse" and "elliptical".

Time and again, we read that in Garab Dorje's Ati Yoga, active striving is rejected. We read also that visualization is not a suitable practice for students of these highest teachings, because sustained recognition of consciousness itself is the meditation and the view of the yoga. Trekcho (abiding in recognition of bare awareness) is the principal practice. Nothing could be more simple and stark.

However, although reliance upon mantras, mandalas, ceremonies and rituals is quite absent in Garab Dorje's original Ati Yoga tantras, all of these came to be considered prerequisites by the Nyingma yogis of Tibet. Typically, Dzoghen would not be taught to anyone who had failed to complete hundreds of thousands of prayers, mantras, mandala offerings and rounds of guru yoga. This method of making Dzogchen an add-on to Vajrayana was probably starting to develop even in Vairochana's lifetime, toward the end of the eighth century, and it has some sound precedent in the way Sri Simha taught Vairochana himself, passing on the Mahayana teachings by day, and the Ati Yoga teachings secretly by night.

Some of the Longde (Space Section) and many or most of the Upadesha (Whispered Instruction) tantras show this importation of tantric views and practices into the original Semde teachings (which I refer to as the pure, original source texts of Ati Yoga). This results in a strange situation where things rejected in the Semde texts are recommended in Upadesha texts, and both kinds of texts are thought of as Dzogchen Source Tantras. The Dzogchen that came down to Longchenpa, and that comes to us from Tibet is actually a hybrid of Semde and Vajrayana. The pure, original Ati Yoga of Garab Dorje is very clear on ten points, which constitute the essence of the path:

1. There is no view on which one has to meditate.
2. There is no commitment, or samaya, one has to keep.
3. There is no capacity for spiritual action one has to seek.
4. There is no mandala one has to create.
5. There is no initiation one has to receive.
6. There is no path one has to tread.
7. There are no levels of realization (bhumis) one has to achieve through purification.

8. There is no conduct one has to adopt, or abandon.
9. From the beginning, self-arising Wisdom has been free of obstacles.
10. Self-perfection is beyond hope and fear.

Most of these points are antithetical to Vajrayana as found in the eight yanas of the Nyingmas. And yet these are still taught as unavoidable preliminary practices that must precede any introduction to the nature of mind or Dzogchen.

The Dzogchen which Tibetan lamas brought to Europe and North America in the twentieth century is therefore not the pure, original teachings of Garab Dorje, Manjushrimitra, Sri Simha and Vairochana. Tibetan Dzogchen is by and large drawn from lineages which amalgamated Ati Yoga into active Vajrayana-Tantra practices and made hundreds of thousands of mantras, mandala-offerings, prayers and prostrations into required preliminaries. Rarely will a student be introduced to Dzogchen by a Tibetan lama unless that student has spent years doing these active practices. This is the opposite of what Garab Dorje taught, as the Semde source texts make clear.

It helps to remember that Garab Dorje was essentially neither a Tibetan, a Buddhist, nor a monk. Outwardly, for decades, he lived the life of a yogi hermit. Inwardly, he was a realized being, later hailed as a direct emanation of Vajrasattva. Inwardly, such a being is not a "Buddhist" seeker, but rather a fully realized being *(vidyahara)* in his own right. Because Garab Dorje's writings come to us through Tibetan Buddhist channels, we may forget that Garab Dorje was essentially a fully realized hermit yogi who lived and meditated in remote caves and cremation grounds for much of his life to consolidate the realization he had from birth. He moved and lived in a Buddhist world, and so as a teacher it suited him to make use of a Buddhist frame of reference and background culture such as we find in his writings. Ati Yoga is not incompatible with Buddhism, but it is not essentially Buddhist either, and it is certainly not Vajrayana.

As a respected authority of Ati Yoga in eighth century Tibet, Vairochana presumed that students who had the good fortune of reading his Great Perfection translations would already be qualified seekers. They would ideally be individuals who had authentic insight into emptiness of self (and other), who understood the significance of non-striving as found in the practice of Trekcho, and also the implications of the Chittamatra "mind only" teachings.

Students with such qualifications would already have arrived at the realization that, apart from the mind's habit of conceptual designation, there can be no such thing as a "thing" (discreet object). Such insight would make it easier for Vairochana's Ati Yoga students to understand that (contrary to the Nyingma eight-yana teachings) concentration or visualization directed at deities forms no part of the pure, original Ati Yoga that we find in Kunje Gyalpo, for example. In Ati Yoga, it is not merely a concentrated mind, but rather a completely thought-free mind, effortlessly sustained, which is the basis of non-dual contemplation.

Repeatedly, Garab Dorje makes it clear that, for one who is qualified to begin Ati Yoga, there is no need to keep busy making merit or to go on chanting mantras or building up mental imagery of a deity. In fact, Garab Dorje clearly states that content of any kind which might arise within the conceptual, dualistic mind, however fascinating, is irrelevant to the authentic view and praxis of Ati Yoga. The texts make clear that an instantaneous recognition of the nature of mind rather than gradual transformation of the *adhara* (body/mind) is the essence of the yoga. This key point is conveyed with uncompromising clarity in the source tantras.

In his original Semde Source Texts, Garab Dorje positions Ati Yoga as the highest and purest form of yoga, beyond the eight yanas (vehicles) of Vajrayana. It is untainted by active practices such as striving and visualizing, and free of complicated intellectual views. It is this pure, original form of Ati Yoga from which the Vajrayana-hybrid 'Tibetan Dzogchen' with its demanding preliminaries later developed. This is the Dzogchen that is normally taught these days all around the world. Namkhai Norbu has been the most prominent of the Tibetan Lamas in recent times to clarify that the Ati Yoga of the original source texts constitutes a complete, stand-alone path unto itself. Sadly, he is no longer with us.

For Garab Dorje, the original transmissions which he received directly from Vajrasattva are known as Ati Yoga. This is consistently made clear by Sri Simha and Vairochana in their collaborative renditions of the Semde Source Texts, the best known of which is Kunje Gyalpo. It is sometimes called "the Dzogchen Bible", and is a detailed, comprehensive compendium for correctly understanding the pure, original Ati Yoga of Garab Dorje.

In contrast to the complexities of scholarly Mahayana Buddhism as promulgated in the great universities of eighth-century India (Nalanda comes to mind), Garab Dorje's teachings were considered to be simple, concise and very direct, leading to sudden awakening and the rainbow body in one lifetime. Garab Dorje, Manjushrimitra, Sri Simha, Vairochana and others attained the rainbow body, a fact which validates the claims made for Garab Dorje's Ati Yoga.

Garab Dorje frequently points out that a meditator will go astray if the yoga is attempted on the basis of a wrong view. In fact, The Magic Key touches upon all manner of possible misunderstandings and clarifies the ultimate view with regard to them all.

Rigpa (awareness) is the view. Full stop. This has stark implications for much of what was being taught in Garab Dorje's time and is still being taught in Mahayana and Vajrayana to this day.

Readers who feel drawn to Garab Dorje's Wisdom will appreciate the fact that it is becoming more readily available as new translations appear.

I share his story and his teachings with the hope that some understanding of the pure, original Ati Yoga will reach and touch the minds and hearts of those who experience the power of Garab Dorje's words.

Something worth remembering: although the bridge from India through Tibet to the modern western world is long, the crossing can be startlingly sudden. Recognition of Bodhichitta arises in an instant and is never farther away than the distance from your mind to your heart.

BOOK ONE:

A Marvellous Birth

Hundreds of years had elapsed from the time of the passing of Shakyamuni Buddha until an emanation of Vajrasattva took human form and was born in the land of Oddiyana in the north-western regions of what was at that time India. His mother was the princess Sudharma, daughter of King Uparaja and queen Alokbhashvati.

Sudharma had been drawn to the spiritual life from a young age, and being the daughter Dhahena Talo, ruler of Oddiyana, she had many personal attendants. She became a meditative recluse who kept her vows with great purity and care. She had chosen to live in retreat on a small island in the middle of Lake Dhanakosha, where she was attended and assisted by many ladies in waiting.

One day, she had a vision of all the enlightened beings from on high sending rays of light, entering through the crown of her head and passing down to the soles of her feet. The following day, a divine being appeared before her, touched her heart three times, and then in the form of the seed syllable HUM, melted into her. She showed no signs of pregnancy, but after nine months a child was born.

The birth of the infant who would later be known to the world as Garab Dorje is said to have occurred on the eighth day of the first summer month in the year of the Wood Ox. Some have placed this in the year 120 BC, but the Shahi kingdom of Oddiyana did not exist at that time. For this reason, other scholars have inclined to the belief that the Wood Ox year of 665 A.D was the real date of his birth.

The symbolism of the early accounts is clear. They indicate that a special incarnation of a divinely enlightened one took place, the birth of an emanation of Vajrasattva, the buddha of clear light Wisdom. The boy was examined by a Brahmin who declared that he would realize and hold the teachings of the highest spiritual vehicle. Initially, his mother named him Akasavajra (Diamond of Space), but that was soon to change.

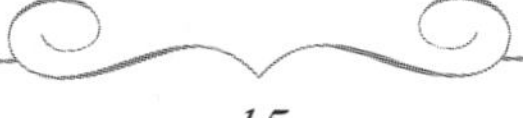

His body bore all the marks of an enlightened being. But because his mother, Princess Sudharma, was unmarried and reluctant to draw attention to his birth, she made an attempt to conceal it. Fearful of her father, the king, she kept secret the birth of her son from the world for seven years.

He was by all accounts a child of great physical beauty who gave joy to the hearts of all who met him. When at last his mother summoned up the courage to present her child to the king, he was not at all angry, but rather pleased.

There had been a prophecy that a great spiritual being would be born into the royal family, and because Pramodavajra (or Prahevajra) had all the attributes of a great being, he was publicly recognized by the king as an emanation of Vajrasattva. The young boy brought tears of joy to the king's eyes, and so he called his grandson Delightful Vajra (Garab Dorje in Tibetan).

If we consider which of Garab Dorje's many teachings is the most important, it has to be Kunje Gyalpo (The All-Creating Monarch) and within that text, chapter 30 which is known as the Dorje Sempa Namkha Che (The Spaciousness of Vajrasattva) is considered to be of special significance. This is actually not considered a tantra, but rather a *lung*.

In Ati Yoga, a text that contains all complete explanations of the base, path, and fruit is called a root tantra. It must be a text that covers the base, path, and fruit clearly and in detail to be considered a complete root teaching, which Kunje Gyalpo certainly is. A *lung*, however, contains the most important points of a tantra clearly and briefly summarized. Dorje Sempa Namkha Che is a *lung* and has always been considered a quintessential teaching of Ati Yoga.

Legend has it that, as a child of only seven years of age, Pramodavajra began to speak the words of The Spaciousness of Vajrasattva (Dorje Sempa Namkha Che). These fifty-five verses, in translation, read as follows:

Listen, oh virtuous one:
I will show you the truth of your being.
You are, and always have been Vajrasatta, the Infinite Consciousness,
Living Presence and creative Power of the Divine,
The vast spaciousness of Being, always good,
The Way of Liberation for all beings,
Beyond appearance and disappearance,
And beyond the grasp of the intellect.

Love being our essence, attainment is already complete,
And there is no need to strive at practicing Great Compassion.
Love being the supreme good,
There is no need either to extol the many splendid
qualities of Compassion.

Phenomena are not other than the True Condition.
Without input on our part, they appear and disappear.
Naturally arising Wisdom need not be actively sought.
Self-liberating by nature, it reveals the Way.

Earth, Air, Fire and Water are the indwelling Divine.
Despite our mistaken notions,
Liberation dawns from within our own being
And is not dependent on others.

Supreme Wisdom is difficult to realize
Except by way of Wisdom itself.
Dependence on others is merely notional
Since bliss actually arises naturally from within.

And yet, the miraculous is not beyond our recognition.
Due to intuitive insight into the natural state,
Our innate capacities and spiritual powers
Come to the fore naturally from within our own inner depths.

Real meditation is effortless letting go in the true condition.
This true condition never appears to us as something which can be seen.
Striving to grasp it,
We prevent the recognition of its true nature.

Nor can the supreme secrecy of the primal continuum
Be revealed by hearing about it,
Nor can words reveal its nature
Even in the barest measure.

The suffering of sentient beings is only consciousness,
Intrinsically perfect energy in varied forms.
Beyond movement, unshaken,
It abides equally in all.

People talk of karma.
In truth, there is only consciousness, beyond all our notions.
For those imprisoned in the ups and downs of thought and emotion,
The pristine continuum of awareness remains hidden.

The mind of awakening gives rise to all appearances.
Being unborn, it is indestructible.
This timeless space of pure Being
Is beyond the reach of thought.

The deepest meditative tranquility
Does not think of itself as this or that.
There is no need to conceptualize or to purify the mind of concepts,
Although Wisdom may, as it comes to the fore, take the forms of concepts.

Some meditators strive to put their minds into a thought-free state
Thinking this gives them access to something subtle.
They isolate themselves in lonely places.
Examined closely, this is seen to be a form of conceptual meditation.

Thinking in terms of causes and results,
Such seekers strive to transcend this world.
They reject the bad and accept the good,
Although nondual Wisdom already transcends dualities like bad and good.

Clinging and indifference are concepts.
So too, echo-like, is anything in-between.
Joy and sorrow arise from the same source –
So declares Vajrasattva, refuge of all.

Where else could aversion, attachment and anger arise,
Except from the luminous energy of mind?
Objects of pleasure are also just this -
Formations of the energy of the light of Wisdom.

Concepts are like space, but
Neither space nor concepts ever come into true existence.
Abiding in spacious consciousness, beyond desire and directed intent,
One's condition widens to infinity.

Concept-free equanimity is the ground of being.
But like the moon reflected on water, it cannot be grasped.
Through the divine creative energy,
The vibratory sounds of speech are manifested.

The mantric sounds of Ah and Ta
And Pa and their many elaborations
Express the creative power of infinite consciousness,
And figure forth the mind of light.

How amazing! The enlightened realm
Is never found by seeking
And can never be perceived by the six senses.
Those who seek it in this way are like blind ones grasping for the sky.

A graduated spiritual path of purification
Is at odds with the effortlessness of the true condition.
Realization does not come by following such a path.
That is like searching for the end of space.

The true condition being what it is,
Revealed as it is, cannot be seen as a path to travel.
The state of effortless enlightenment is the source of all.
Its manifestations are all marvelous wonders.

Past and present abide within the true condition.
The eternal now of consciousness is the path for all.
This is suchness, the light of Wisdom,
The realization of enlightened beings both past and yet to come.

This living Presence is the universal Way.
The moon and its reflection on water are non-dual.
The mind of awakening is not to be found by those engrossed in
Fabricated features and stages of the Way.

Focusing attention on present pleasures
And their future consequences
Is a limiting way to follow any path.
It is something to avoid.

Past, Present and Future are one, not three.
Only the Present has endured throughout time.
The nature of Reality pervades the whole of creation,
Its wonderful qualities everywhere to be found.

Everything that appears in all the worlds
Derives from karma, is rooted in concepts and is phantasmal in nature.
Even the situation of a universal emperor
Is merely a training ground for dealing with illusion.

Those who meditate using the time-bound intellect
Will never be liberated within the timeframe of their imagining.
For those whose practice is rooted in prayers and striving,
Everything said about emptiness fully applies.

The Essence is one, unstructured, unborn,
And the way of the yogi is like
The path of a bird in the sky.
How then can we suppose that phenomena actually exist?

Inner and outer phenomena are both the one real condition,
Which is not an object to be grasped by the conceptual mind.
The things of this world are mere names based in mistaken concepts.
And so it is, we fail to experience the equality of deep contemplation.

The outer and inner spiritual commitments that we take up
Pertain to the constituents and senses of the body-mind,
Which has never been other than the true condition.
There is therefore no benefit in talking about spiritual commitments.

Appearances, symbols of the All-Good,
never change into something other than Presence.
Never being other than Presence, appearances are therefore Wisdom.
In the absence of grasping, nothing has a self-identity.
Absent rejecting, there is only the equality that transcends speech.

All possible circumstances, and all beings in them
Arise non-dually from the Pristine Continuum.
In the purity of Divine Presence,
There are no such distinctions as "male" or "female".

In the domain of Reality, there is no talk
Of getting somewhere by means of effort,
And yet some say that by using the powers of sound
One can generate the bliss of a magical illusion.

The True Condition cannot be grasped conceptually,
But appears in varied ways, according to how one views it.
To strive for bliss, desiring it to manifest,
Only generates obscurity and confusion.

Meditating on the appearances of a deity
Is like meditating on the reflections of the Moon in water.
Although such meditators strive to be undefiled and unattached,
Their practices are like child's play.

One may even identify fully with a wrathful deity
In a mandala of wrathful attributes,
And unmistakenly manifest the seed syllable,
And yet not experience the suchness in which concepts disappear.

One may crop a palm tree or burn a seed
To prevent them proliferating,
And some teachers even advocate such a destructive approach
For students who wish to overcome their emotional problems.

Moreover, there are hundreds and even thousands
Of methods for practice, and they all blossom in their own way,
But since pristine awareness is beyond characteristics,
It is not revealed by practices such as these.

Blessed are the yogis
Who abide continuously in the True Condition,
Not discriminating between self and other.
They enjoy the magical illusion, while abiding in the Great Perfection.

All phenomena are perfect and complete, nothing excluded.
The true condition is equality, beyond change,
Spaciousness without limit,
Beyond dependent arising, beyond causes and conditions.

Incomparable Wisdom alone
Knows the blissful continuum of self-perfection,
The domain of the ultimately real, which does not arise
From extraneous causes and conditions.

This insight is easy, so easy in fact that it seems difficult.
Though all-pervading, the continuum is invisible.
It cannot be pointed out by saying: "This is it",
Not even by Vajrasattva himself.

This amazing, wonderful display of energy,
Spacious by nature, transcends action.
From within our deep unknowingness, beyond thought and thinking,
These dynamic potentials suddenly arise.

The energetic radiance of consciousness
Dwells in all and is the way for all.
For those lost in ignorance, confused by obscurations,
It is like a medicine in search of a doctor to prescribe what is needed.

From within the field of our understanding, bliss arises,
Revealing the ordinary world as pristinely pure.
When lights from all directions come together in one's heart,
One realizes omnipresent divinity, above, below, and in all directions.

From the colours of the rainbow,
The primordial families and their qualities are manifest,
Compounded moving parts in the uncompounded, unmoving base,
Along with deities of the five elements that animate creation.

Notions like "past", "present", and "future"
Cannot comprehend the nature of the Unborn, Unceasing.
In truth, nothing arises, nothing ceases.
The Wisdom of Source unifies all and dispels any such notions.

Equal in all its manifestations, there is nothing to gradually arrange.
All forms being one in Reality,
nothing needs to be dedicated in any direction.
We may accumulate and arrange our various offerings,
But since they occur naturally, they need no arranging or distribution.

The true condition being intrinsically perfect,
There is no need to make offerings.
Pure from its inception, the pristine continuum is already Wisdom-nectar.
There is no need for our minds or our senses to visualize or intend.

All phenomena are already arrayed and consecrated
By the mind's judgments.
The spiritual power of clear seeing
Is the equipoise of contemplative stillness.

Even an instant of this contemplation is Divine Union.
The satisfaction of this union fulfills all spiritual commitments.
Going through the dance steps of various spiritual practices,
One is, in Reality, offering the state of union non-dually.

Non-grasping is already the perfect offering
Beyond any need for practice,
the consummation of all practices which is already present.
Non-conceptual Wisdom eliminates every obstruction.
Contemplative equanimity is the perfect mantra.

To honour spiritual teachers, practice generosity,
And perform all manner of merit-making activities
Becomes a form of ignorance when performed in the absence of
Equality and non-attachment.

The Wisdom conveyed by this teaching
Gets obscured by active striving.
When envisioned by conceptual grasping,
The true condition cannot be realized.

At about this time, the child Pramodavajra engaged the panditas of the royal court in debate and was victorious. For this, they gave him the name Prajnabhava, or Wisdom Being. However, his grandfather preferred to call him Acharya Prahevajra (the vajra of supreme delight), or in the Tibetan language, Garab Dorje. And that is the name by which he is best known to this day.

BOOK TWO:
Enlightenment

After becoming a monk, Pramodavajra lived a disciplined life for many years, which prepared him for the contemplative life. He studied many texts and scriptures, but over time he gradually turned away from books and studies to explore the depths of contemplation. He meditated in his cell and in the caves and forests of the Kingdom of Oddiyana.

At a certain point in his spiritual trajectory, Pramodavajra received the transmission of the *Mahayoga* Secret Matrix Tradition (*Guhyagarbha-tantra*), with full blessings and empowerment, from the distinguished saint Mahasiddha Kukkuraja. Then, he retired into retreat on the slopes of Mount Suryaprakasakara at a location where many lost spirits roamed about at will. There he spent the next thirty-two years living in a small hut thatched with grass, devoting his life to contemplation.

Kukkuraja's instruction to Garab Dorje entailed a teaching of the Three Vajras in relation to Vajrasattva, Atiyoga and the Kulayaraja Tantra. His words were very pointed: "Everything without exception is the Body-Speech-Mind of the Enlightened State. This Body-Speech-Mind is all-encompassing. Know your true identity. It is none other than Vajrasattva, the Body-Speech-Mind of the state of Enlightenment. When everything is seen as the Great Self Identity, this is known as Ati Yoga."

Garab Dorje took these words to heart and devoted himself to realizing their true import. At the end of his life, when he encapsulated the whole of his Wisdom in three precepts, the second precept was: "Decide on one thing."

In his thirty-second year of solitary practice, Prahevajra attained full realization.

As dawn was breaking on the eve of a Full Moon, the illumining Presence of Vajrasattva descended fully into Prahevajra and he realized the timeless Reality of his true identity.

Simultaneously, a rainbow appeared in the clear sky, symbolizing the fact that he had opened his being fully to the Wisdom and the light of the infinite consciousness.

He sat in samadhi for seven days. Then, having completed his spiritual journey, he arose and began a new phase of life. He now knew that 'Mind's nature is and has always been the Buddha.'

Garab Dorje received all the tantras, transmissions and instructions of Dzogchen from Vajrasattva and Vajrapani in person and became the first vidyadhara (Wisdom holder) in the Dzogchen lineage.

BOOK THREE:
The Writings

As an enlightened sage, Sri Prahevajra could channel the ultimate Wisdom of his realization into his intellect and words. He received many Ati Yoga illuminations in pure visions. When finally written down, his spiritual testament would consist of over six million lines (according to tradition) of Sanskrit verse summarizing the nature of Ultimate Reality, the path of unfolding the fullness of human potential, and the most direct way to enter the state of full enlightenment. Nothing of these Sanskrit documents has remained, but translations into Tibetan have come down to us and on these this book is based.

On the summit of Mount Malaya, located in the Salt Range south of Oddiyana, together with three women of high spiritual attainment (Vajradhatu, Pitasankara and Anantaguna), Garab Dorje spent three years composing the Tantras which would later be known as source texts of Ati Yoga. As mentioned earlier, writings from this period are called Tantras, although the content is not tantric in nature, and the teachings are in many ways unlike Vajrayana or Mahayana Buddhism.

Of the three sections of the Dzogchen canon, the Mind Section (Semsde) is most likely to be synonymous with Garab Dorje's Ati Yoga Tantras. The Mind Section is generally considered to be comprised of eighteen texts, although there are three additional texts frequently included for a total of twenty-one. These texts circulated individually or in small collections such as the Five Early Texts which were translated into Tibetan by Vairochana shortly after his return to Tibet.

The unifying theme at the center of these earliest Ati Yoga writings is Bodhichitta, or the "mind of enlightenment." In Dzogchen parlance, this term refers to the true nature of a person's consciousness, which is nothing other than the enlightened state of a Buddha. To enter and abide in this pure state of awareness is the ultimate aim of the various methods of the various Buddhist paths, but Ati Yoga fulfils their intent and surpasses these approaches in being more direct. The Theravada, Mahayana and Vajrayana paths of Buddhism are gradual and depend on cause and effect such as accumulating merit and striving for progress through active practices such as mantra, ritual, chanting, prostrations and so on. The meaning they attach to the word "bodhichitta" also differs slightly from what we find in the Semde Tantras.

The Space tantras are reported to have been brought to Tibet by Vimalamitra, an Indian pandita who was a contemporary of Padmasambhava and Vairochana. In Tibet, he passed the seventeen tantras of the Space Section to a small circle who circulated them in relative secrecy for several generations, hiding them at times, and then recovering them until they were more widely disseminated in the eleventh century.

The texts of the Upadesha, or Instruction Section share the perspective and vocabulary of the Space section. In contrast to the Mind Section, the Space and Instruction Sections of the Ati Yoga Source Texts pass on quite a few active techniques found in Vajrayana, at the same time introducing other original methods of practice. The purity and integrity of Garab Dorje's teachings is considered to be most concentrated in the Mind section, which eschews the active practices of Vajrayana. It is not altogether surprising that certain elements of the Nyingma lower yanas crept into the Space and Instruction (Upadesha) source texts. But this differentiates them from the pure, original Source Texts of the Mind section, whose authorship is most confidently attributed to Garab Dorje.

Vairochana, Vimalamitra and Padmasambhava lived, translated and taught at the same time in Tibet, knew each other well, and collaborated in bringing the Great Perfection teachings to the Himalayan Kingdom. The Mind Section is considered to have come directly from Garab Dorje via Manjushrimitra and Sri Simha, and then via Vairochana and his assistant translators back in Tibet. Vairochana had collected a number of Sanskrit originals and had begun his own translations during the time he spent with Sri Simha inside the gandhola at Dhahena, India.

As mentioned in the introduction, the cultural background and literary conventions of the Ati Yoga Tantras display a quite different mindset from that of university-educated seekers from North America or Europe. The ancient Greek of the four gospels is far easier to render into modern English, and far easier to understand when translated, than the Buddhist writings of eighth-century India and Tibet, where we find unfamiliar metaphors and endless repetition to be the norm.

It is often the case with ancient source texts that literal translations result in a version which is far too daunting for the average reader, and this is where a condensed paraphrase can be useful.

If the modern reader has to think like a scholar before attempting to read the pure, original Ati Yoga source texts, the deepest purpose of these texts will be subverted, for it is transcendence of thinking activity altogether which the teachings advocate, not the development and deployment of more and more scholarly mental conditioning.

Ati Yoga does not require that its practitioners have special intellectual, linguistic and scholarly skills. It requires only a capacity to discern the real from the unreal, and to see through the thinking activity of the mind. The words of the masters are intended to facilitate this.

For this reason, I have decided to render teachings from major works like The Force of Wisdom Tantra (Great Tantra on Uncomplicated Clear Meaning), which comes to us with the name of Garab Dorje as its author, as condensed 'pith teachings' (as opposed to literal translations with copious footnotes). This is nothing new. We know that Garab Dorje condensed certain Tantras into much shorter versions (*lung*) that focused on the most important points exclusively.

A pith teaching takes the essence of a long passage and reduces it to a few sentences, in order to expound concisely what is of greatest importance. Known as *menok* in Tibetan, and *upadesha* in Sanskrit, a pith teaching is the honey distilled from nectar, the quintessence concentrated from the essence. Pith teachings use simple, direct language to focus the mind on what is most significant in any given teaching or topic.

If we want to understand Garab Dorje's clear intent in his major Tantras (such as the Force of Wisdom Tantra), then the "pith teaching" format (with occasional paraphrase) has many advantages over more literal types of translation. Even the best translations, painstakingly faithful to the original Tibetan language, have a tendency to limit readership of Garab Dorje's teachings to the select few whose scholarship is equal to the challenge, and who have spent years in training to understand the symbolism, specialized vocabulary, arcane references and so on.

The Force of Wisdom Tantra is the Root Tantra of the Yangti (dark retreat). It comes from Garab Dorje, who taught it to Manjusrimitra, who taught Sri Simha, who instructed Padmasambhava, who brought it to Tibet in the Eighth Century AD. There the text was hidden until it was re-discovered by Lama Chowang who made it available to the wider world.

At the outset of the Force of Wisdom Tantra, Garab Dorje states:

> *In the past, teachers such as Shakyamuni taught the eighty-four thousand Dharma Teachings including the nine yanas... but they did not teach the sudden penetration of awareness. I (Vajradhara) ask you (Garab Dorje) to teach the sudden penetration of self-awareness.... I, the great Vajradhara, the personal intuition of self-awareness, teach you (Garab Dorje) what has not been taught previously or by another, the meaning of which does not depend on hearing, thinking or meditating, the Dharma of little effort and of ease in understanding the great meaning. I teach the sudden penetration of the Dharmakaya of self-awareness, which all inferior minds realize by the mere teaching, and which is the great essential meaning of all the Dharmas. It is the root of all the vehicles of samsara and nirvana, the unification of transmission, sutra, and sacred instruction, the essence of the Tantra. It is the sudden penetration of self-awareness, the condensed meaning which severs extremes and severs reification.*

In the thirty-eighth chapter of this Tantra, Garab Dorje gives his reader a short, clear summary of his life and his core intent in bringing these teachings into the world:

> *I was first born with the body of an eight-year-old child. Then, for eight years I rotated the wheels of the five Wisdoms at the life-tree of profound knowledge. Through inspired insight, I was liberated. I have (already) commented on these, my inspired experiences. For eight years I brought many manifestations into the world and focused on my purposes, clearing away the suffering brought about by my entourage in the first abode of the gods. I put a string of precious pearls on a thread of silk and used this to turn the outer wheel. Motivated by compassion, for the sake of liberating others, I have contemplated the deep meaning of the enigmas of life and explained the teachings of the lower vehicles. At the pinnacle of Burning Fire Mountain, I fully realized the truth of the enlightened ones and explained the Dharmas concerning the emptiness of all appearances. Then, at Vulture Mountain, I released from my heart the great Tantras, secret and astonishing. I wrapped them in the vase of my throat, exposed them on the lotus of my tongue and displayed them by means of the*

consciousness which has five aspects. I made clear the meaning of The Cuckoo of Awareness with a melodious voice imbued with the sixty qualities of a Buddha's speech. I brought closure to the doubts and complications in the minds of my followers. In my twenty-fourth year, on the occasion of my nirvana, I made clear the three parts of my testament (to humanity). For the sake of those who are to come, I have revealed the Uncomplicated Clear Meaning. Secondly, I revealed One Knowledge: Total Liberation. And thirdly, I revealed A Condensation of All Precious Things. For those who go forward on the path I have revealed, who do not have the good fortune to meet with me in person, for these I have set this down (in writing). I lay down the reliquary of the three kayas and pass away completely into nirvana. For the sake of those who are to come, in the future, speak these words. (Chapter Thirty-Eight, the Force of Wisdom Tantra: How We Work for the Sake of the Nirmanakaya)

I have tried to pick out sections of the text which best explain the topic of the chapter. I have not provided commentary or analysis to make the material more lucid for the reader. Rather I have tried to express the original in a clear, comprehensible way, keeping paraphrase to a minimum, but using it where necessary to make the meaning apparent. It is always a balance between being too literal, and interpretive, my guiding principle being that unless a reader understands what he or she is reading, to the point of being able to paraphrase it, the text has failed in its purpose. I am working from a translation of the text by Christopher Wilkinson, published under the title Clear Meaning, this being the only complete translation of this work available at this time in English.

THE CLEAR MEANING TANTRA

Originally written down in Sanskrit by Garab Dorje, this work was transmitted to Manjushrimitra, from whom it passed to Sri Simha, who in turn transmitted it to Padmasambhava. He brought the tantra to Tibet and hid it at some point in the mid to late 700's AD.

Centuries later, Guru Chowang (1212 – 1270) found the book and published it, which made possible its preservation in the collection known as the Hundred Thousand Tantras of the Ancients (Nyingma Gyubum). Christopher Wilkinson did a paper on this tantra for his master's thesis in 1988, and later published his translation of the work in 2019.

The full name of this tantra in Sanskrit is the *Tilaka Duhakala Tradu Tilaka Tantra Mahatantra.* In Tibetan, it is known as *sPros bral don gsal chen po' rgyud ces bya ba.* In English, it is referred to as the "Tantra of the Great Unreified Clear Meaning" and also underline "Clear Meaning Tantra."

The first few pages of the Tantra indicate how its Wisdom was sourced from the inner world and transferred to Garab Dorje (Prahe Vajra) directly from the enlightened beings of the Buddha realms. The description of the setting is filled with spiritual references, symbolic imagery and colourful details that would be unfamiliar and possibly irrelevant to the modern reader.

This Tantra is a long and comprehensive treatise touching upon roughly one hundred and twenty-two aspects of spirituality, which makes it a sort of 'Dzogchen Abidharma'. Most of the chapters are short expositions, and each one deals with a selected topic. Most of these topics are summarized in a page or two. However, some of the chapters are longer and cover their topics in greater detail.

The perspective or basic assumption behind this Tantra is that a thorough knowledge of spiritual cosmology (such as the five elements, the three eons, the eight vehicles, the five Wisdoms, the three times, and so on...) is meaningful for a serious student of Ati Yoga. This is not a point of view that modern teachers and students of Ati Yoga (especially those of the western hemisphere) generally share. However, the Clear Meaning Tantra is rich with insights and jewels of Wisdom for the reader who perseveres and makes the effort to explore its many topics, which run to over five hundred pages in Christopher Wilkinson's newly released translation.

I have presented selections from the first twenty-five chapters of the Clear Meaning Tantra in clear and simple English with a focus on the core content of each chapter, and clarity of meaning in modern English. A literal translation of the ancient Tibetan words would be altogether puzzling to the modern reader, but nonstop paraphrasing is also not ideal. A balance between these two must be found and is not always easy.

The early portions of this compendious tantra focus on the Ground of Being, (or Base), and the Force (its energetic radiance), topics that are basic to Ati Yoga. However, the further one progresses into the later chapters of this tantra, the more it reads like an exposition of Nyingma cosmology, and this makes the lion's share of this text of interest for scholars rather than lay practitioners of Ati Yoga.

There is no doubt that disciples like Manjushrimitra had comprehensive and scholarly minds more than capable of assimilating the fullness of the detail which is to be found in this tantra. Also, because he collected and preserved and wrote tantras on all aspects of Ati Yoga, we must assume that Garab Dorje too had a mind quite capable of scholarly exposition in and around the topic of Ati Yoga. But for most modern readers, it is the jewels of insight which will be of most interest, and I have presented select portions of the tantra in the style of "pith instructions" with this in mind.

(1) BROACHING THE TOPIC

Awareness is inherently beyond complexity. Perfection dawns when we simply abide in the Dharmakayta (Ground of Being).

There is no 'true condition' to be realized by paying attention to the contents that appear in the mind. Thinking, praying, and formulating opinions are all activities of the intellect.

No matter the energies in play, once there is familiarization with the nature of the mind, there is liberation.

Reading leads to understanding. True comprehension communicates to us the Reality of Dharmakaya in an instant.

The knowledge we have is obscured by our ignorance. Use the lamp of Wisdom to dispel these obscurations.

Subject-object thinking is an iron chain that shackles the spirit. Apply the key of Wisdom to be free of such chains.

Grasping at flawed ideas is a habitual disorder. Apply the remedy of Wisdom to be free of this illness.

We waste our time in generalized opinions but do not recognize the truth of our being. I request you to teach (yourself) the sudden recognition of your true nature.

Wisdom is a higher seeing; do not get dragged down into the obscurity of a meditation which is overly passive.

Using the lamp of words, reveal the pure gold of the true meaning. The noble instructions which lead to a true understanding of these matters ties together word and right understanding simultaneously. To read the words (of the Victorious Ones) is to arrive at right understanding.

(Request to the Teacher) Please elucidate for all listeners the Wisdom of this incomparable tantra which sets forth the secret whispered instructions, source of every precious jewel, the uncontrived clarity of the ultimate knowledge.

(Vajrasattva's request to Garab Dorje) Teachers of the past such as the Buddha taught the eighty-four thousand (shastras) and the nine yanas as a cure for all emotional difficulties. But they did not teach sudden recognition of pure awareness. I request you to teach the sudden recognition of pure awareness. This is the heart-essence (not reliant on study, reflection or meditation) of uncontrived purpose, the sudden recognition of Dharmakaya.

This is the heart-essence of all dharma teachings, supremely important, the source of all the paths we follow, both in samsara and in nirvana, this sudden recognition of the pure awareness that is our true nature.

(2) AN OVERVIEW OF THE TEACHINGS

For the sake of those to come, for fit recipients, I request from Vajradhara a tantra that we can comprehend through teaching, and that we can understand by reading, one in which all manner of varied tantras are combined in one, something both deep and comprehensive.

The path of liberation has four elements: the view, the meditation, the practice, and the outcome. In the end, I will teach you how it is that we dissolve into the Ground of Being.

There is a certain way that we experience our existence on the Dharmakaya plane. It is like this: The awareness is clear. We do not reflect on it. Although we merge, we are not confused. There is no clinging to the sense of existing as a separate self. We are inseparable from Source, but not blended. There is openness, but not to any extreme. We transcend all extremes and identify with no fixed position. We are beyond sorrow and joy, but the blissful flow is unimpeded. We are past hope and fear, naturally and effortlessly realized, not by seeking or striving, and not through dependence on anyone else. Our delusions have disappeared, making return to samsara impossible.

I will teach you firstly how to exist identically with the Ground of Being, and you will recognize that this is the mode of existence of all that is, all the way to final attainment.

(3) THE MODE OF EXISTENCE OF THE GROUND OF BEING

The Ground is an undifferentiated mode of existence, a self-originating continuum of being where there is no beginning point and no prior or subsequent (reference points). Nothing good or bad exists to accept or reject. There is no boundary or center, no point of reference or preference.

This is our original state of being, incorrupt, uncomplicated, beyond comprehension, delusion or knowledge. Our unique characteristics are not yet manifest. There is no good or bad in the non-dual equanimity of the Dharmakaya, and no truth, untruth, being or non-being, nor ideas nor (individualized) minds. Our existence (on this plane) is formless and clear like the sky. There is no appearance or emptiness, permanence or impermanence, singularity or duality, liking or disliking. Thus, there is no such thing as grasping for reference points or opposites.

Unfabricated, it is the ground of all. Self-generated, spontaneously self-realized, it is the source of all. It is the undefiled heart-essence in all, the all-inclusive purpose of all, and abides beyond all.

Here, there is no experience and no non-experience, no application or non-application, no emptiness or non-emptiness, and no point in seeking any of it.

The immaterial heart-essence within us all is the ground of all, and transcends craving and non-craving, actions and actors. It is beyond change and beyond conditions which could be susceptible to change. It cannot be something seen by our way of seeing.

To abide non-contrivedly within our own being is Bodhichitta, naturally self-realized, a storehouse of all that is precious.

Ignorance of our true nature propels us into the samsaric realm of (fixation on) evanescent forms.

(4) THE GREAT VISION OF THE GROUND

The vision of the Ground is the significance of all the appearances that arise from it. Always remember this!

When we see our authentic core, we become living expressions of who we are in the truth of our being. The Ground of Being is not a subject that we can investigate or analyze.

It is called the utterly clear purity of the domain of the enlightened ones, and it is borderless, having no center, no beneath and no above. It is directionless, boundless, having no limit whatsoever to its vastness and no complication. It is changeless spaciousness, ineffably pristine, uncreated, uncontrived, beyond the limits of blame or praise, uncorrupt, beyond faults or flaws, uncaused, unconditioned, unrivaled, not prone to change and free of defilements of any sort. It is the essential meaning of all dharmas whether samsaric or nirvanic. Emerging from the domain of our Wisdom, it is not lacking awareness but beyond extremes. It is all-pervading Wisdom held within our awareness.

We do not entertain grasping ideas concerning this awareness, we are not fixated on it, as if it were an object (of attention). Awareness is our very heart-essence, and it encompasses all forms of Wisdom and all manner of virtues. Our essence is like a cloudless sky. In form, it is like the heart of the sun.

(5) ASPECTS OF THE BASE

The Ground of Being, in its essential nature, is nondual. We refer to it as the Ground, or the Base, because all appearances emerge from it, ranging from samsara to nirvana.

By simply being aware, liberation dawns. We let go of preoccupation with physical things and abide in awareness. We let go of anything of substance and come to rest in emptiness. Dualistic seeing clears away, and we are non-dual.

As pure awareness, we are self-originating, so we let go of causes and conditions. Being realized naturally and effortlessly, we go beyond hopes and fears. Being utterly pure, we are rid of defilements. We transcend the extremes of nihilism and eternalism.

We are beyond forms, material atoms, and entities, beyond clinging to any and all appearances whatsoever.

(6) ANALOGIES

The Ground of Being can be compared to the depth of an ocean of stillness. It is all-pervasive, vast as the sky, and empty. It is of pristine purity, like crystal, but beyond grasping, like a reflection in a mirror. It is present in the multiplicity of things, but untouched by any defilement, like a lotus.

Although it does not appear, we experience it in the form of blessings. It is a wish-granting jewel.

We are all unceasing purity in our essential nature. We are like the heart of the sun. We are an un-interrupted flow, like a river, stable as a mountain, a oneness appearing to be many. Being one, we encompass all, like reflected images that appear in water bubbles.

The ground of being is present in all appearances in the same way that a mirror is able to hold an image of the rising sun, or the way that milk holds butter.

Within awareness abides the heart-essence of Reality.

Not generated by any cause or condition, uncompounded like the atmosphere, our true nature, like gold is changeless through all the ages.

(7) WORDS THAT EXPRESS THE GROUND AS PRESENCE AND AS APPEARANCE

The ground of being is the essence of phenomena, whether of samsara or of nirvana. It is the truth of our being, our essence.

We go beyond physical forms, and we transcend ignorance. We rest in the essence of pure knowingness. We abide as awareness.

Self-originated, uncaused in our essence, we did not come into the world of appearances by happenstance, but because of Wisdom, for we are expressions of the primordial consciousness.

Everything comes from the ground (of Being), therefore it is great; nothing was prior to the Ground of Being, therefore the fundamental base was the earliest of all.

Our awareness is not compounded. It is empty, pristine, indivisible clarity.

Our essential nature is free of defilement. The radiance of our innate Wisdom is spontaneous clarity which existed prior to all else.

All appearances are of one flavour in non-dual sovereignty. They are all-good (Samantabhadra).

Reality is radiant, transparent, and from it the effulgent rays of purest Wisdom shine forth.

For us there is no coming and going from pure awareness and the light of Wisdom.

We are inherently enlightened beings, naturally and effortlessly attained.

Pay great heed to this, for if you rightly understand this, your mode of being will be truly worthy.

The Ground of Being is utterly beyond our grasp or comprehension. This alone deserves our consideration, so it is worthy of our attention. And this we do. Effortlessly, we abide in this Presence. This is how we are natural.

All things arise from this Ground, so it is the Source, the seed of all that appears (to the mind), the Wisdom of primordial purity, utterly clear, a precious jewel from which samsara and nirvana arise.

We do not conceptualize the Ground of Being. Our knowledge is not derived from intellectual analysis.

We are simply present in a natural uncontrived way, abiding in awareness of our true condition. This is our ineffable Wisdom.

(8) RECOGNITION OF THE GROUND

The clarity of our awareness and the emptiness of our awareness are non-dual. This we refer to as pristine.

Awareness moves freely like the wind, having the ability to impart mobility to appearances (in the mind). It is beyond polarities such as nihilism and eternalism.

Differences such as understanding or misunderstanding are not something that we discriminate. We do not fixate on anything, whether of consciousness or of obscuration, distraction or non-distraction, existence or non-existence.

We do not fixate on names or other referents. We exist in the simplicity of cognizant awareness.

The force which flows from the Ground is indeterminate and we are unsure as to outcomes.

When we have conclusive familiarity with the Ground of our Being, we will instantly understand the significance of view, meditation, practice and reward.

There is no teaching like this in any of the other vehicles. Moreover, it is not suitable for all.

We seem not to know that clear seeing has no need for grasping. We are comfortable in a kind of conceptual ignorance where we are always making determinations.

We are attached to the notion that Wisdom and sentient beings are poles apart.

We experience the energetic aspect of the Dharmakaya and mistakenly construe a Sambhogakaya which we think of as its body. From the union of these (presumed) two, we mistakenly impute a Nirmanakaya, which we then think of as its speech.

It is because we do not understand the external aspect that we are born in the six classes of sentient beings.

Our bodies inhabit the sphere of our acquired habits. This is best understood when imparted as instruction by a guru.

When we live and work for the wellbeing of all, clarity arises and we spontaneously realize the three bodies. This arises here-below in minute detail and is something necessary to comprehend.

(9) RECOGNITION OF WISDOM

A clear understanding of the Ground of Being, outlined earlier, is not mere information. It is Wisdom. What then is Wisdom?

In essence, Wisdom is non-conceptual clarity. The natural purity of the Wisdom inherent in the Ground of Being is utterly pure and non-material. This is our essence.

Our Wisdom is free of extremes such as subject or object. This is its essence. The entire range of samsaric phenomena appeared out of immaterial awareness, utterly pure from its inception. This Wisdom abides in emptiness in the Ground of Being. Awareness is not different from or other than emptiness although we think of them distinctly. Our Wisdom is able to conceive of things individually. This Wisdom is not something substantial. It is a Wisdom that accomplishes through its force, which comes into play unimpeded and directionless.

This is the Wisdom of awareness, self-originated, not created, inseparable from our existence, the Wisdom of our heart. This Wisdom, abiding in the Ground of Being, brings about all appearances and is therefore like a precious jewel.

(10) THE WORDS THAT REVEAL WISDOM

In this tradition, the statement that 'every deed will happen' indicates the Wisdom of the base. As we practice in emptiness, we enter the Wisdom of domain of Dharma. Practice without hesitation is the Wisdom which is like a mirror.

When it is said that something is non-dual, this is the Wisdom of equality. When our practice is perfect and without flaw, we say of our clear awareness that it is the Wisdom which considers things individually.

The words 'unimpeded Wisdom' refer to the Wisdom that accomplishes things. The phrase 'beyond the limits' refers to Wisdom that is not still. The terms 'clear light of awareness' and 'self-awareness' refer to the superlative Wisdom of awareness.

(11) THE FORCE

Pristine, immaterial awareness arises as the five Wisdoms. The Wisdom of radiant light is clarity as blue. The Wisdom of equality, based in a condition of indivisibility (non-dual consciousness), is clarity as yellow. The Wisdom of conceptual activity, based in a state of knowingness, is clarity as red. From a space that is unimpeded, the all-accomplishing Wisdom manifests its clarity as green. Finally, there is the unhindered radiance of the mirror-like Wisdom that expresses its clarity as white.

At all times, and in all conditions, we abide in the magnificence of an immaterial purity. Our un-obstructed, pristine clarity is ever-present.

(12) THE ARISING OF THE FORCE

The energetic radiance of awareness arises as five Wisdoms, their five light rays and their five elements, namely Space, Wind, Water, Earth and Fire - each with its qualities and functions. Each of the lights supports a special function within the body. Each of them appears both inwardly and outwardly.

That which gives rise to all is called a great marvel. A vast variety of appearances arise like phantasms lacking any true nature, and we have no notion of their being clear light.

(13) A BRIEF TEACHING ABOUT THE FORCE

The Force, in essence, is unbroken. It is called "force" because it has the power to manifest (all appearances).

(14) ORNAMENTS AND PLAY

Something that is beautiful is called an ornament. The three bodies are the ornament of Reality.

The ornaments of the Dharmakaya are the South and the North. The five Wisdoms are the ornaments of these. Ornamented by compassion, the Wisdom of the Dharmakaya is a perpetually beautiful wonder.

Non-dual union is the source of playfulness which arises from within and expresses through us.

The playfulness of Reality comes from a continuum of unfabricated purity. When we enter into a state that is unmoving, the true condition reveals itself, unhindered in a vast spaciousness that has no pathways. The luminosity of the elements appears and we recognize these appearances to be lacking in any true nature. We abide in the clarity of a magnificently unobstructed luminosity.

Thought and memory are the playfulness of our consciousness; the sounds of our language are the playfulness of our self-expression; perceptible forms are the playfulness of our incarnation.

Those who do not recognize this are attached to their own meanings and live in the play of samsara.

Playfulness and ornaments may appear to wise yogis, but they have no true nature and are illusory.

Ornaments and the play of the Force may appear anywhere. Understand them in light of what I have pointed out here.

(15) SUMMARY WORDS ON THIS TOPIC

Wisdom is the ornament of the Ground of Being. In a body made of five lights, this Wisdom is perfected. The ornament of Wisdom is compassion.

We use words such as ceaseless, arising, beauty, power, transmissions, teachings and so on to discuss these matters.

(16) ANALOGIES

Analogies are used to exemplify the nature of Reality. It is said, for example, that the sun and moon are placed in the center of the sky. Another analogy is placing turquoise in a golden setting. These refer to the ornamentation of the Dharmakaya.

The five colours of a peacock egg, the crystal of five bodies, the ceaseless five lights are analogies for the Dharmakaya being ornamented by Wisdom.

When a crystal encounters its surroundings it radiates an appearance. An egg cracks, the baby matures and the work of externalizing takes place.

From the light of the sun, rays of light emanate. This analogy indicates pure Wisdom ornamented by compassion.

Ocean waves ebb and flow. Because practices are illusory, a variety of reflections appear.

The mystery of unhindered play is that it can appear as anything whatsoever. There are many analogies for this, but they are summarized in the above.

(17) THE ORIGIN OF DELUSION

We do not understand the (cosmic) Force and its (whimsical) play. Our mistaken sense of things is that there are subjects and objects and the play of samsara is (consequently) what happens to us.

The Ground of Being is eternal, and we have been enlightened from the beginningless beginning, free of habits rooted in delusion.

The non-dual state of the Ground does not alter. Because of its inherent good qualities, it appears. The positive energies of the Ground appear (to our deluded minds) as many things. We experience the appearance of flaws and faults. Those who have a clear understanding of this process are freed from their (mistaken) notions about vices and virtues.

Reality is empty but arises as Wisdom. In the end, our grasping thoughts are numerous. Proliferating thoughts appear, but there is no heart-essence in them. The way our minds objectify by thinking is one form that ignorance takes.

In the beginning, awareness shines uninterruptedly. Then, we start grasping at its radiance. The thinking-activity of our mind flickers continuously and we have many ideas. This creates a basis for the confusion of our minds.

Initially, awareness emerges from spaciousness, then it becomes the "space of Reality" and further on we have habitual patterns based on it.

Awareness provides a space for our mental delusions to appear.

Prior to the appearance of sentient beings, Earth, Water, Fire, Air and Space were superior. Prior to these, the exalted heavens were all-surpassing. From the spaciousness of ultimate Reality, these have always been, from the beginning of time, pristine.

(18) THE CAUSE OF DELUSION

Ignorance is the root cause of delusion. Ignorance is dullness and clinging to what is not there.

We are not aware of our innate Wisdom. The ongoing fabrication (in our minds) causes us to be oblivious of the domain that is unfabricated.

Our conceptual ignorance is rooted in our notions about objects.

The extent of our knowledge is limited because the body is limited. If we had perfect knowledge, the objects we see would be recognized as the five radiances of Wisdom.

(19) THE DELUSION OF OBJECTIFYING

The (primordial) cause (of appearances) is unqualified awareness. The (primordial) condition is the emptiness of (the nature of) Reality. The hallmark of Dharmakaya awareness is direct knowledge of the unity of awareness and emptiness.

Our fivefold Wisdom arises rainbow-like in the sky (of mind) and then immediately ideas arise (in their wake).

These ideas are the precondition for (the appearance of) a self. Then, in the very next moment, we see forms as objects. Because we are grasping conditions, thinking-activity comes into play. These are the factors that lead to our delusion.

Our ideas about object and subject will not make clear the five natural lights (of our Wisdoms), for (in following ideas) we rely on our mental conditioning.

To our way of seeing, Reality is like a mirror.

The authentic spirit of our five elements (Wisdoms) is held in pristine Wisdom, miraculously engendered.

From the Ground of Being the Force emanated, from which awakened and un-awakened beings came to be.

Relative to the level on which we live, this Ground may be called 'unmoving'. Our grasping makes things appear as something they are not. It also obscures the five lights (of our Wisdom).

Our true nature is clear, but we are unable to be clear. Nevertheless, the authentic nature of our obscurity is clarity.

Whatever is in play, just that is what we are to know.

(20) THE FORMATION OF THE INNER CONTENTS

Like wind moving through the empty sky, the powerful gales of our thinking activity roam in all directions. Using our eyes, we see whence this world comes. Using our hearts, we know the source to be beneficent and beauteous. We develop attitudes of attachment, but in and through our many thoughts, we never lose our awareness.

(21) THE FIVE ELEMENTS APPEAR

We experience a wide range of emotions because we grasp and objectify the appearances that arise in consciousness and impute significance to them. We operate within the limitations of our conceptual minds, and we envisage content fabricated by our own minds. Our pristine awareness cuts through all of this.

The cause of our samsaric experiences is our emotions, whether this takes the form of the desires of humans, the disputes of the asuras or the delights of the gods.

(22) A SUMMARY OF THE FIVE ELEMENTS

The five elements arise as the force of our awareness. Nirvana and samsara appear from this force. There are two aspects to these: radiance and corruption. The five lights are the radiance of the elements, and Earth, Water, Fire and Air are the four corruptions. Our very flesh and bones are corruptions of the radiance. You can see the radiance in the five colours of the rainbow. It is not unlike the rays of the sun, or the light that appears in a pure crystal.

(23) THE WAY WE RISE AND THE WAY WE FADE

Earth is hard. Water is fluid. Fire is hot. Wind moves. Sky is expansive, spacious.

Radiant white light rays, when corrupt, appear to be earth. In the same way, there are four kinds of light rays from the radiant elements and each can appear in corrupt form.

A radiant element is firm but not hard and condenses without being liquid. It shakes without moving, burns with no heat. There is a kind of radiance that is not pervasive in its action. The Reality of Dharmakaya is unchanging.

Just as the firmness that is not hard, Reality and Dharmakaya are non-dual, pure, pristine and uncorrupt. Everything is encompassed by this.

In the same way that water condenses without being liquid, Reality and Dharmakaya are non-dual. Because it does not move, it has no barriers....

Reality and Dharmakaya being non-dual, supreme Wisdom abides in its own radiance, beyond conceptualization that could make it appear as something else.

Nothing burns in the absence of heat. We are clear within ourselves without any appearance of another. In particular, we are allied to the radiance of Wisdom, which is the radiance of spaciousness, which is not encompassed by anything whatsoever.

The corrupt elements are liberated within the five lights, and these lights meld into a dimension of radiance. This is how we indicate them, but they arise gradually.

(24) THE THREE EONS

An eon is an impermanent (time-space) continuum where the five elements appear and function.

Originally, only the eon of Reality existed. Then, due to grasping at thought-forms, the light of Wisdom faded within us. This gave rise to the eon (continuum) which makes possible the appearance of the world. Finally, we have the eon of perceiving and grasping.

(25) DHARMAKAYA AWARENESS

All appearances emerge from one source, namely awareness. This awareness is the sovereign, all-encompassing view.

Numberless are the noble qualities of this awareness. It is is uncaused, sovereign, compassionate, timeless and of a knowledge that liberates. It is consciousness and emptiness non-dual. It is an unshackled knowingness that is the essence of our five forms of knowledge.

Words are used to embody for our disciples what for us is ceaseless knowingness.

Because our very own awareness is ineffable, pristine from its beginningless beginning, and sublime, we say it is great.

BOOK FOUR:
Teaching in India

Having set down the teachings and installed them in in the archives of a cave-temple known as the Dakiniabhivyaktabhava, in the safe keeping of the wise woman named Cittassana, knowing that these supremely precious teachings were secure, the Vidyahara then travelled to Vajrasana, or Bodh Gaya, the site of the Buddha's enlightenment.

Subsequently, Pramodavajra, (Prahevajra) along with his shakti the Lady Suryakirana, took up residence in the Cool Grove (Sitavana) cremation ground which is about thirty kilometers northwest from Bodh Gaya. A large white stupa was located in the cremation grounds, and at its base, we are told, the Master would sit in meditation and from time to time give teachings to all who sought his presence and his instruction. Here, and at various spots in and around Bodh Gaya, Sri Pramodavajra (as he was known in India) spent the remainder of his days, teaching, inspiring, and guiding the seekers.

According to the Vairo Drabag, other realizers who received teachings from Garab Dorje during his human lifetime included King Dhahenatalo, Prince Thuwo Rajahati, Princess Barani, Lui Gyalpo Jogpo, Nodjingmo Changchubma, and the first Kukuraja. These were all part of his spiritual circle.

We actually have written records in which these jnanis summarize their understanding of the essence, as they had been taught by Garab Dorje. For example, King Dhahenatalo says the following about meditation:

Meditation means being undistracted in the ultimate nature that knows no center or border.

Thuwo Rajahati has this to say about enlightenment:

As everything is ultimately nothing but mind (consciousness), its very nature is dharmakaya: if you understand, this is the state of enlightenment!

From the first Kukuraja, we have the following:

It is thought that creates the duality of mind and object; it is Wisdom that perceives them as non-dual. Meditation means understanding that there is nothing to enter or to exit from. Not grasping what appears is the state of self-liberation!

Word travelled far and wide that the sage Sri Prahevajra from Oddiyana was teaching a new doctrine, a non-causal approach to spirituality by means of which, with small effort, enlightenment could be realized in one lifetime.

Not everyone was pleased that a doctrine which disagreed with Mahayana was being taught, and among these was a highly placed preceptor, or Mahapandita, at Nalanda University known as Manjushrimitra. He travelled to the Cool Grove with the intention of debating and discrediting Prahevajra, but in the end he surrendered and requested to become his disciple.

He spent the next seventy-five years living with Garab Dorje, meditating and receiving instruction, becoming his chief disciple and lineage holder. Manjushrimitra received the complete teachings in written form and passed them down to Sri Simha.

BOOK FIVE: The Three Precepts

After transferring all of his teachings and Wisdom to Manjushrimitra, at the time when he dissolved his physical form into the Body of Light, Garab Dorje left his "Final Testament", a small casket of gold which he dropped into Manjushrimitra's hand. It contained the "Three Principles which Penetrate the Essence" (sometimes called the Three Precepts) which are the essence of Garab Dorje's Wisdom. These three verses summarize the whole of the Ati Yoga path. A word-for-word rendering reads thus:

Meet your own face directly.
Cut one rope directly.
Go with confidence and release directly.

However, in English the three statements are often presented more clearly like this:

A direct introduction into the nature of mind
Prioritize the state of Presence
Carry on abiding in the nature of mind with full confidence of liberation

Or, this:

Recognize directly your own nature.
Decide directly on one option.
Continue directly with confidence in release.

Or this:

Direct awakening to how it is.
Doubt-free clarity that this is how it is.
At ease in unchanging liberty.

Garab Dorje's Three Vajra Verses encapsulate the essential points of Ati Yoga and are the most famous and significant of all his teachings.

Garab Dorje's rainbow body realization transformed his physical body into an immortal body of light which could appear wherever and whenever needed to give spiritual assistance to sentient beings. His disciples Manjushrimitra, Sri Simha and scores of others have transitioned from life in this way.

A Short Commentary on the Three Statements of Garab Dorje by H. H. Dudjom Rinpoche:

I. As for the direct introduction to one's own nature: This fresh, immediate awareness of the present moment, transcending all thoughts related to the three times, is itself that primordial awareness or knowledge (ye-she) that is self-originated intrinsic Awareness (rig-pa). This is the direct introduction to one's own nature.

II. As for deciding definitively upon this unique state: Whatever phenomena of Samsara and Nirvana may manifest, all of them represent the play of the creative energy or potentiality of one's own immediate intrinsic Awareness (rig-pa). Since there is nothing that goes beyond just this, one should continue in the state of this singular and unique Awareness. Therefore, one must definitively decide upon this unique state for oneself and know that there exists nothing other than this.

III. As for directly continuing with confidence in liberation: Whatever gross or subtle thoughts may arise, by merely recognizing their nature, they arise and (self-) liberate simultaneously in the vast expanse of the Dharmakaya, where Emptiness and Awareness (are inseparable). Therefore, one should continue directly with confidence in their liberation.

(Translated by Vajranatha Baudhnath, Nepal 1978)

BOOK SIX: Manjushrimitra

Manjushrimitra was born in the Magadha district in India located West of Bodh Gaya, to a Brahmin family. In India, prior to meeting Garab Dorje, he was named "Siddhi-garbha" and "Samvara-garbha." The name Manjushrimitra was conferred on him by Garab Dorje when he imparted empowerments and transmission of the full Ati Yoga teaching.

He entered Nalanda University and quickly rose to a high position in that august institution. In a vision, Manjushri instructed him to travel to the Sitavana charnel ground in India if he wished to reach enlightenment during his lifetime.

In Manjushrimitra, we see two outstanding qualities, total sincerity, and outstanding aptitude. His sincerity was demonstrated when he recognized the mistaken notions he had cherished, surrendered publicly to the superior Wisdom of Garab Dorje and became his disciple, renouncing his scholarly career at Nalanda University. This sincerity extended through the seventy-five years during which he sat at the feet of his guru, assimilated the teachings and mastered all aspects of the path.

These two qualities made him a suitable vessel to be the lineage holder of all Garab Dorje's Wisdom, the recipient of the full body of his teachings, which had been written down over the years, and the leading authority on Ati Yoga after Garab Dorje's passing. Manjushrimitra became the teacher of Sri Simha, who taught the Indian pandit Vimalamitra and the Tibetan translator Vairochana in the late eighth century.

When they first met, Garab Dorje asked Manjushrimitra: "What do you want?"

Manjushruinutra gave up any idea he had about debating Garab Dorje or trying to prove him incorrect. He expressed regret for his arrogance and was prepared to cut off his own tongue to atone for his mistakes.

On seeing this, Garab Dorje spoke:

> Unconfined equality, spontaneous perfection, greatest bliss,
> This is the essence, the awakened condition of all.
> And yet, the six classes of beings grasp their objects
> And by clinging they are bound.
> Extremists misconstrue the nihil and the eternal,
> Fixating on two extremes.
> Clinging to ideas about what truly exists and what does not,
> The followers of the eight vehicles remain bound to duality.
> With bias and with ambition,
> They cling to points of view about the base as if it had sides.
> They break up the nature of equality into divisions,
> And ignoring what they have, they go questing elsewhere.
> They exert effort to seek for a spontaneous presence,
> And they hope, in some distant life,
> To arrive at the enlightened state of their own minds.
> Equanimity is never realized by narrowminded, grasping views.
> I feel compassion for all who entertain such views,
> They are so tiresome and so conceited.
> Be free from biases like these.
> Cut off the two horns of grasping and clinging.
> Embrace the blissful path of boundless equality!

Garab Dorje advised him to 'seek a teaching that is superior to the teachings based on cause and effect, and in this way to be purified' (of wrong views)

Manjushrimitra requested from Garab Dorje a teaching which would bring about realization of the unconditioned nature in a single instant, and full enlightenment within one lifetime. Garab Dorje placed his right hand upon the crown of Manjushruimuitra's head and intoned the mantric sounds "A HA HO I." In this mantra, the sound A refers to that which has never arisen; HA means the unceasing; HO signifies the nondual, and I means the indivisible.

Manjushrimitra immediately realized the true nature, and stayed for days in deep samadhi, at rest in the peace of consciousness-existence, beyond concepts or words. When he came to, there was an uninterrupted continuity of realization and an abiding Wisdom concerning the self-existing wakeful condition, the intrinsic nature of consciousness that is the essence of all beings and all things.

Sri Pramodavajra began the re-education of Manjusrimitra by instructing him as follows:

> *"The nature of your own mind-essence is, from the very beginning, none other than Buddha. This mind, in and of itself, is both birthless and deathless. It is simply like the sky. If the intrinsic truth of the nonduality of all phenomena is understood in its totality, and if this view is merely sustained in faith, without making any kind of effort, then that is how one should practice meditation."*

Upon hearing this, Manjushrimitra stated:

> *I am Manjushrimitra*
> *Who has obtained the siddhi of the Lord of Death.*
> *Having understood the complete equality of samsara and nirvana,*
> *The Wisdom of omniscience has arisen in me.*

After Garab Dorje's parinirvana in about the year 740, tradition has it that Manjushrimitra organized the teachings he had received into three series – Mind (for those who are established in meditative equanimity), Space (for those who are free of worldly activity) and the Secret Precepts or Upadesha (pith instructions for those who focus exclusively on the essence). (Note: We need to remember that many of the Space and Upadesha tantras were written later, in some cases centuries later, which suggests there would have been relatively few of these available at the time.)

Manjushrimitra had not yet met anyone suitable for receiving the full transmission of these teachings, so he hid them under a boulder marked with the sign of crossed diamond scepters which was situated to the northeast of Vajrasana (Bodh Gaya).

Like Garab Dorje, Manjushrimitra took great care concerning the written tantras of Ati Yoga, collecting them, studying them exhaustively, and preserving them for posterity. Manjushrimitra himself is credited with being the author of thirty-four works. The best known among them is the famous Meditation on the Bochichitta, or Bodhicittabhavana (in Sanskrit, in which it was originally composed), also called Extracting Pure Gold from Ore. This is one of the twenty-one principal tantras of the Semde, or Mind series of pure, original Ati Yoga.

MEDITATION ON THE BODHICHITTA

Unconditionally, non-conceptually, I dedicate myself to the blessed one who has realized the emptiness of both self and other, who has realized pure awareness undefiled by concepts and who is established in the continuum of unconditioned existence-consciousness.

I dedicate myself to the equanimity of the true nature of all appearances, and to the supreme path beyond acceptance and rejection;

I dedicate myself to those who are one with the Vidyaharas, possessing the ten powers, never turning back;

And I dedicate myself to the identity of the three places of refuge which are equal in the nonduality of unconditioned consciousness.

All teachers give praise to the supreme state of existence-consciousness, the light of this world, the radiance of youthful Manjushri. Being the mother of all realizers, this is the sole path for all Victorious Ones, and the foundation for the oceanic ways by which limitation is transcended.

When a discerning person has made this Presence real and living, it is what the teachers call the pure Bodhichitta, the supremely excellent abiding in the Real.

This is known as the eye of discernment because it is ultimate knowingness.

This Presence is ever-fresh awareness, non-conceptual, ultimate, indestructible.

The supreme freedom of the Noble Ones comes about by realizing the fullness of this Presence; its various powers come into play from that.

This is the supreme path of liberation, for without this Presence and without their total commitment to abiding in the authentic nature of mind, the immortal, exalted and noble lineage could not have come into existence.

How, then, is one to cultivate this continuous commitment to the Vajra-nature?

This path of the great realizers is beyond ideas such as thought and non-thought. It is subtle, not easy to comprehend, being beyond verbal conventions, difficult to point out and not easy to investigate.

We do not come to it by means of words. It is not in the domain which ordinary people experience, or accessible except by a valid approach.

Therefore, rely on the oral instructions of your master and the authoritative instructions of your teacher.

We generally think about entities within a limited conceptual framework in which affirmation and denial figure prominently.

We continually grasp experience by means of thought. We use thought to validate and then to invalidate. Limitless are our ideas, unending our research. But since grasping by thought is empty, how can it lead to higher knowledge?

For this reason, the conventional methods of studying topics by mentally conditioned minds is unnecessary on this path.

The starting point for inquiring into this path is (recognition of) the characteristics that generate our limited notion of "entity" (or "thing").

Things are not what they appear to be in our minds. By using the six kinds of grasping, we arrive only at delusion.

If this mistaken way of knowing by grasping really worked, more sentient beings would be free, like the arhats who simply deny the existence of entities.

Since seekers are tormented by their frustrations and ground down by time, it is obvious that they are self-deceived. If the various senses could provide true knowledge, no one would be in need of the authentic path.

Ordinary awareness limited to the senses (and thinking activity) does not overcome human frustrations. Rather it obscures the stream of pure awareness.

The Victorious Ones have made it clear that the thoughts and perceptions of samsaric sentient beings are deluded.

How is it, then, that these deceptions, arising from our grasping at appearances, impress themselves upon us?

Our innate potential for experience gets into the habit of trying to grasp experience through thought. It is automatically compromised by this grasping activity. The clarity of awareness becomes obscured, and a certain lack of clear awareness settles in. The varied forms which appear to the senses and thinking mind then seem to exist in and of themselves, independently.

The obscuring power of this habitual tendency grows over time. We are caught up in this obscuration. Our innate potential for experience presents itself as these appearances. This happens in a way similar to meditation on the human form as consisting only of bones; over time, one begins to see only bones in place of normal human forms.

Due to this continuing stream of accumulating tendencies, the mind also objectifies its own being and imagines it to be a distinct "self". But such a self does not actually exist.

This mistaken way of structuring all experiences is no longer seen for what it is because of the habit of being caught up in experience, and because of the obscuring tendency of this habituation. Our conceptualizing hinders us, and as a result we no longer see clearly.

We lose the true perspective on appearances due to our continuous efforts to grasp experience by means of thinking. Concepts such as "self" and "entities" proliferate due to this unstable grasping activity.

We do not see how this fundamentally structures our experience, how our mental conditioning and habitual tendencies lead to the idea that there is a self, along with notions about liberating this self.

The continuum of existence-consciousness makes possible an unlimited variety of actions, making the duration of our habitual tendencies potentially endless and beyond our reckoning.

When these karmas mature, a human body with human mental conditioning appears. In a similar manner, other tendencies lead to other forms of life, such is the power of this process of change.

Some believe that all this happens due to a divine being like Shiva or Indra, but this way of thinking does not lessen anyone's suffering or result in liberation.

Failing to understand how this structuring of our experience comes about, doubts arise in our minds, and the opportunities offered by a yogic path are missed.

By imagining a self, one completely obscures one's potential and separates from the lineage of the blessed ones. Imagining that entities (and things) truly exist, we open ourselves to many kinds of vexation, including being born in the lower realms.

We tend to fixate on certain qualities in the field of our experience. Perception then seems to be eightfold, just because of this, although it is not so in its essential function.

In the first moment of sentient experience, our body and its varied functions are present, but due to thinking about and fixating on objects of attention in our habitual way, in later moments, experience flows accordingly.

For unevolved people, and for the wise as well, nothing exists but the continuum of experience. The kind of experience that arises for each of the six types of sentient beings arises due to their habitual modes of seeing.

Since the continuum of awareness is intrinsically without demarcations, to call it "one" is meaningless. All the innumerable fields of experience are in Reality one's own being. The form we designate as our own body may appear likewise in the infinite fields of the bodies of other people.

Our minds and habitual tendencies are not one, nor are they many, and so it is exceedingly difficult to arrive at a fixed determination about anything whatsoever.

All that appears unfolds according to dependent origination, things born eventually coming to an end. However, as with a burnt seed, a nonexistent result cannot arise from a nonexistent cause. Ultimately, there is no such thing as cause and result.

Our minds are obsessed with 'real things'. Therefore, we think of these 'real things' in terms of cause and result, and in terms also of causes and conditions.

However, cause and effect do not exist. Nor do originations and cessations. Nor do self and other.

And because there is ultimately no transformation and no death, permanence and annihilation are also nonexistent.

This being the case, neither samsara nor nirvana truly exist either.

Since our habituating tendencies are produced by trying to grasp experience with thought, something completely mistaken, these tendencies we have spoken of do not truly exist. If these do not exist, their area of operation does not exist either, and the fundamental structuring of experience, including perceptual and cognitive activities cannot be said to truly exist. Boundaries and demarcations to not actually exist in our actual perceptual experience, and so a specific location for anything does not actually exist either. How then do cognition and perception arise?

The nature of experience is beyond all our limiting notions of existence and non-existence and cannot be understood as either a unity or a multiplicity.

The arising of clarity from within our confused self-deception comes about when Presence makes itself known. It becomes apparent to those who have been deluded.

The ground of being cannot be found, even when sought. Nor can awareness. Yet they purify all the concepts raised up by the thinking mind.

Because we use thought to grasp and because we objectify the field of appearances and the positive activities connected with pure awareness, we imagine that "things" really come into existence.

Since the ground of being and radiant awareness are not to be found when investigated, and thus do not exist, they must be understood to be incapable of bringing about outcomes.

Since we cannot demarcate and identify this radiant awareness, how then can we speak of momentary events (that presumably depend on it?)

Since the source of all pure, positive qualities (Samantabhadra) cannot be found or proved to exist, how can radiant awareness, which pertains to worldly matters, be validated either?

There is nothing to accept or reject since Presence and lack of Presence cannot be said to exist or non-exist.

There is thus no state of an awakened one to attain, and no status of a samsaric being to reject.

We use terms such as nonduality, beyond thought, openness, Presence, the ineffable, and so on, all of them conceptual designations.

When Ultimate Reality does not exist (except by way of conceptual designation) then neither does a state lacking in clarity (except conceptually).

To say that anything is ultimately real is itself a kind of obscurity, not clarity.

Since there is no actual field of appearances and meanings, and no meditator who fully comprehends, the duality of true and false does not exist. Therefore, being doubt-free regarding what is real, or doubt-possessed due to lack of insight are both baseless. The nonexistence of both meditator and object of meditation means that there can be no doubt and no authentic insight.

When we investigate our notions about the existence of "things", we find them to be nonexistent, even as mere appearances.

There can be no non-existence if there was no existence in the first place. (Although we can talk of them), none of these are ever found.

Our limiting notions about existence and non-existence are fantasies. Therefore, the middle between these two fancied extremes cannot be held to truly exist either.

When all things are seen to be alike and present in sameness (by the nonconceptual, nondual mind), there is no need to reject anything.

Seeing deception where there is only sameness is itself a deception.

Even false views and teachings and wrong actions need not be judged and rejected.

Since skillful action and wise discernment do not truly exist, engaging in them is a kind of limitation.

If there is intellectual pride, attachment and aversion are sure to arise, and then disputes are bound to follow. The lack of awareness (implicit) in all of this means that the real point is not recognized (concerning the merely notional status of concepts like "true" and "false").

Agitation of the mind is limitation.

The practice of abiding in Presence is subtle.

One does not (need to) rest in a state where there is absence of the movement of thoughts, nor in the absence of non-movement of thoughts.

When there are no deceptive appearances, it is known by the awakened ones as "the primordial continuum of pure Presence".

If you strive to go beyond grasping at form, identifiable traits and wishful thinking you are likely to fall into extremes of acceptance and rejection.

But nonconceptual cultivation is without acceptance and rejection. Form itself is open-dimensional; desire is not different from absence of desire, and there is nothing to eliminate.

Elimination of attachment, aversion and ignorance while seeking nirvana is an activity of limitation. This kind of practice fails to comprehend the equanimous nature of everything.

There is no samsara to eliminate and no nirvana for which to strive.

Apart from the path of abiding as Presence, there is no other way to realize the freedom of the enlightened ones.

True cultivation does not require a thought to be eliminated upon arising. Nor does one generate a support for the mind because of the non-arising of thoughts. Nor does one realize or attain any ultimate Reality or any goal.

If even the slightest thought stirs that is not the Wisdom of Manjushri, that too is still the domain of gnosis. But we do not strive to remain in this or any other condition.

It is impossible to obtain a (point of reference which could serve as a) basis for meditation.

Nor will one obtain a result from meditation.

Grasping experience by conceptual designation, which is how the egoic mind operates, is itself the energetic display of the nature of Reality (dharmadatu). Objects that appear in the mind are also the radiant display of the ineffable.

Beings wander in samsara because they fixate on identifiable characteristics, and freedom from this grasping activity is freedom from samsara.

Once we are free from fixating on perceptions, there is nothing that is superior or inferior. To be free from fixating on preferred perceptions, there being none that are better and none that are worse - this is the path to cultivate!

Conditioned events are unborn in that they do not come about by external causes and conditions. Thus, they are beyond the domain of frustration and suffering.

When one has thoroughly understood that there is no such thing as a "thing", (entity, sentient being, etc.) then everything that arises is without defect and incapable of causing frustration, confusion, ignorance or suffering.

This is the supreme state of having overcome all emotional problems and their roots

Space cannot be objectified. It is a mere name.

Nothing arises or appears which is either positive or negative for anyone.

In true cultivation, the mind does not seek or strive, nor is it directed toward anything. There is freedom from knowing and freedom also from not knowing.

There is no application of antidotes in meditation, no delight in acceptance or rejection of anything whatsoever.

Nothing is objectified, and there is unbroken awareness and understanding of sameness, and no creation of duality. The mind is at rest beyond the domain of words. Neither is there activity or inactivity, or accumulation of merits or downfalls due to defilements or (as a result of) mistakes.

The mind is not seeking anything. One is not disturbed by anything.

Knowing the basic sameness of all appearances, there is no concern about being entranced by objects or attachments to anything whatsoever.

One neither avoids nor dwells on anything that may arise in the mind.

In this practice, the overcoming of limitation is known; the nature of Presence is known; the face of ever-fresh awareness is known; the underlying undifferentiation of all appearances is known, and imperturbability in all kinds of conditions is known.

Cultivation of Dharmakaya is the path. If one's cultivation strays from this, transparent clarity does not arise.

Recognition through symbols is also Presence as the Teacher has made clear. Symbolic means are in fact a basis for the cultivation of Presence itself.

Symbolic encounters such as the sky, the heart mantra, and so on are the action of the Awakened One and bring direct encounter with the primordial continuum.

By cultivating this commitment to vajra-Reality, all paths are unmistakenly cultivated.

Nothing that is positive, whatever it may be, needs to be thought of as outside the action of the all-good.

That which is not taken up becomes a form of limitation, and it will ultimately come to an end and be exhausted.

Even the activity of so-called limitations is the action of pure Presence for one who is a knower of the Presence.

Strong interest in the primordial Presence is itself praised by the Victorious One as Presence in action.

Having firsthand experience of the pure continuum of Presence, one overcomes all limitations and transcends all objects of veneration in the three worlds.

This hidden activity of those who are fully consecrated to abiding in Presence is the highest form of skillful action.

If the primordial Presence did not exist, then the Victorious ones could never have appeared, and the various paths and teachings would never have been taught.

In a mere instant the power of trusting confidence is such that one becomes the youthful Manjushri.

All commitments and ethical undertakings are fulfilled by full commitment to Presence.

If the merit of Presence had form, then even the boundless extent of space would be too small to contain it, as the Victors have made clear.

Individual sentient beings have been, will be, and are being born in various life-forms and have come under the power of the stream of birth.

Not understanding how the mind is forever grasping at experience by means of thought, not knowing the implications (of this habitual

activity), sentient beings are deceived. The flow of thoughts never ends and there is thus no chance of their turning away from delusions.

By the power of illusions these beings lose their happiness in the same way that a dream is imagined to be real.

Those who live under the sway of dreams reject the path of liberation and look to other paths which are extreme. They teach these paths as "unerring" in a way that resembles those who pronounce stone to be gold.

These deserve compassion, the spontaneous compassion that arises in the hearts of the noble ones.

Sentient beings who suffer due to worldly conditions, and who do not exercise right discernment, have difficulties in understanding this pure teaching. They rely on the words of the teaching, but do not understand their meaning.

Various points of view arise, each confirmed by individual minds according to their capacities. A river of misunderstanding separates such sentient beings from the nectar of the pure teaching.

For this reason, though primordial experience of pure Presence is the unexcelled way taught by the Victorious ones, and also the field of activity proper to all realizers, I have (personally) undertaken to validate the truth of this teaching for myself through long experience and by valid avenues of approach to the supreme knowledge.

Through the composition of this work on the unexcelled path of nonduality, and for the sake of all sentient beings, may all obstacles diminish, and may the primordial experience of the Victorious Ones spread far and wide.

Manjushrimitra wrote the Bodhicittabhavana, in order to explain Ati Yoga to the Mahayana Buddhists who were in the majority in India at that time, and in particular to his fellow scholars from Nalanda University. Experts have determined that the work is written in the style of a learned Indian scholar, using the philosophy of post sixth century A.D. Mahayana Buddhism. Meditation on the Bodhichitta presents the Ati Yoga Semde teachings in a logical, intellectually cogent way with a high level of scholarly coherence. In this work, Manjushrimitra emphasized that intellectualism and logic do not bring about enlightenment and that "Those who seek the Truth should embrace direct experience if they hope to acquire realization." We can see that Manjushrimitra has gone far beyond the concept of Bodhichitta found in Buddhist sutra and tantric writings and arrived at an understanding of Bodhichitta as presented in Ati Yoga (where it means the essential nature of mind, or awareness).

Mihai Derbac, in his doctoral thesis on the Five Early Translations comments as follows: "In 1987, Norbu and Lipman translated Byang chub sems bsgom pa'i rdo la gser zhun in Primordial Experience: An Introduction to rDzogs-chen Meditation. This text is attributed by the rDzogs chen tradition to Mañjuśrīmitra (an early rDzogs chen patriarch from India), and Norbu and Lipman claim that this text is the rDo la gser zhun, one of the five texts under consideration. Preliminary text-critical research suggests, however, that this text is a philosophical treatise that is based on another text, a root text, and is not the text that can be found in the Kun byed rgyal po." In consideration of this, two texts have been included in this book; scholars have been at pains to work out their provenance and to differentiate them, and it is an ongoing research. (1)

When the Semde teachings were translated into Tibetan, eighteen texts were identified. The eighteen texts consist of the first five to be translated, which were by Vairochana, and given the name the 'Five Early Translations', plus the thirteen texts translated by his disciple Yudra Nyingpo, known as the "Thirteen Later Translations of Semde," coming to a total of eighteen. When the 'Three Major Tantras' of Semde' were then added, it came to a total of twenty-one. Meditation on the Bodhichitta was actually one of the Five Early Translations, which shows that Vairochana considered it to be a work of importance.

After Vairochana received the Ati Yoga Source Tantras from Sri Simha, he returned home and transmitted the tantras to the Tibetan king Trisong Detsen, to his assistant Yudra Nyingpo, and to others. Although these teachings were reserved for the limited few who had the capacity to make use of them, the Ati Yoga Tantras gradually spread throughout Tibet where, for centuries, they were copied and recopied and preserved in monastic libraries. They were never widely taught or dispersed, but reserved for those of special aptitude.

After the passing of his master, Manjushrimitra went to the Sosaling cremation ground to the west of Bodhgaya where, in the company of other yogis and yoginis, for a quarter of a century he taught his many followers and in particular his foremost heart-disciple, the lineage-holder Sri Simha. He would often sit in a meditative posture on a throne supported by carved stone lions, remaining in contemplative samadhi for extended periods of time, with occasional breaks for discussion and word-of-mouth teachings for his students.

In the end, like Garab Dorje, Manjushrimitra dissolved his physical body into light and entered parinirvana demonstrating the fullness of his mastery by this victory of consciousness over matter. Manjusrimitra is said to have briefly appeared in physical form to at least one of his disciples after his death.

His final testament to Sri Simha (circa 680 – 760 AD), which he passed on at the time of his transition via the rainbow body, was a jewel casket containing a brief text called "Six Meditation Experiences" (*Gomnyam Drukpa)*. In translation, they read:

O Noble One, if you hope to experience the true nature of mind, nakedly unveiled, then:

(1) Attend to pure Awareness as the object of your meditation;

(2) Press the points of the body by means of the mudra (using the vase breath);

(3) Exercise control over the inhaling and exhaling of the breath;

(4) Direct attention at the crown bindu;

(5) Cultivate immobility of body, eyes and consciousness;

(6) Enter the vast openness of absolute Awareness;

This is the final statement of Sri Manjushrimitra.

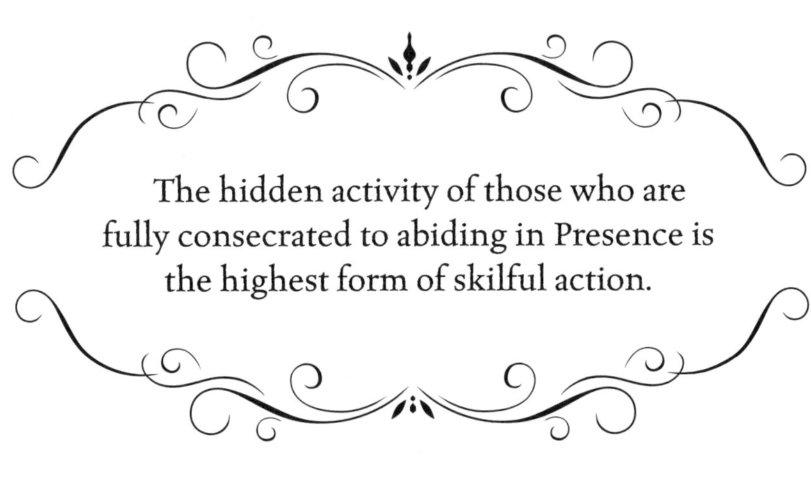

The hidden activity of those who are fully consecrated to abiding in Presence is the highest form of skilful action.

BOOK SEVEN:
Sri Simha

Born in what is today Myanmar, Sri Simha at a young age had a vision of Avolokitesvara in which he was advised to travel to the Sosadvipa cremation ground in India. Thirty years passed before he followed this indication, time which he spent learning the tantras on Wu T'ai Chan mountain in China. On travelling to India, he met Manjushrimitra and studied under him for twenty five years.

He was able to rescue the Tantras of Garab Dorje which Manjushrimitra had hidden under a pillar near Bodh Gaya and arranged these teachings into outer, inner, secret and uttermost secret cycles, graduated according to the degree of their conceptual elaboration. From Sri Simha, these teachings were passed to Padmasambhava, Jnanasutra, Pagor Vairochana and Vimalamitra, who at one point worked with Vairochana in translating the well-known five early texts of Semde into Tibetan. There exists also an early testimonial to the effect that Garab Dorje appeared to Vairocana directly and personally in the cremation ground called "Place of Smoke" (du ba'i gnos) and transmitted to him all 6,400,000 verses that comprise the complete Ati Yoga source teachings. One is curious as to just how this transference of so much material might be possible.

Longchenpa lists the first five texts as:

1. The Cuckoo of Presence
2. The Great Potency
3. The Great Garuda in Flight
4. Pure Gold in Ore
5. The Victory Banner that Does Not Wane – The Total Space of Vajrasattva

He tells us that the later translated texts were:

6. The Supreme Peak
7. The King of Space
8. The Encrusted Ornament of Bliss
9. The All-encompassing Perfection
10. The Essence of Bodhichitta
11. The Infinite Bliss
12. The Wheel of Life
13. The Six Spheres
14. The All-penetrating Perfection
15. The Wish-fulfilling Jewel
16. The All-unifying Pure Presence
17. The Supreme Lord
18. The Realization of the True Meaning of Meditation

These eighteen major *lungs* constitute the foundation of Ati Yoga. The first five texts and the Kunje Gyalpo or All-Creating King are particularly esteemed. The first five texts appear as separate chapters within the Kunje Gyalpo. We have previously noted that the Dorje Sempa Namkha Che or Total Space of Vajrasattva is considered the root and core of all the Semde teachings, and that it constitutes the thirtieth chapter of the Kunje Gyalpo. This tantra summarizes the key points of Ati Yoga Wisdom.

We have several stories of Padmasambhava's meeting with Sri Simha and these make clear how very special the Ati Yoga Teachings were. Upon meeting Sri Simha, Padmasambhava asked, "Great master, I beseech you to grant an instruction that enables the material body to disappear within this very lifetime, brings forth the vision of the sambhogakaya realms, and awakens one to Buddhahood in the realm of dharmakaya."

Sri Simha replied, "Excellent, noble son! I have an instruction that is the pinnacle of all teachings, the innermost of all views. It transcends all the vehicles and is the heart essence of all dakinis, the subject of extreme secrecy more secret than ordinary secrets. It is the great vehicle of the luminous Vajra Essence, beyond thinking, devoid of the intellect, and outside the domain of dualistic consciousness. It does not lie within the confines of existence or nonexistence and transcends the ranges of view and meditation, development and completion (of Vajrayana). It is the mother of all the victorious ones of the three times, the short path of all the great vidyaharas, the ultimate and unsurpassable instruction through which one can attain the enlightenment of the buddhas within three years. I shall teach it to you!"

Sri Simha then bestowed upon him the appropriate empowerments with scriptural instructions on how the teachings were to be applied. And, as supportive teachings, he transmitted the eighteen Semde Tantras. This accomplished, and having received profuse thanks from Vairochana, Sri Simha advised his pupil as follows:

> The instructions I have given you have the power to enable you to understand all of samsara and nirvana and actually to perceive their essence. So take care of them as if they were your own eyes. They are the root of all the teachings, the peak of all the vehicles, the essence of the mind of all the enlightened ones; take care of them as if they were your own life and your own heart. As they are the source of all the siddhis, the supreme siddhis and the ordinary ones, take care of them as if they were the wish-fulfilling gem.

At a later point in time, Yeshe Tsogyal requested the profound pith instruction of the Heart Essence in Actuality, for awakening to enlightenment in this lifetime. Padmasambhava replied:

> Tsogyal, it is extremely excellent that you make this request. It is an instruction unlike any I have given in the past, the summit that transcends all the nine gradual vehicles. By seeing its vital point, conceptually created views and meditations are shattered; the paths and levels are perfected with no need for struggle; and disturbing emotions are liberated into their natural state without any need for correction or remedy. This instruction brings one to realization, the fruition of which is not produced by causes. It instantly brings forth the spontaneously present realization, liberates the material body of flesh and blood into the luminous sambhogakaya within this lifetime and enables you to capture within three years the permanent abode, the precious dharmakaya realm of spontaneous presence.

These references afford some idea of how highly treasured these teachings were, and why they remained sacred and secret for so many years, being passed on only to those qualified to make good use of them.

Sri Simha advised Vairochana to learn the art of "fast walking" in order to return swiftly and safely home. This he did, and immediately undertook to translate the Kunje Gyalpo and the first five of the Semde texts which he taught in secret to the king. Years later, he transmitted all the teachings he had received to his disciple Yudra Nyingpo, who was the reincarnation of his former travelling companion. It is through him that the lineage and empowerments passed on from Sri Simha to Vairochana have been transmitted down to the present time. These Semde teachings explain the meaning of the primordial state and are rich with instructions that enable a sincere student to recognize and realize the true condition. It is these words and these teachings which we can most confidently attribute directly to Garab Dorje, as passed on through Manjushrimitra, Sri Singha and Vairochana.

It is important to understand that the term "primordial state" means the same thing as the term "Bodhichitta" in these texts. This latter term has several meanings, and they vary from Sutrayana to Vajrayana and Ati Yoga. As used in the Semde texts, Bodhichitta designates the mind or intention addressed to the attainment of enlightenment (bodhi). Generally speaking, in the Ati Yoga source texts, it is also used to mean direct intuitive recognition of the true nature of phenomena and of consciousness itself, including insight into emptiness (*sunyata*). It is fair to say that the Semde texts are all about Bodhichitta. It is the essence of enlightenment (also called Buddha-nature). The way to realize Bodhichitta is to remain in pure non-conceptual recognition of nondual suchness, beyond the flow of thinking activity. Direct encounter with the true nature of one's own consciousness fulfills the first of Garab Dorje's three-part description of the path, and is often called "direct introduction".

Whereas in Mahayoga and Anuyoga the gradual path to realization involves striving, active practices and the process of transformation, working with the chakras and kundalini energy, the fundamental approach of Ati Yoga is self-liberation. The Kunje Gyalpo makes clear in many ways that Ati Yoga is an effortless path based on recognition of pure, non-dual presence. In Ati Yoga, recognition is sudden, not gradual, and this takes place at the beginning of the path, not as its culmination.. In fact, in Ati Yoga, the path, the practice and the goal are identical. Kunje Gyalpo makes clear that in Ati Yoga,

1. There is no view on which to meditate;
2. There is no commitment or samaya one must undertake;
3. There is no capacity one must seek or develop;
4. There is no mandala one has to create;
5. There is no initiation one must receive;
6. There is no path to tread;
7. There are no levels of realization to achieve through purification;
8. There is no special conduct to adopt or abandon;
9. Self-arising Wisdom has always been free of obstacles;
10. Self-perfection is beyond fears and hopes, so there is no need for striving.

The nature of mind is already naturally present and self-perfected, so there is no need to seek Presence and perfection from without. To simply abide in total relaxation, minus effort, is the direct path to realization.

At the time of his passing, it is said that Sri Simha dissolved his body into rainbow light, as had Manjusrimitra, and that he left his disciple Jnanasutra a final testament, known as The Seven Nails. This has remained a significant text in the Ati Yoga tradition until the present time. Jnanasutra was not present at the time of his master's death, but he is said nevertheless to have received this last testament from the hand of his master in person, for Sri Simha appeared bodily before him at the time of his entry into the rainbow body. The text of The Seven Nails, in translation, reads as follows:

Homage to Absolute, union of uncreated Clear Light and Emptiness.

This self-existent Awareness,

Encompasses all and abides in all,

Being open and beyond partiality.

Therefore, affix the original immutable Ground of Being

By using the seven nails of the Path of the
Nonduality of Samsara and Nirvana.

Thus shall primordial Great Bliss arise in your consciousness.

1. *Affix the non-separation of Samsara/Nirvana with the nail of boundless radiant Awareness.*

2. *Affix the non-separation of Observer and Observed with the nail of radiant Clear Light.*

3. *Affix the non-duality of Self and Other with the nail of innate pure Beingness.*

4. *Affix the inseparability of Nihilism and Eternalism with the nail of liberation from Views.*

5. *Affix the juncture of Phenomena and Ultimate Reality with the nail of absolute Awareness (vidya).*

6. *Affix non-duality of calm abiding/agitation with the nail of letting-go-of-sense-stimuli.*

7. *Affix the juncture of Appearances and Emptiness with the nail of primordial embodiment [of the Absolute].*

Colophon

This is the last testament of Sri Simha.

THE MAGIC KEY

The Magic Key is an Ati Yoga text on which Sri Simha and Vairochana collaborated. It would have been translated from a Sanskrit original, and it is almost certainly an Ati Yoga Tantra originally passed on from Garab Dorje, likely to Manjushrimitra and then to Sri Simha. The following is a condensed version of the full Tantra, in other words, a "lung" which touches upon the key points of the original.

Taking Up the Topic

The essential significance of Reality is beyond letters and words. We do not come to it by verbal pronouncements. Our true condition is ineffable. However, without appropriate words as indicators, we fail to understand our intent. For this reason, dharma is taught by means of (verbal) symbols. Through verbal affirmations, we manifest our intent.

Our Own Mind Is Our Teacher

Our true mind is the revealer of that which we seek. True mind is also the attainment. That which we are reveals its own Reality. Those who imagine that Wisdom is conceptual make statements about nirvana and samsara. They calculate the sources of happiness and grief. They work from their notions about good and evil. They inculcate mindfulness and encourage faith. They take up an attitude of faith to inculcate diligence. Gurus who proceed with great diligence contemplate the significance of Samadhi. Their Wisdom expands by growth of the power of Samadhi.

Our knowledge is uncontrived knowingness and we are (inherently) natural embodiments of the Dharma. The best of teachers do not instruct by means of spoken or written words. Their own essence conveys the true Dharma. They entertain no concept of 'self' or 'other'. They use their own essence to communicate the Dharma.

The Method To Explain The Core Meaning

The Reality we call Bodhichitta exists. There is only this one. It exists within the appearances of the perceptible world.

We do not teach the existence of a distinct essence. Reality, the Bodhichitta, resembles nothing at all by means of which it could be expressed and is beyond any object that can be imagined.

Differences Between Four Yogas

There exists a knowingness that does not conceive of objects or senses. Not conceptualizing things and senses is known as Sattva yoga. When we open to the divine Wisdom, that is our own pure spirit. This is Sattva Yoga.

Aspiration to know the pure Wisdom of our own spirit, with no graduated contemplations on the levels of Samadhi, is also Sattva Yoga. The Bodhichitta that is not taken up or laid down is Sattva Yoga.

Of course, the gradual paths, Maha Yoga, Anu Yoga, and Ati Yoga all have their own distinct approaches to Samadhi and the Bodhichitta.

Discernments

All conceptual designation is an activity performed by the mind. Everything we grasp, fabricate, discuss and ponder is of the mind. All appearances and realizations occur within the mind. These are all formations brought about by the mind by virtue of the power of thought.

Real power is the power to turn away from all such delusions. This places us beyond conventional notions of great and small, good and bad, and so on, which taint the minds of sentient beings.

Doors of Entry

In the limited space of our minds, the matrix of all that appears, there is a precious jewel. It is obscured by various obstructions, the gross and the subtle things that we think we need to understand, our notions about grasping and appropriating appearances, the eternal hunger to know and to experience.

The precious jewel that is deep within is obscured by our notions about accepting and rejecting, seeking, and working on things, and our need for a practice of our own. We tend to settle into ourselves, and then seek for something else. This can go on for eons, with no result. It amounts to a kind of prolonged blindness.

As for our approach (in Ati Yoga), we settle our uncontrived minds into Reality, just as it is. We settle into non-dual Wisdom as our experience, and from this we do not move. This is the fulfilment of all samayas and the greatest refuge.

Our awareness is self-luminous. This is the jnana we recognize, this, just this, and no other dharma beyond this.

The View

The Great Perfection (Dzogchen/Ati Yoga) view is a pristine perfection beyond all things and rejects none. Being limitless vastness, no intellectual perspective can express or grasp what it is.

Reality is not something fixed. The way things appear is the way Reality appears. In the absence of certainty that our essential nature is one, we cannot embrace a specific view. The views and perspectives of the eight yanas give rise to confusion. But Suchness has no confusion concerning great perfection Wisdom. Reality is perfection.

We (students of Ati Yoga) do not have a view based on an intellectual perspective. We are beyond all such. We take no fixed position. We recognize no view of this sort. Appearances take on the characteristics of our discordant thoughts. This is why things appear as they do to individual minds. For this reason, we allow nothing whatsoever to circumscribe our realization of vastness.

The View Beyond Perspectives

The real nature of the sky is beyond male and female, nor is it neuter. It is beyond colour, form or flavor. It is not to be found in any of the directions, nor is it inner or outer, shiny or obscure, one or many.

Our view falls into no intellectual position, no notions of bad and good, big or small, joyous or grievous, virtuous or flawed, and all the rest. It is in this way that we never depart from the Bodhichitta .

Teaching the Perfect View

Relative truths do not confuse our view of the ultimate truth. In its position, all that is relative is absolutely perfect.

The great mandala remains perfect because we do not mix the five varieties of coloured sand. Similarly, in weaving we do not mix up the various grades of silk.

We are not bewildered by relative truths because in our view of the ultimate truth there is only perfection.

We are in the position of being a subject, but with regard to our view of Reality, it is quite perfect. Taking up intellectual perspectives can be confusing, but not for us. Delusional understandings do not confuse us because our view of non-dual Wisdom is perfect.

The views and practices of the lower yanas do not confuse us because the view of Great Perfection is completely perfect.

The Key

We use analogies like a "magic key" to unlock the secret meanings to which our words point.

The suchness of appearances that may arise in the sky does not confuse our perception of appearances that arise in the ocean. They are both perfect.

The variety of dharmas does not confuse the image we hold of non-dual Wisdom. All is Great Perfection.

The lucidity of the ocean does not take on confusion because of forms that appear in the sky. No rejection is needed, nor grasping. Sky-forms neither possess nor diminish the scope of the oceanic lucidity.

Just so, non-dual Wisdom does not take up the many dharmas, rejecting here and grasping there. Wisdom has no need either to reject or to appropriate. Nor can it in any way be diminished.

Reflections in the sky and reflections in pure water are not different. They are non-dual.

In the same way, the pristine continuum of awareness and its energetic radiance are not dual. Rather they are one and undifferentiated.

A single form in the sky can result in innumerable reflections in water down below. Just so, non-dual awareness can manifest innumerable powers and expressions. Awareness is the ground of all appearances. Its power is spontaneously self-emergent.

Reflections in water are not possessed of a "true nature". Nor are the varied appearances arising from the radiant energy of consciousness. Colours that are mixtures of various tints cannot be called "a single thing." In truth, there has never been a division of the One into the many.

Freedom from the tyranny of multiplicity should never be forfeited. Wisdom brings together all dharmas into a singularity. But just by saying this, we do not necessarily recognize how it is true.

There are no real divisions that generate real individuals. There is nothing that could cause us to relinquish our freedom from multiplicity.

Dharmas appear to be many, but they are non-dual in Wisdom. In the absence of many names for dharmas, we are all one in the domain of the non-dual.

Whatever their forms and names, all things made from gold are in essence gold. We may conceptualize and name an endless variety of dharmas, but in essence they are one. Mind is one, but varied appearances give rise to a seeming multiplicity of individuals.

One in essence, the six classes of living beings appear to be distinct. But we never change from our true nature and cause, which is always one. Thus does our world come about.

The nature of Reality neither appears nor disappears. What is medicine for some may be poison for others. Even so, our essential Wisdom may appear as desire, ill will or dullness depending on our thoughts.

Absent Wisdom, our Bodhichitta nature takes the form of ignorance, but when non-dual Wisdom arises, we experience the bliss and blessings of Dharma lived.

Yogis may live individually before realizing Reality, but afterward they become one in realization, blissfully inseparable from the Dharma.

Meditation reveals the Buddhahood that is present in the heart of all sentient beings. At least, this is the belief of those who strive for attainment in the lower yanas.

Dispensing with Flawed Views

When we try to grasp our essential nature by means of conceptual fabrications, we generate flawed views based in separation. Eternalism and nihilism are examples of such flawed views.

The uncontrived Reality exists just as it is. Some take this as a cause for renunciation. Others become preoccupied with purification. Still others take this as a reason to become immersed in studies.

For some, their views and their actual practice do not square. Others are spiritually acquisitive. And yet others get preoccupied with accepting and rejecting.

In Mahayoga, the purity of spirit is emphasized. Anuyoga teaches that cause and outcome are dual. Mantrayana practitioners believe in the two truths, conventional and ultimate, the Reality of other worlds, the building up of merit and the importance of applying the power of generation. The need for blessings, conceptual frameworks and the existence of some uncreated condition of perfection as a goal are all taught to those who follow the Mantrayana. All of the above are mistaken views.

If we squint a certain way, we can see two moons in the sky although there is really only one. In the same way, delusional understandings arise from mistaken views. Duality is seen where it does not exist. For as long as we cling to duality, we will lack authentic insight into non-duality.

Relinquish the desire for manifold intellectual views. The sky is without parts, whatever cosmologists may think and say. The mind of awakening has no "practice sessions" Nor is the authentic Dharma composed of many aspects.

The View that is Worthy of Belief

All dharmas are in Reality the mind of awakening, or Bodhichitta, for it is their very heart-essence, and with this we can reveal what is un-manifest.

It is not dependent on causes or conditions; therefore, it is self-sprung Wisdom's certainty. It is not something to be sought, but rather a naturally arising certitude.

It is the ordering principle and the light behind all our teachers and scriptures. It lights up the pattern-of-the-whole. It is thus the highest of ten yanas, the royal path of all the enlightened ones.

Consciousness subsumes all and is the root of all. All that arises does so in consciousness. It is the foundation and origin of everything.

Since consciousness gives rise to all, it is the essence of all. Though imperceptible, it pervades all. It is beyond change and beyond concepts such as "one" or "many".

The real nature of the Dharma is the basis of all views. It lives in us but is not easy to comprehend. Thus, we hold it to be a secret and sacred transmission.

Hope And Fear Cannot Compromise The View

The Great Perfection View makes hopes and fears irrelevant. The bird that soars on high has no fear of elevations and valleys in the land below. Those who have certainty with regard to awareness have no concerns about the ups and downs of samsara. There may be signs of progress or no signs arising from their practice, it hardly matters.

For those who know the deathless state, compound forms may or may not be permanent, it matters not. For those who know the non-dual Reality, it is of no concern how ideas may be grouped in the mind. Good may be separated from evil by way of conceptualization, but if equality has been realized, it hardly matters.

On the pathless path, one's abode may be high or low, it makes no difference. We are beyond the implications of concepts and narratives.

For Whom Is The Teaching Meant?

A sacred offering may be poured into a precious vessel, and later poured into inferior vessels where it is wasted.

It is well known that ambrosial nectar can only be consumed by the healthy; for the unhealthy it only aggravates the digestive system.

The nectar of the highest view is positive for those of clear intellect, but for the confused it compounds bewilderment.

Bodhichitta Encompasses All

The contemplations of the Buddha are many, but the Bodhichitta is one. How is this to be understood?

Everything, including the teachings of the Buddhas, is equalized in the Bodhichitta. In the Bodhichitta, all things are held, because there is no good or evil, no acceptance or renouncing. The practices of Ratnasambhava, Amitabha, and Vairochana have the same intent: the Reality of the Bodhichitta.

The whiteness of the sky, by analogy, can hold all the various colours. Bodhichitta is the Reality that holds all possible meanings. Its self-arising Wisdom is all encompassing and eternal. All varied appearances are but permutations of the Bodhichitta.

We do not conceptualize this and so we are at peace. This is called the contemplation of the sky. Nothing that appears do we grasp by way of concepts. We may use words and meanings, but we do not fixate on them, and so we have nothing to conceptualize or narrate. Our minds settle into the unfabricated tranquility of Reality as it is, the spaciousness that is called "the contemplation of the sky".

The Great Perfection View

How are we to separate or distinguish the beingness of the Dharma from its radiance? Are they to be considered as identical or different? The body of the Dharma and its form – are these identical or different? The Dharma-body and Wisdom, are they the same or different?

Ignorance and Wisdom, are they the same or different? A fixed perspective and the ultimate view, are they the same or different? Buddhas and samsaric beings, are they the same or different?

The Dharma's existence and its radiance are like the sun and its light, neither identical nor different. Dharma's body and its form are like the moon and its reflection on water, neither identical nor different. The Dharma-body and Wisdom are similarly one in essence.

A fixed perspective in the mind and the real nature of mind are both vision, one impure and the other pure. They may appear to be different, but they are not. Nor are they identical. Buddhas and samsaric beings, good and bad delusions and the rest are neither identical nor different.

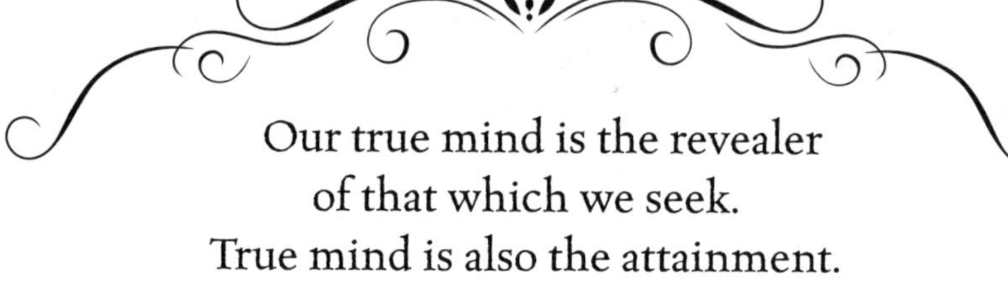

Our true mind is the revealer
of that which we seek.
True mind is also the attainment.

That which we are
reveals its own Reality.

BOOK EIGHT: Vairochana

The best known of all the translators and preservers of the words of Garab Dorje was Vairochana. More than any other figure, he is considered the one who introduced the original Semde teachings of Ati Yoga into Tibet. His writings come to us with a sense of freshness and immediacy, conveying a genuine transmission of power and presence.

Vairochana lived during the reign of King Trisong Detsen, who ruled 755-804 AD, and is held by the Nyingmapas to be one of twenty-five principal disciples of Padmasambhava, who recognized him as a reincarnation of an Indian pandita.

He was among the first seven monks ordained by Śāntarakṣita, after which he was sent by the king to Dhahena in India, to retrieve and translate the Ati Yoga teachings of Garab Dorje. Trisong Detsen entrusted a considerable amount of gold to Vairochana so that he could cover travel costs and make offerings in exchange for the teachings.

Setting forth with only one friend, Lekdrub, he experienced many hardships and close passes with death before he got to Dhahena and met Sri Simha. Shechen Gyaltsab mentions in his Pond of White Lotus Flowers that before meeting Sri Simha, Vairotsana had encountered the Wisdom forms of the two vidyadharas Garab Dorje and Mañjuśrīmitra in a miraculous pagoda at Dhahena. After he had presented a huge offering of gold, they imparted their blessings to him along with an indication that he would receive the full body of teachings from Sri Simhaa.

Sri Simha did not have the texts that Vairochana sought, because the local king had sealed them up at Bodhgaya in order to keep them secret and prevent them being taught. It became necessary for Sri Simha and Vairochana to sneak in by night and abscond with the books, so that their contents could be studied, translated, and brought back to Tibet.

At Dhahena, Sri Simha taught the meaning of the Semde Ati Yoga texts to Vairochana in secrecy. In Vairochana's biography, The Great Image, we read that after several years of study and translation, working with Sri Simha, Vairochana returned to Tibet and continued with his translations of texts originally passed down by Garab Dorje. There were many Ati Yoga Tantras belonging to the Mind Section which Sri Simha passed on to Vairochana. These are listed and briefly described in Chapter 14 of The Lotus Born (Shambhala Publications).

We know of several texts that Vairochana worked on translating while with Sri Simha. One is a Manjusri Yamantaka Sadhana, another is The Great Tantra of Vajrasattva; Equal to the End of the Sky, another is the Force of Wisdom Tantra, and yet another is The Magic Key, a *lung* (abbreviated summary) of which is to be found above. These three are some of the earliest translations of Ati Yoga teachings into the Tibetan language, where they were preserved long after the originals disappeared in India, possibly during the Islamic invasions.

Although Buddhist language and themes are often found in Vairochana's translations of Ati Yoga source texts, there are many passages where the language and ideas are not typically Buddhist. Concepts such as oneness, non-duality, the error of cause and effect, and the wrong views that lead to striving and active practice are examples.

In the Semde source texts, we often find thinking typical of the Upanishads and Advaita, but couched in Buddhist terminology. It is impossible to study the early Ati Yoga Tantras without seeing the many ways that they contradict the orthodoxies of Hinayana and Mahayana Buddhism of the day. For this reason, many Ati Yoga Tantras were not included in the collected teachings of the Buddha or Kagyur.

Although Garab Dorje's teachings were embraced by many Vajrayana practitioners in Tibet and came to be considered by the Nyingmapas as the highest of all their teachings, and although Garab Dorje is often portrayed by Tibetan sources as a Buddhist, the fact is that he was an enlightened being who transcended religious categories and norms. One reason why Dzogchen teachings were reserved for the very few for many centuries in the monasteries of Tibet may be that in many instances they directly contradict certain tenets of Mahayana and Vajrayana Buddhism.

Although the eighteen major tantras of the Semde (Mind Section) were taught by Sri Simha to Vairochana and his travelling companion Lekdrub of Tsang, Vairochana received many other transmissions from Sri Simha, tantras from both the Mind Section and the Space section of the Ati Yoga Source texts before he returned to Tibet. Through his studies, meditation and time with the great master Sri Simha, Vairochana attained realization.

Eventually, Sri Simha told Vairochana that he was not the keeper of the complete tantras, scriptures and instructions and that the time had come to bring those he had shared to Tibet. At this time, he conferred upon him the spiritual name Vairochana, replacing his Tibetan name Pagor, by which he had previously been known.

Upon his return, Vairochana focused his energy on translating what Sri Simha had given him into Tibetan. But certain highly placed court officials had taken a dislike towards him and spread rumors causing the king to exile Vairochana to a region of Tibet known as Tsawarong. Before being exiled from the Tibetan court, Vairochana had translated five of the works passed on by Sri Simha. The remaining thirteen were later translated by Yudra Nyingpo and the great Indian pandit Vimalamitra.

Vairochana did not attribute these Ati Yoga source texts to himself, but rather to Garab Dorje, who was revered as a full emanation of Vajrasattva in human form. Vairochana's first five translations stand on their own as jewels of Wisdom, the core teaching being always the same: the luminous, natural, non-dual mind of Great Perfection itself. All five of these early translations were included in the Kunje Gyalpo (All-Creating King, or Kulayaraja Tantra). The list of five includes:

8.1 The Cuckoo's Song of Awareness (Rig pa'i khu byug)
(Ch. 31 in KG)

8.2 The Great Potentiality (rTsal chen sprugs pa)
(Ch. 27 in KG)

8.3 The Great Garuda in Flight (Khyung chen lding ba)
(Ch. 22 in KG)

8.4 The Refining of Gold from Ore (rDo la gser zhun)
(Ch. 26 in KG)

8.5 The Un-waning Victory Banner (Mi nub pa'i rgyal mtshan)
(Ch. 30 in KG)

In introductory comments to his doctoral thesis on the Five Early Translations, Mihai Derbac makes the following comments:

> *The sNaga Ingda texts (early translations) are not descriptive in their approach (telling us what is the case) or prescriptive (telling us what we ought to do), but rather suggestive. They hint and allude, inspire and evoke a particular experience. They provide what could be called a rDzogs chen "vision" of Reality through heuristic devices, such as metaphoric expressions and apophatic discourse. This vision refers to Reality as-it-is, a Reality that is not filtered through human prejudices, habits, and preconceptions: a Reality that reveals itself spontaneously in a rich variety of possibilities. Awareness, in this context, is not a matter of some altered states of consciousness, but of being present to the wonders that life and the world have to offer. A close analysis reveals that all rDzogs chen texts have been conceived in such a manner that they not only say something but do something as well. A text's "disclosure" provides illumination and inspiration for a spontaneous insight, a direct experience of awareness.*

This is a very sound assessment of Vairochana's early translations, their style and thrust. It is worth adding that the suggestive nature of early Tibetan sacred writings may frequently lead to what a modern reader from the West might deem vagueness or imprecision of conceptual clarity of the sort considered to be a core virtue of well written modern English-language prose. The western reader often wants to pin down exactly what the writer is trying to say. Looking for the clear meanings inside the suggestive prose of the originals is a constant challenge. It is one of the biggest difficulties in translating early Tibetan Semde texts into modern English or rendering modern translations into a clear and comprehensible prose such as we find in the Christian gospels. When comparing translations (there are at least four translations of Kunje Gyalpo in modern English) one often finds that the same passage can be rendered in several different ways, with distinctly different meanings.

The modern reader may well feel the need to distil the suggestiveness of the original prose into a clear meaning, which usually means a conceptual nutshell of precise intellectual content. It helps to be reminded that illumining insight is the real goal of these writings, not clearly etched power points of spiritual philosophy. It helps also to recognize that clear and simple English prose can also stimulate illumining insights and lead to spiritual awakening.

The Cuckoo's Song of Awareness, while only six lines long, has been translated into English in a number of different ways. Here are a few examples:

The infinite diversity of experiences
and their actual nature are non-dual.
Yet the actuality of each particular occurrence
is beyond judgement.
What is known as 'as it is' is untouched by thought
Yet the forms of appearance are unobstructed,
being complete as they are.
Being intact we are free of the sickness of effort,
Spontaneously abiding and so everything is settled.

The true nature of infinite diversity is non-dual,
Since each phenomenon is free of conceptual elaboration.
The so-called state of "just as-it-is" is non-discursive,
Since all manifested forms are ultimately self-perfected.
As everything is already accomplished,
by giving up the affliction of striving
One finds oneself naturally abiding in the effortless state.

Diversity and nature non-dual:
Specific apparitions, each beyond judgement.
'As it is', neither concept nor conceptualisable:
All manifesting is perfect, complete in itself.
Intrinsically complete, untouched by the disease of effort:
Spontaneous presence, unchanging.

Diversity essence, non-dual:
Apparitions specific, beyond judgement.
'As it is', not concept, not caught by concept:
Manifest, perfect; the common good.
Complete in itself, the disease of effort discarded:
Spontaneous presence, settled.

The second of Vairochana's early translations, The Great Potentiality, while not long, is packed with significance:

THE GREAT POTENTIALITY (RTSAL CHEN SPRUGS PA)

From the very beginning, the nature of Reality has been inclusive of all appearances, both outer and inner. In the domain of primordial perfect purity, there is no distinction between enlightened beings and samsaric sentient beings. How, therefore, could there be anything in need of correction by way of paths to follow and antidotes to apply?

Since the true condition has no place for desire or striving, there is nothing to be attained. The nature of Reality is naturally self-perfected and free from activity. In the dharmadatu (true condition), notions and analyses are non-dual. How then could this dimension possibly be affected by the behavior of unwise people and their mistaken views?

Non-dual bliss can be experienced by all. Even mistaken paths contrived by deluded seekers are not (in essence) different from the all-encompassing path, as already pointed out. Whoever knows this equality is the master of enlightenment.

The third of the five early translations is The Great Garuda It has two parts in Keith Dowman's view. Verses one to sixteen contain information on nonmeditation, and verses seventeen to twenty-six are about being a yogi.

THE GREAT GARUDA IN FLIGHT (KHYUNG CHEN LDING BA)

[1] The non-conceptual condition has no location or support. To fabricate subtle experiences (in meditation) based on hopeful intentions is pointless. This is essentially a conceptual approach to the manifestation of Reality. Self-sprung primordial awareness abides in the suchness of its own nature, beyond the grasp of our thoughts.

[2] Being beyond activity, it (the nature of mind) is not some kind of object (that is perceivable), and it is not in need of corrections or antidotes. If sought through perceptible phenomena, it can nevertheless only be appreciated in non-conceptuality. Being the essence of all, it reveals its presence spontaneously. Being the nature of Reality, it is not to be found elsewhere, or apart from appearances.

[3] The true condition is undivided and abides beyond the ten directions. Being the pristine continuum of bare awareness that is self-originating, it does not abide in anything. Moreover, it is the very heart of non-conceptual and immediate experience. Those drawn to this pure path will assuredly attain the ultimate equanimity.

[4] Unvarying, beyond conditionality, there is nothing to which one could become attached. There being no object to grasp, there is in consequence no place for the grasping mind. Those who strive to experience, happily attached to such (conceptually grasping) meditation, will never attain the direct experience of authentic equality due to their attachment to such (a fixating) form of meditation.

[5] The domain of oneness is all-pervading, and there is nothing which can be added (to it). Being endless, there is also nothing to be subtracted from it. There is no (such thing as a) concealed state that abides beyond our manifest Reality. The domain of self-originated greatness is always just what it is (i.e.: suchness).

[6] To see that there is no "thing" to be seen is to see the ineffable. Since the ultimate Reality transcends all representations, there is nothing to be heard either, the (so-called) correct and the incorrect being all comingled and equal. There is no way that what we call ultimate Reality could possibly be described.

[7] Our conceptual delusions cannot shape the path of utter purity. The primordial continuum of purity is beyond the limits of speech. Like shadows cast by physical forms, conceptual thoughts appear to the mind directly, experienced from within the timeless perfection of this continuum.

[8] It (the pristine continuum) is neither non-existent nor truly existent. Inner Reality seems rather to manifest as absence. Emptiness abides in the domain of emptiness but is not empty. Awareness comes into being from within the nature of spaciousness. Without hankering after bliss, we enter the experience of bliss, liberated from activity (such as striving).

[9] The continuum of pure awareness cannot be made apparent to the mind in the same way that objects can appear to the mind. If the mind becomes fixated on its notions concerning ancient masters, one comes to experience the agony of striving and struggling. The all-knowing state comes to the fore only by entering the way of essential Reality.

[10] Those who cling to their own notions about the true condition make meditation into nothing more than a conceptual process. They yearn for supreme bliss but fall prey to the debility of craving. If they do not administer the cure, which is abiding in the state of timeless equanimity, then their ascension to higher domains is fraught with confusion.

[11] This is a path wherein there is no path. Thus, those who strive for specific goals end up like a deer in pursuit of a mirage. The objective is not a thing which can be acquired, not a product or a formation to be found in any of any of the three worlds. Even reliance on a belief in the ten directions is an obscurity as regards pristine purity, the true condition.

[12] Void of notions, the ever-present continuum of pure awareness is like a priceless gem appearing among spiritual companions. Beyond change, though it is unseen, by its inherent nature it fulfills all cravings.

[13] Upon scrutiny (while meditating), we find nothing at all. Left to itself, it (Presence) manifests extraordinary qualities. It fulfills all wants even though it is invisible. It is a supreme teacher, even though it is beyond self and other – a priceless treasure indeed! Belonging to the domain of complete perfection, it (suchness) can be made apparent only by unconditional compassion.

[14] It is unmoving. It cannot be perceived. There is nothing to be found within it. It is not an object to which anyone can become attached. Authentic, compassionate selflessness is not a condition that one can enter, or that can emerge (take form). It is always present, beyond delusions of separation, and beyond appearance (or disappearance).

[15] To crave the experience of bliss is to abandon bliss. Bliss being already present, bliss is to be sought by recognition of its

non-absence. To seek for something external is to misunderstand what great perfection really is. To grasp perceptions is to be forever separate from realization.

[16] There being no such thing as enlightenment, the name enlightenment does not refer to anything that is real. It is a mistake to use a conceptual designation to indicate enlightenment. To look for enlightenment from others is to follow a path of folly. Not even the barest teaching can be given concerning the experience that is beyond form.

[17] Innately peaceful, liberated from cravings, non-material, formless, the essence of this nectar cannot be grasped by thinking activity.

[18] The boundless, wonderful and incomparable teaching is a cure for everything trivial. When its greatness brings about the state of equanimity, all notions of greater and lesser are left behind.

[19] Teachings, the primordial continuum, perceptions and appearances are like phantasms conjured by a sorcerer. Covering up the revelation of pure awareness, these lead to further rebirths.

[20] This (the nature of mind) is the ultimate path, the foundational nature that makes all things possible and clings to none. It cannot be conceptually grasped. It cannot be the object of desire. And it does not engender even the slightest degree of clinging and hankering.

[21] Like a magnificent Garuda soaring in spaciousness, beyond elaboration, beyond conception, it seeks nothing and fears no loss whatsoever.

[22] Always present, like a great oceanic expanse, it (pure awareness) gives rise to all dharmas (phenomena). Its nature resembles that of space, having no beginning point.

[23] Unexpectedly, the nature of mind reveals itself as unequaled contemplation. In appearance like an incomparable ocean, being non-conceptual it is infinitely spacious.

[24] The realm of the All-Good is beyond change and origination. The twelve stages of cause and effect are only notional

narratives fabricated by those who still entertain fear. Those who are wise will remember this for the sake of those who live in confusion.

[25] Although six classes of deluded beings have appeared, this (unconditioned consciousness) is to be seen as the primordial path. If endowed with compassion, whose who are caught up in their cravings may even yet orient themselves toward the pristine continuum by any means they choose.

[26] Those who kill and butcher animals or sell their bodies for pleasure, those who have committed the five most serious transgressions, and whose actions are defiled are abandoned by the world. But the well-intentioned, the self-perfected ones, understand that even these miscreants are not different from the supreme bliss. They know the nature of mind, and so they understand all its varied appearances as well.

[27] To seek the true condition by relying on the true condition would be like space seeking for space, or the sky seeking (to grasp) the sky. To think that one can find the true nature by relying on another is like trying to put out fire by means of fire. These are notoriously difficult things to do!

[28] The heart of the non-conceptual state is not hidden away in the depth of anyone's personal experiences. Those whose lives are beyond conceptual grasping, whose actions accord with flawless purity, continuously abide (unobstructedly) in the true nature of Reality.

* * * * *

The Sun of My Heart is a book of instruction for students of Ati Yoga, composed by Vairochana and based on his five early translations. It is included here as part of the Gospel of Garab Dorje because it is one of best sources for understanding the approach to practice in pure, original Ati Yoga.

THE SUN OF MY HEART

Those fortunate ones with favorable conditions should begin with physical cleansing. Then they are to be seated on a comfortable mat. In this way, they are to continue on and sustain the Bodhichitta by placing the mind in a state of unbroken equanimity. They should continue thus, even though they may not yet have a full understanding of the path.

As to settling the mind into its natural condition, there is no information in our view, and nothing to ponder in our meditation. We abide without reflecting on any topic whatsoever. Nor do we think about not thinking. The equanimity of suchness is sustained by this very freedom from compulsive thinking.

In the pristine continuum, there are no thoughts whatsoever. If we have not been overcome by sloth and torpor, we will go beyond the bubble of our thinking-activity and enter the abode of great bliss, illumined by a Wisdom far beyond all our opinions and notions, which are then clearly seen to be something completely irrelevant.

The meditation we perform brings the karmic mind into its true condition. The essential feature of this meditation is that we are freed from all complexity. Complications belong only to the karmic mind, whereas Reality, in its essential nature, is a condition of utter spontaneity.

The pristine continuum of the natural condition is unborn and unending. It cannot be understood by means of the intellect. It is beyond dualistic categories of thought such as permanence and cessation.

Illumined by Wisdom, we become clear concerning our true goals in life. The awakened consciousness leaves no residue of anything at all that thinking-activity could grasp. It is impossible to symbolize the true nature. This is the way it is, concerning the continuum of Wisdom, as the wise ones have stated.

The pristine continuum which is our essence cannot be augmented or diminished. The mind takes up its abode in a vast inner space. By means of a diligence in which there is nothing whatsoever to do, nothing tires or depresses us, for we are free of thinking-activity.

We meditate for short durations which are frequently repeated. When we arrive at the point of being neither slothful nor agitated, we find ourselves transported into the pristine continuum of pure being. Thereafter, with minimal exertion we can easily dispel any tendency to stray, and in this manner, we continue on in dhyana (meditative focus).

In the beginning, we abide in the true condition for short periods of time, then, perhaps for half a day, and later for a day or a night. We come to a point where it is possible to take unbroken refuge in the pure continuum of being.

The Great Perfection is free from striving and seeking. Be very clear on this important point: No matter how much you seek, there is nothing to look for. In the absence of (conceptual) grasping, there is nothing to seek.

Live spontaneously. It is the best of all accomplishments. To abide in the true nature is the way of happiness.

When we have not reached familiarization with the true nature, we become agitated, lost in thoughts of past and future. We give up regular practice and simply grow old. Depression, tiredness and other shifting states of mind such as attachment to alcohol and lust all arise from lack of familiarization with the true state.

Appearances go on by themselves; making efforts to change this is futile. Do not try to stop the flow of ideas. Just allow everything to settle into the condition of suchness. Ideas appear and get pacified by themselves. As Wisdom dawns, there is no need to give up normal activities, for life simply and effortlessly unfolds as the natural radiance of the all-good.

On the pathless path, everything comes together without any need to control or conceptualize the process. Understanding the holiness of intuitive feelings, we are under no compulsion to produce some state where we are beyond feelings altogether. What is essential, however, is to end the sickness of seeking.

There is no kind of activity which we need to take upon ourselves, and none we need reject. We simply let go of the disease of seeking and come home to the equality of dhyana. In this way, we are never separated from our inner sources of inspiration, no matter what we do. Established in the equality of the true condition, we are indistinguishable from the victorious ones.

We go beyond having nothing to do, nor do we actively seek for a path. To strive for enlightenment is exhausting, and there will never be a time for completing such a project. Do not get lost in paths of active striving. Extended meditation will definitely bring about signs of attainment, and in this process obstructions naturally disappear.

We come to the natural state without seeking it. Equanimity eventually reigns supreme. We no longer resent samsara and karma, nor do we fear death, or rebirth. Our hopes and fears come to an end. However intense our sorrows, we no longer encounter them in sadness. We take no joy in words. Like the spacious sky, we are beyond agitation, and this stage of experience comes about in its own way, in its own time.

Just as ripples on water disappear by themselves if we do not interfere, so our obstructions get cleared up naturally, on their own, with no need to seek them out and purify them. When we have given up the ailment of striving for results, defilements fall away all by themselves.

Wisdom bears fruit in a life lived spontaneously. The mind of the meditator is the real wish-fulfilling jewel, the primordial source of all results, and beyond comprehension. For this reason, we do not look elsewhere. We understand that Wisdom and the spontaneous life are not acquired by disciplined striving. They have always been there, and simply come to the fore in the absence of obscurations.

The state of natural abiding is not something that comes by being sought and it is not something that can be improved by striving. It is beyond any levels of attainment that could be elaborated or explained, having been an uncaused, pristine Reality from the beginningless beginning.

For us, fruition is a spontaneous meditation where view, practice, samadhi, cause and result all merge and are as one. We go beyond any kind of view that can be asserted with words. The spontaneity of the Bodhichitta, the dharmata, is our unique Reality, and our practice centers solely on this great perfection abiding in the core of our hearts.

For us, the victorious one is the sum total of what we hold most precious, and thus we have eliminated all forms of contrived striving. Garab Dorje has explained the bodhicitta-way in his teachings. His Wisdom is there to draw on by those who are wise. Additionally, for those who are truly prescient, it is evident that our own primordial consciousness is the living Reality of the victorious one himself.

BEYOND SEEKING

In supreme Samadhi, there is no active meditation, no thinking activity whatsoever. Primordial Reality entertains no hopes or goals whatsoever. Wishes, fears and fabrications of all sorts are incompatible with the boundless spontaneity of the true condition.

However meritorious he may be, a novice on this path must be saturated with the Wisdom of the Upadesha teachings. Anyone who has grasped the profound meaning of the pith instructions and who cares for nothing else deserves our full support. We embrace those who are marked by destiny (to follow such a path as this).

Having many ideas and many active practices is a tendency only to be seen in those who are immature. Activities externalize one's attention, preventing one from settling into the true condition. Our meditation, on the other hand, is to abide in the supreme Reality, which is nothing less than direct recognition of awareness itself.

Any form of visualization tends to focus one's understanding on a limited object of attention, and this can only result in a lesser kind of samadhi. The Victorious Ones did not favour such visualizations. Visualization is an unsatisfactory approach to recognizing and abiding in the true view wherein all things are known to be primordial enlightenment, and where cause and fruition are one nondual Reality, not two.

The enlightened state and the condition of a samsaric sentient being are not two things. Nor are evil and good two things. Nor is there any duality of self and other. Authentic Wisdom shines through all appearances in such a way that our experiences and our Wisdom are non-dual.

In the great bliss of all-surpassing wholeness, there are no concepts such as samsara or nirvana. We do not allow the mind to wander or become preoccupied by grasping at objects or fixating attention on interesting forms. This is the true perspective, the foundational insight which is at the core of this path.

There is no need to conform the intellect in any special style of meditation. The mind is not to be engaged with conceptions or non-conceptuality, with visualization or non-visualization, with rest or non-rest or any other conceptual dharma. The mind is not placed on any dharma (phenomenon) at all. What appears in the mind, petty or vast, can be left just as it is.

The non-conceptual state is the quintessence of equanimity. To seek for enlightenment is to entertain notions about what this enlightenment might look like, even though the enlightened state cannot by any means be represented by thought. The activity of seeking will never bring the mind into a non-conceptual state of pure abiding.

Primordial Wisdom is self-arising and self-recognizing. Any notion concerning obstruction is simply a contrived issue cooked up by the intellect itself. In its actuality, Wisdom is beyond being either obstructed or un-obstructed.

Seeing through the mind's contrivances, we will never find even a single problem which requires our attention. Our meditations will be flawless when we have no notions about achieving some kind of positive result. Simply put, presence is peace - which is Reality, even when Reality seems to assume varied appearances due to thinking-activity.

Active practices based on conceptual notions do not evoke what is ultimately true, and for this reason they are delusory.

Being contrived, they constitute an obstruction and will never lead to enlightenment.

Complication and complexity arise only because we have taken the approach of seeking for some outcome or result. Remember this: outcomes based in activities such as seeking and striving remain limited to the three worlds of mere appearance.

To simply remain in the samadhi of suchness is to attain total fulfilment. No active striving or searching is required. To seek for a goal is to be unsettled. Simply refuse to depart from the natural state. Abide in the true condition by refusing to follow your thoughts. In this way, you will remain settled in clarity, equanimity, and non-attachment.

Let your mind abide in the natural state. Avoid grasping. Do not imagine that awakening into awareness will make you special and different. Drop any notions about the state of your attainment. Ideas about attainment are merely verbal and notional, whereas the natural state is a direct experience of oneness.

You find that your thoughts decrease, your mind becomes blissful, your body becomes light, your mood becomes joyful. You will not care about words, but rather about meanings. You will have inspired dreams, and you will lose interest in your cares and concerns. You will go beyond fixed opinions and your emotional problems will melt away.

You will have no concerns about future births. You will become skillful about avoiding involvement in various projects, and without any effort you will be released from any and all tendencies toward spiritual seeking.

None of these developments come as a result of striving or aiming for results. Self-arising Wisdom carries with it no sense of resistance toward samsara.

Authentic Wisdom entertains no notion of attainment. It is nothing other than recognition of bare awareness, the natural state. In fact, the true meaning of all these teachings is nothing more and nothing less than your very own consciousness.

THE SOARING OF THE MAGNIFICENT GARUDA

Free from any compulsion to expand or contract, our true nature soars in the sky of mind. Receive this aural transmission concerning a practice where self-centered goals are completely absent, for we have no interaction with objects that appear to the mind. Of all forms of engagement, this is the best!

Obstructions arise because of deviation from the view. Be clear about this point from the very outset and you will experience the dhyana of unmistaken view. When we practice with an interest in getting results, we will have karmic thoughts about appearances which we take to be real.

When we transcend attachments, the ground of our practice will be seen to be utterly pure and there will be nothing in need of purification. In that which is changeless, there is no thing to which one could become attached, no object, no grasping, no placement of attention. Objects upon which to settle the mind simply do not exist. The ground of being itself proclaims this truth.

There is no need to relinquish dependently originating things and render form into emptiness, for the ground of all appearances is innately pure already. Truth is indivisible, and dharmas are inseparable. People talk of some ultimate and "higher" Dharma, but it does not exist.

Bodhichitta has always been inherently perfect. Meditations of generation, separating nirvana from samsara and the rest, are all contrived. Teachings and visualizations based on such inventions lead nowhere. Samsara and nirvana are not dual, nor can their essence be visualized, nor will appearances cease to appear as a result of practice.

From what is primordially pure, only purity can appear. All forms express their heart-essence. Permanence and impermanence are both its expressions. Changeless, unfabricated, undiluted, the light of Wisdom is not a path that leads from one place to another, nor is it revealed by seeking, nor as the outcome of striving and practicing.

The mind tries to fathom the nature of Reality with concepts such as permanence, impermanence, unity, plurality, emptiness and appearance. Avoid any attempt to express the nature of Reality with words or to grasp or cling, as if it were a material thing. Appearances conform to our pre-determined notions and intellectual capacity. None of this reveals the nature of Reality.

Samsaric mind never succeeds at samsara, never becomes a Buddha. Reality is beyond the extremes of words. It is not an essence to which we must be attached, nor an awareness which a yogi must develop, or sustain. The view entails no subject who attains, nor is it some kind of goal to be sustained. There is nothing that needs to be said or done, nothing to seek or reject. Being non-dual, Reality is intrinsically clear. It affords the intellect nothing to contemplate.

We make way for a presence that lies beyond our thoughts and our excessive speech, and we meditate in the unwavering state beyond internal and external appearances. In this, we continue on, without giving up. Once glimpsed, the true view precludes thinking about anything else. All things are but the luminosity of pristine awareness and cannot be grasped or expressed by words such as "this" or "that".

Other than our minds, from the beginningless beginning there have been no dharmas. There is no Reality located elsewhere on which to meditate and no refuge other than mind itself. This is the crystal palace, and this is the wish-fulfilling jewel. It is the holy dwelling place of enlightened beings and meditators alike. We abide like the sky, nothing to contrive, nothing to conceptualize, nothing to do or to attain. All things inner and all things outer are but the radiance of awareness.

What we call "heart-essence" is not something to be visualized or pondered. Thoughts and definitions of the sky will never convey its nature, so we relinquish all such forms of conceptual grasping. There is nothing, no "thing", whatsoever on which to meditate. Anything we might do by way of meditation is not the way of Great Perfection. We do not conceptualize luminosity.

The sky that is our mind is by its very nature an equanimous continuum of conscious clarity, un-qualified, complete and perfect. In this undefined and indefinable sky of our very own consciousness, we become liberated from seeking, as from pondering the significance of the truth.

Experiences of the absence of thought do not bring us any closer to recognition of the inconceivable. Nor do altered or higher states of consciousness. Once we understand that ignorance is Wisdom, why relinquish higher perception? Knowing that our concepts are the luminosity of Wisdom, why try to avoid peaceful abiding? Reality will go on generating appearances, in any case. Thoughts too are but the radiance of awareness, so there is no need to relinquish or acquire them.

Knowing the heart essence of all appearances, I need not feed the hunger to know what things mean. I have nothing to reject or to acquire, no fascination with samadhi or gnosis, no aversion to being active upon occasion. The natural state cannot be fabricated or contrived, and all dharmas are its liveliness.

From an undisturbed state of consciousness, we settle into the dhyana where there is nothing to do. So-called "practice" appears by itself, and when it does our only responsibility is not to drift away from it. This does not require that there should be a cessation of appearances which in any case are but the body, speech and mind of the Supreme Reality.

There is no end to the process of accumulating merit, and we are easily trapped by the practices we undertake and the karma we generate in all these seemingly virtuous ways. Understand decisively that Buddhahood is not to be attained by active striving.

MEDITATING ON THE BODHICHITTA

To know the nature of mind is to know the nature of all its dharmas. On this, the supreme path, our freedom is infinitely beyond description, and beyond our efforts to limit or foster, embrace or reject.

We go beyond the mind that pre-occupies itself with thinking, speaking and acting, and our dhyana is beyond directed intent as well. Bodhichitta is uncontrived, inherently luminous, beyond visualizations and strategically directed meditations.

There is no requirement to take upon ourselves certain dharmas and reject others. We are beyond the strategies of thought, problem-solving, visualizing, and struggling with samsara. Nor are we trying to meditate our way to nirvana.

The natural state makes clear to us that there is nothing, no thing, about which to think. This is the intrinsic suchness of Reality, and not just a notion that we imagine. Direct recognition of awareness itself, as distinct from its contents and topics, makes this evident. The clear light of awareness will not be recognizable to minds that cannot comprehend this point.

The way things truly exist is beyond the reach of our conceptual designations. Ideas like "self" and "other" have no basis in Reality. Buddhahood is not an objective to seek. Consciousness itself is the view and goal of Ati Yoga, and non-seeking is the practice. Our meditation is simply a matter of abiding in recognition (of Bodhichitta).

We rest in the nature of mind which, although it is one, appears in many forms and is not some fixed thing. We abide in the natural state, free from any hankering for possession of the One or any of its many appearances, neither visualizing nor seeking. Freedom from the hunger for experience infuses the sacred stillness of our abiding.

Our samadhi and our realization are not compromised by the fact that appearances continue to present themselves to the mind. Whatever the appearance, we do not fixate upon it. The flow of our awareness is like a river wherein there is no possibility for fixed understandings (or perspectives) to arise.

In the sky of mind, there are no thoughts for the intellect to grasp, or understandings to be known or unknown. How then could it be possible to hanker after some kind of "definitive experience?" Freedom from striving is freedom indeed. Anything conceptual is a complication for this, our Ati Yoga Dhyana. Air dissolves in air. What concept of it need be entertained? What practice need be engaged, or what mind-placement, and in what?

The radiance of the Real is uncontrived. We are under no compulsion to fashion something out of the way it shines. The luminosity of the real has no place for contrivance, whether by way of meditation, visualization or other. Intentional practice misses the mark, for there is nothing to be done.

To recognize the nature of mind in every appearance (that arises within our minds) is to be free of contrivance. Appearances are self-arising and self-liberating. We need not interfere. The appearance of every thought is Reality's radiance, and the passing away of thoughts is also the natural way of things. So too, the equanimity of Wisdom dawns in its own time, bringing with it the meditation of effortless equanimity.

Set aside time to meditate in four sessions: early morning, afternoon, twilight and evening. Gradually extend each session. Take care not to upset your health, and if need be, reduce the sessions and take extra care with food should you feel imbalanced.

Settle the mind into a state of steady tranquility, free from the two extremes of agitation and sloth. When the mind is settled, clear, and problem-free, extend the duration of your sessions until they are days or even weeks in length. By trial and error, learn how to develop and sustain a stable abidance in the Wisdom of equality.

The natural state is uncontrived because there is no inclination to think about the details of the appearances that arise in your mind. Arriving at a stage of natural freedom from thinking activity, stabilize the mind by resolving not to revert to any form of conceptual activity whatsoever, except for your studies. Let go of the idea that there are things needing to be done, and avoid the distraction of keeping busy with activities.

A joyful mind will develop, with no need on anyone's part to seek it out. This happens simply by abiding in the natural state. Varied conditions will come and go, some of them seemingly obstructive, but they do not corrupt our samadhi. The pulls and pushes of the external world will in no way dislodge our minds from their rest in the natural poise of our true nature.

We cling to no dharma whatsoever, including the pleasure of meditative absorption. We have no fear of hell or hope for happiness whether it be worldly joy or transcendental delight. There is nothing to reject and nothing to grasp. Our minds are free of seeking, and we abide beyond such notions as self and other, absence and presence and all the rest.

Knowing Reality to be like the sky, we take no interest in forms that can be visualized or in the placement of attention on any dharma (phenomenon) whatsoever. Abiding in equanimity through all contingencies, we entertain no notion that there is anything to be done or undone. Obstructions disappear on their own, and auspiciousness comes unsought.

The Ati view is obscured principally by clinging to the notion of being a separate self. Direct perception of awareness is the essence of our dhyana and continues on unhindered by the varied appearances which arise and self-liberate in the space of the mind. Obstacles to practice clear up by themselves, and we need not wrestle with them. Miracles and wonders will also appear and vanish over time. We neither crave nor reject such things.

Wisdom perfects our samadhi when dhyana (meditative practice) has thoroughly familiarized us with Bodhichitta. Our inborn knowingness is itself the non-conceptual Wisdom of full attainment, and we are all Buddhas primordially. Giving up all other distractions for the sake of this, we abide free of the mind's desires, and come into the fullness of the perfected state.

THE UNFAILING ROYAL INSIGNIA: THE MAGNIFICENT SKY

Primordial Reality affords us no objects which could be a basis for vows. It is like the sky, whether we take vows or not. Knowing this, we may or may not choose to take vows. Either way, Great Perfection is not contradicted, there being nothing to seek and nothing in need of doing. Our way of meditating is not sought, not cultivated, and is beyond any notion of there being objects and objectives with which to be concerned.

We settle our minds in equanimity, but not by way of the mistaken practice of visualization. We do not imagine Primordial Reality to be an object that we could picture to ourselves in our minds. We do not fixate on objects or forms as the basis for striving and seeking a fixed objective. An unmistaken path such as Ati Yoga unfolds naturally in its own way and is neither contrived nor fabricated. Generating and then meditating on conceptual constructs is not the valid approach to enlightenment.

We do not conceive of any entity such as a separate self, or for that matter, a separate deity. We do not engage in notional practices such as non-conceptualization. We are not searching for an invisible Reality on some higher plane. There being primordially no such thing as an entity, what point would there be to such visualizations or indeed to meditations that concern the mind with non-visualization, for that matter?

Our meditation is not founded on conceptual predicates. We do not meditate conceptually, nor do we meditate on non-conceptuality, nor on abiding and non-abiding. We entertain no conceptual designations at all. Primordially, there is nothing whatsoever to which conceptions could attach, or on which visualizations could be developed.

We settle ourselves naturally into concept-free equanimity, and we do not take upon ourselves the burden of active striving. The pristine continuum of Suchness is beyond the domain of the conceptual mind where words and meanings appear and disappear. We do not seek the experience or the form of some special Reality. Rather we rest naturally in the equanimity of primordial awareness, the heart-essence of Vajrasattva. This is a domain beyond conceptuality, a self-illumining, and pristine continuum void of objects to cognize.

Here in the heart of Vajrasattva, it is not as if there are no conceptions, but we refrain from thinking about them. The purity of this continuum permits no such possibility. In the primordial continuum, there is no such thing, as an object which could be contemplated, only our sustained non-distraction in gnosis. Later, when we apply the mind to study, we assimilate the instructions which point unfailingly to the magnificent sky of Bodhichitta.

We do not cling to samadhi, for we have understood the complication which comes from grasping. We do not use the intellect to meditate on the view, nor are we caught up in our own ideas and definitions concerning the nature of Reality. So, for example, we need not picture our mind to be some kind of luminous emptiness or sky-like spaciousness. We need not conceptualize who and what we are in our inmost essence. Nor do we settle into equanimity with some strategic motive in mind, such as avoiding this or that responsibility.

When we cherish fixed beliefs about the way things are and entertain speculations about their true essence and so on, we are going astray. To conceive of emptiness and then meditate on it also misses the mark. All dharmas are mind-only (consciousness). Reality is not to be found among the extremes of our polarized concepts. Self-luminous awareness is alone real. We rely on nothing from the intellect, no lights that we may perceive here or there in any region of the earth, inner or outer.

To conceive of some pure spaciousness like the sky is not necessary. The ultimate view of the great spirit itself entertains no conceptions such as dharmas, persons, meditators and the rest. Impermanence liberates all appearances, and we need not reject them or give them up. There is no such thing as a thing, outwardly, inwardly or anywhere in existence. We have nothing with which to be preoccupied, nor to fear nor to want. All dharmas (phenomena) are equally empty.

Only the self-arising Wisdom of our natural state is true. When controlled by some different mode of consciousness, the pristine flow is obstructed. The Wisdom of enlightenment does not conceptualize. Thus, the true condition remains pristine, authentically present. All dharmas, from the perspective of Wisdom, are identical to the true nature. Awareness and appearances are non-dual. Failure to perceive this means being caught up in conceptuality.

The complications that arise from conceptualizing simply disappear when we abide in the true condition. Clinging to thinking activity brings unhappiness, acquisitiveness, calculation, restlessness and on occasion even extreme elation.

We begin the Ati Yoga meditation-path by sitting in five sessions daily, namely three sessions during the daylight hours and one each at dusk and dawn. When we are adapted to this, we develop a capacity to meditate for half a day, and later on we can sit for a single session lasting for a full day. In this way, we gradually develop our capacity to abide in dhyana.

We enter into a state of equanimity, and abide in a superposition of infinite potential, where there is no compulsion whatsoever to strive or to attain. When tired, we take a break. When we feel unwell, we shorten our sessions and take extra care with our diet. In certain extremes, we may even set aside our practice in order to re-balance, and when we are well again, we gradually re-engage and extend the time of sitting until a single session may last a month or more.

The duration of sessions is dependent on the stability of our experience, and gradually we develop the mountain-like poise of perfect non-distraction. Our diligence is a matter of sustained non-doing underpinned by a non-seeking whose hallmark is to be free of intentionality or strategic motivation of any sort. If there is no doer, then how do striving and seeking make sense, and for whom?

We settle the mind in equanimity, its natural state, until it finally reaches stability. The pristine continuum of awareness is already perfect, as we discover simply by relaxing into tranquility. We find here all virtues, perfections and attainments with no need for anything conceptual. Our personal notions have no place in the immaculate continuity of non-distracted abiding.

The kind of happiness that the mind derives from appearances is an obscuration. So too is a belief in getting results by taking actions. The wish to generate some kind of satisfaction which we can lay hold of and secure (for ourselves, as an achievement) is problematic as can be seen in those who get attached to the bliss of samadhi. Knowing that there is nothing to reject, cultivate or contrive, we come to a dhyana that is free of ulterior motives.

If you ask: "What is the essence of Ati Yoga?" it is this: a naturally arising peace undefiled by contrivance. The freedom of this condition appears in its own way and in its own time, unrelated to our notions or intentions. By following our feelings, we only develop an attachment to the experience of samadhi. Beyond the pulls of hope and the pushes of fear, beyond imaginings, free of contrivance and fabrication, we settle into the natural peace of the true condition, an unceasing flow of Wisdom's Presence.

Vajrasattva offers us no teaching that can be set forth in notions or words, or in such thinking-processes as "This is this", and "That is thus." The peace of existence is beyond verbal formulation or intellectual conceptualization. There is no way that ideas or words can adequately express the nature of Reality, concerning which there is really nothing that can be said. You will never be able to formulate or reveal the nature of Reality by using words. The effort to do so is futile.

THE MIRACULOUS OCCURRENCE OF THE BODHICHITTA

To understand the miracle of the Bodhichitta is to realize and embody original nirvana, the state of full enlightenment. In dependence on our understanding of this tantra, rooted in our practice, we fully penetrate the view and go beyond the need for further study. Our samadhi is itself a superlative practice that requires no thinking and no intentional, directed effort.

The primordially pure awareness of all sentient beings is inherently pure. It needs no refinement, knows no enlightenment and cannot be an object of intellectual understanding. For it, there is no arising or cessation, no worlds or events, no improvements or losses. It is the sky-like singularity of the Bodhichitta itself.

This has always been the blissful abode of all enlightened beings, and the ineffable, supreme Reality of all dharmas. Here, in the sky of Wisdom, the heart is truly happy and has no need of intellectual understandings. The Wisdom of the view shines unimpededly and requires no practice, being beyond intellectual and worldly, or even planetary, domains of experience.

The sincerity of our aspiration determines the quality of our understanding. In this yoga, by virtue of sincerity, we are beyond the poison of doubt, the disease of hesitation and the weakness of divided interests. We have compassion toward all, but our minds take no interest in their worldly concerns. We feel no fear or aversion for bad places and we are not touched by sorrow. We entertain no longing for happiness or worry about its absence. The continuous flow of the light of Wisdom is our effortless and non-intentional practice.

All appearances are instances of the magical presence of the Bodhichitta, the ground where Wisdom's light shines unobstructedly. This self-luminous awareness is the Supreme Being, the great spirit, the authentic Reality of all notional selves. Knowing this, we are not burdened by hopes and fears, or distracted by protracted and distracting searches. We do not wander from place to place. We simply abide in the true condition.

By way of preliminaries, we establish right relation with a wise, spiritual friend and mentor, we request the whispered transmission, we eliminate inner and outer attachments, complete the accumulations and gather whatever practical supports we may require, such as medicines, doctors, special foods and so on. We are determined to clear away any obstructions, enemies, or unfinished business that could be a source of distraction, and we take care in selecting a suitable meditation retreat, not too hot or too old, free of distractions, and pleasant.

In actuality, the real refuge is not a physical location but a state of awareness where things are seen and known as they really are.

All appearances already inhere in, and are not other than, the primordial continuum of being-consciousness. There is nowhere to which we need relocate when we recognize this to be the case.

Failing, however, to understand the real nature of Bodhichitta (pure awareness), people envision an alternate realm and then pursue it. We internalize our notions about Reality and make efforts to settle the mind in some form of congenial experience, hoping or assuming that it corresponds to the view. We conceive of a goal which we deem to be worthy of our expended effort and we strive for success within the framework of our notions. We represent to ourselves that we are not actually visualizing a reified goal, or even non-visualizing it as a form of practice, and we like to believe that we have gone beyond such contrived techniques and desired outcomes.

In the background, we may not have understood that the longing for enlightenment obscures the primordial enlightenment that we already embody. How then can we settle the mind into its true condition?

Those who have arrived at unmistaken comprehension of Garab Dorje's true meaning do not enter into the world of conceptual designations. In nothing whatsoever do the wise ones engage their minds, for they well understand that Ati Yoga dhyana involves no settling of the attention on anything.

In this yoga, there is nothing to reject and nothing to cultivate. The Bodhichitta does not practice intentional (goal-oriented) meditation. The mind of the ultimate view is non-dual, non-conceptual bare awareness itself. There does not exist any such thing as a place into which something else, such as a meditator's mind, could settle. And yet our intellects continue to churn out understandings, thoughts and suppositions, which we need not struggle to hinder, because these too are all woven from the light of Wisdom.

The starting point where most seekers make a beginning is rarely noticed. It is a mistaken idea that the meditator is separate from the goal of meditation. From this a further mistaken notion follows - that effort is needed to get to the experience of Reality.

But what is true of the Bodhichitta is also true for all of us: Reality is non-dual and non-conceptual and requires no striving from anyone. There is thus no need for a contrived dhyana, as all appearances are already composed of the light of Wisdom, inseparable from the awareness which is the meditator's abiding nature primordially.

The equanimity and the spaciousness of the sky do not require fabrication or upkeep on the part of anyone. This natural and un-strategic spaciousness, transcends intellect and offers nothing upon which the thinking mind could settle. Unmoving, uncalculating, it is the primordial abode of our dhyana. Here there is nothing to ponder, nothing to reject nor any such thing as a gain or loss, or anyone to experience either. Where no thoughts arise, how could there be the emergence of a contrived view?

The sky of mind presents nothing that requires improvement or cultivation, avoidance or acceptance. It provides no scriptural validation concerning what is right or wrong, and no byways for deviation. In this, the simplest of approaches, without thought, naturally relaxed and with nothing to contemplate or do, we merely abide. We are not peering into the beyond or hankering for special feelings or visions. We refrain from grasping at what is ineffable or conceptualizing what is by its very nature inconceivable.

The sky of mind does not crystallize into anything that could be a source of hope or consternation. This being the case, we simply sit, relieved of any motive for thinking-activity.

When this becomes our lived experience, then all appearances, both inner and outer, are recognized as waves of the ocean of infinite consciousness. We allow them to appear and self-liberate, knowing that there is nothing to work for, and nothing that needs to be visualized. We simply sit, free of thought, in the luminosity of ever-shifting appearances.

Experience makes clear that the contrivances of our mind are phantasmal. When we outgrow their relevance, we will come to experience the bliss of a samadhi so profound that we will be reluctant to let it go.

But this too will be transcended, until we come to abide beyond all pulls and pushes, all (impermanent) states of consciousness and all dharmas (phenomena). It is the light of Wisdom flowing like a river which is the real doer of all such notional practices. There is nothing for which we need search, no motivation which would lead us to fabricate intentional practices, no tendency to hunger for preferred experiences, or beneficial outcomes.

With nothing whatsoever to do, we simply and naturally abide in though-free spaciousness. We have no desires and no reason to practice austerities. We have no concern about the body or its health, having accepted the body just as it is. We have no fear of being a mind-stream that will be reborn or experience the process of dying, for we have gone beyond hopes and fears and the reach of sorrow.

All of this unfolds naturally and effortlessly from within as a vividly lived experience. That which is real and true reveals itself from the heart, effortlessly, in its own way and its own time.

The truth of our being is primordially enlightened. In this recognition, we release all possibility of striving and all notions of accumulating merit. Our obscurations disappear on their own, even before we are fully familiar with the truth of our being, due to the miraculous Bodhichitta that is the essence of our dhyana. All our doubts are reduced to dust and alchemized into the luster of the wish-fulfilling jewel.

Abiding in the peace of a vast interiority, we know no object of attention. Our senses are empty of their objects, and we neither arrive nor depart from the equanimity of the true condition. We do not think about anything, for we have no goals. Moreover, this inner freedom is stable despite the ever-changing alterations of samsara and nirvana.

That which is true and real is not a multiplicity. It has no parts, perspectives or degrees. It is the unity where explanations converge and dissolve. Its own Reality touches us as a flow of Wisdom, instantly present, though transcending all the thought-forms by means of which we try to figure it forth.

The pristine continuum of ultimate Reality cannot be expressed. In the non-dual, non-conceptual plane of being, we find no way to designate any experience by means of fixed concepts. Although the delight of the natural state cannot be expressed or revealed, we find it to be the ultimate in terms of inherent perfection. We are under no compulsion to objectify what this is all about, and in this there is perfect freedom.

Appearances will continue to arise in the mind, but because of awakened Wisdom we will be free of their implications. For example, we will easily be able to harmonize and balance our practical requirements, and we will not be inclined to think about personal issues and sorrows. We are not pulled or pushed inwardly by a desire to be free or to separate from certain causes of stress. We may have lofty visions, but we are not attached to them. We will not fear demonic influences, but we will have a spontaneous good will towards all. We will not be invested in speech, but we will have dreams, experiences and glimpses that reveal a higher Reality.

When we have no interest in the information that comes to us via our senses, we will find that the portal of supernatural cognition begins to open. Even the so-called obstructions that we may encounter will be seen for what they are, the luminosity of primordial Wisdom. In all that comes to us, we feel no motive to achieve, to repel, to reify or to grasp. In this light we will see that, except for our conceptual designations, the so-called obstructions never actually existed.

What we sought to attain was always there as the very ground of our being. We are thus primordially freed from the need to search within for something we imagined to be missing, like the Wisdom of consciousness-existence.

The essence of our being is already perfect, and fully present with no need to produce, improve, contrive or demonstrate anything whatsoever. This is the heart-transmission of the all-good Garab Dorje. Hold to it as you would your very life.

Summary Perspective

Samten Migdrön (first published in the west in 1974) is considered by many present-day scholars as one of the most important early sources on Ati Yoga to have appeared in the twentieth century. According to traditional accounts, the text was written by gNubs chen Sangs rgyas ye shes (Nubs-chen), who flourished at the end of the ninth and the beginning of the tenth century AD. In Samtan Migdron, Nubs-chen gives us the earliest description we have of Dzogchen as it existed in the eighth and ninth centuries in Tibet. He makes it clear that in Dzogchen:

> [one] does not engage in reasoning, does not examine, does not conceptualize, does not actualize, does not investigate, does not measure; he does not [purposefully] do anything whosoever. Rather, in the manner of non-postulation he posits... in non-knowing he knows, in non-acquirement he acquires, in non-achievement he achieves, in non-seeing he sees, in non-realization he realizes, in non-attainment he attains, in non-visualization he visualizes, and in non-experience he experiences.

Nubs-chen makes the point that even "suchness" is nothing but a label. It is nothing more than a name that should not be grasped or reified.

For a mind confused on this key point, much time and effort could be spent writing down descriptions of spiritual cosmology while missing the essential insight that there is nothing at all that could possibly be grasped by the intellect.

Pristine awareness (Tib: rigpa) is the view. *There is no conceptual reference point that actually exists* in the first, or any other, place. The cosmic Reality cannot be understood using words and narratives. It can only be experienced as identical to the nature of mind in the light of non conceptual Wisdom.

There is wide consensus that Five Early Translations are the Semde texts most likely to have been translated by Vairochana as a result of his time in India with Sri Simha. They are in verse form. Their content is not philosophical but rather focused on direct experience of the nature of mind. These tantras are not concerned with cosmology or with speculation but are focused on the mind of awakening and its realization. In these early translations, intellectual narratives of all stripes are rejected. The recognition and realization of rigpa is placed front and center over and over as the sole concern of the yoga and the point is repeatedly made that this cannot be attained by conceptual thinking or analytical speculation. It is only by direct, personal experience that this can be known, and only direct knowing through experience leads to realization. These works corroborate the point emphasized by Nubs-chen, quoted and commented on above.

Semde writings which remain focused in realization through direct experience come closest to the illumining insights that distinguished Garab Dorje in his own day and age from other masters who followed gradual paths of active striving, or who veered into philosophy and cosmology.

Not all Ati Yoga Source Texts sustain the radical purity of understanding that rigpa alone is the view, practice and goal. Certain early texts that carry Padmasambhava's or Garab Dorje's name by way of attribution turn out to be inconsistent in this decisive characteristic.

THE GREAT TANTRA OF VAJRASATTVA EQUAL TO THE FARTHEST REACHES OF THE SKY

Vairochana's career is closely connected with the religious plans and projects of King Trisong Detsen, who ruled from 755 to 804 AD. When Vairochana was still a young man, the king selected him to travel to India in search of teachings which promised effortless enlightenment within a single lifetime. In India, Vairochana met with Sri Simha, a qualified teacher of what came to be known as Ati Yoga and spent years studying with him. There are two translations which have come down to us from this time, the Manjushri Yamantaka Sadhana and the Great Tantra of Vajrasattva, Equal to the Farthest Reaches of the Sky, which makes this work one of the earliest translations of an Ati Yoga Tantra from Sanskrit to Tibetan.

In many ways this material has features of a Buddhist teaching, with its references to Buddhas, Bodhisattvas and the yanas or vehicles. However, it also has atypical features such as talk of oneness within non-duality, its indications that active practice was unnecessary and its insistence that cause and effect were of no importance. It is therefore a work which, while written in the style of a Sutra and teaching along the lines of Buddhist Dharma also has an unorthodox aspect.

This Tantra makes the claim that certain people may achieve enlightenment just by reading and understanding what it says. ("Understanding" in this context means direct experience and insight, not intellectual comprehension alone.) At certain points, the voice of the author comes through, and Garab Dorje is speaking to the reader directly. One such section is Chapter Twenty, What Is To Come, the opening line of which states: "The Tathagata Vajrasattava proclaimed this Tantra concerning the Great Perfection Bodhicitta which has united with The Furthest Reaches of the Sky in my (Garab Dorje) contemplations." The chapter goes on to describe how this Tantra will fare in history, in particular when it has been translated and taught in barbarian lands by persons of insufficient virtue.

1. Introductory remarks.

Many sections of this work are repetitious and redundant, and I have omitted certain passages of the text which repeat what has already been stated.

In addition, I have inserted a word or two here and there in parenthesis to clarify the meaning. It has been particularly helpful to refer to Christopher Wilkinson's 2015 translation of this work which runs to almost two hundred pages. I have tried to avoid any obscurity of meaning and have made it a point to use the English words and grammar best suited to elucidate the intended meaning, as opposed to the literal words or symbolic language of the ancient Tibetan where the meaning was unclear. There is no attempt to echo the structure or the poetic elements of the original Tibetan, only to deliver a text with as clear a meaning as possible in conventional, colloquial English.

The First Chapter sets the scene.

The Second Chapter begins the teachings:

2. The Arising of Wisdom

In the Great Perfection, contemplation is uncontrived. It is systematic. It bears fruit. We embody just this and express it in a voice beyond dispute.

Consider these three things: the real meaning of material phenomena; a path free of seeking, our eternal heart; and the fruition that comes on its own, not due to seeking or striving.

These three are equal and inseparable but require three different modes of setting forth.

The ground, the way and the goal come about by virtue of a Wisdom that is self-existent (uncaused). This Wisdom brings radiant joy to contemplatives, and the light of clarity to their thoughts.

This Wisdom arises naturally in its own way. It is uncreated and uncontrived, present within us primordially, not encountered or lost. It is inherently perfect. It is an unperturbed clarity, a domain that comes into being on its own, a continuum of tranquility of which we become aware, but which we cannot grasp using (intellectual) conceptions.

It is unobstructedly radiant, an awareness of which we become cognizant and which we come to recognize as the essence of our understandings. It is self-luminous, beyond visualization, not part of any object.

The radiant spaciousness of flawless Wisdom cannot be expressed in words. Beyond thoughts of self or other, it is self-perfected tranquility, utterly free of extreme positions.

Nothing need be generated, and there is no reason to practice deity generation. The heart of enlightenment is uncaused and unceasing.

Where all is one, how could there be differences? In the heart of enlightenment, in clear self-awareness is perfection beyond our seeking and striving. There is no need to generate anything, no requirement for causes and results. In the perfection of the heart's core, all is instantaneously self-perfected.

The true condition has no location and cannot be visualized. Uncontrived, self-originating, beyond conditions, there is nothing about it that has anything to do with a material view of Reality. It has no connection to words, representations or expressions as we can see from our direct experience. We see this from our (firsthand) knowledge arising from familiarization. It bears no relation to the extremes we fall into when using conceptual designations.

There is nothing that can designate it, which places it outside the domain of our intellectual certitude or uncertitude. It cannot be expressed by words and their specific meanings, or meanings arising from letters (of an alphabet).

Right from the beginning, the true nature of our Wisdom has been emptiness. Rejecting no definitions, the clarity of our heart's essence sustains its self-perfection. It is ever perfect in a realm completely removed from the fantasy of our thought-bound minds. It is ever present at all times, come what may.

Present in all appearances, a singleness that is uncompromised, it pierces our preoccupation with appearances, and is far beyond anything that could be the object of our seeking.

Because of its invisible equanimity, whatever we intend appears, and although the true condition is nothing (no thing) whatsoever, it can bring forth the appearance of any thing whatsoever.

Like the radiant heart of the sun, it is beyond measurement, relatedness and comparisons.

The precious jewel of mind itself (consciousness) is intrinsically pure, beyond conceptual designations which we use to take in and grasp appearances.

The heart-essence of our Wisdom, sustaining our knowledge, knows nothing (no thing) at all, yet is aware of its very own intrinsic clarity.

This Wisdom, clear within itself, is inseparable from perfection and as we experience it, comes to us as both appearances and consciousness (the light of awareness).

The abode of self-arising Wisdom is a treasure of (precious) gems, a point of entry for many other portals. Though incomprehensible, if rightly recognized it is an abode where we dwell in oneness.

3. Explanation of the Nine Spaces

The supreme secret of the Bodhichitta is a treasury of jewels with many doors and is to be understood through its radiance. Self-radiant awareness is perfection itself and affords us the possibility and method for discussing the blissful heart-essence. This we can do, as regards results, but with no reference to striving and seeking.

The supreme tantra is not written down and has no relation to form, colour, movement and the rest. It may be called the Greatness that has never been captured in words.

This tantra is vast as the sky, a treasury of all secrets. It alone represents the supremely great perfection that makes it possible for us to abide in our way and realize the stages of enlightenment.

This is the most precious preserve of our contemplation, an all-pervading spaciousness. The secret whispered instructions are all summarized in this, and it gives us the impetus to go beyond our book learning.

When we get involved with vows, techniques, samaya, good works, mandalas, stages and paths and enjoy the results of it all, we are inadvertently cherishing and holding on to the small self. We think of the supreme truth in terms of categories and are bound up in our chosen practices. Everything that we appropriate or renounce in this way constitutes a deviation and an obstruction.

The principal point to understand is that by connecting causes to results we go astray. Reality is non-dual. When we get involved in "this" versus "that", we are going backwards. We break up and misunderstand the essential unity of truth. We strive to build up something pure within the emptiness of the invisible clear light, which is a fundamental contradiction.

The ultimate view is utterly unchained from preoccupations here-below. At the same time, struggling against responsibilities in life is a form of delusion.

There are certain dharmas that complicate our lives and dim down our Wisdom. This jewel of a teaching is free of them. Just know that seeking and striving with notions about purity is a mistaken path.

When we seek and strive, we are separated from the inner treasure of our heart's essence.

* * * * *

The Great Perfection view is self-radiant and quite unconnected to what happens on the various planes. There are limitations obstructing the light of Wisdom, but the clear light of awareness is perfected in and through all of this.

The All-Good is endlessly playful. Inherently perfect, unstoppable awareness arises from its own beingness; so it is that the spontaneous play of our uncontrived heart-essence fills the whole of space, beyond all our concepts of center or perimeter. This play is our practice.

The Wisdom of this awareness dawns on us instantaneously. Your spiritual teacher can clarify the timing of this.

Without any action on our part, the perfection of Wisdom becomes obvious (to us).

The samadhi which arises out of this naturally appearing Wisdom comes about spontaneously and is inherently luminous. When it arises, do not let it be disturbed. It pierces through all forms of seeking and agitation.

* * * * *

Samsara is Wisdom unrecognized. Inconceivable fruition comes to its skylike fullness within samsara. Offering all that we have and are, we melt into the self-originating luminosity of Wisdom. Through our spontaneous self-offering, free of calculation, we taste the blissful radiance of the omniscient.

We are to immerse ourselves in this without hesitation.

It is for this that the most secret and sacred teachings, beyond any form of symbolically expressed meaning, have been transmitted to us.

4. The Precious Jewels that Must Be Known

In the domain of the inherent luminosity of all things, we are perfected.

This transmission comes into play on its own, cutting through aggrandizement and aspersion. It is known as the heart-essence and has no center and no boundaries. It is a condition of conscious equanimity beyond all reference points, like a heap of precious jewels. Radiantly present in all, it has no preferences and no (fixed) positions.

* * * * *

The heart-essence is a treasure, boundless as the sky, a wish-fulfilling jewel that abides in its own pristine space all by itself. One who opens this portal of radiant and complete comprehension will come upon a treasure trove of precious gems.

One who is qualified to teach this Wisdom will use his speaking skills to reveal connections between words and their meanings. He will be a master at conveying (true) meanings through (verbal and non-verbal) symbols. He inwardly abides in a domain (of consciousness) that transcends conceptual designations. His intuition is all-pervading like space. His Wisdom encompasses that which is without center or boundary. His is the power of transmission of a contemplation that transcends words (and concepts).

Upon meeting such a one, you will have confidence. His self-awareness is radiant, and his presence manifests it. In transmitting the light of Wisdom, he simultaneously manifests it to himself.

The precondition for our growth in understanding is a transmission that shines light on our learning, our meditation and our contemplation. Its source is the self-arising light of Wisdom, the luminous awareness that grows within us. It is an inexhaustible treasure, a magic treasury of priceless jewels. Now is the occasion to possess the key which opens any spiritual path (you may choose). This Wisdom encompasses all the particulars of the various teachings and paths.

* * * * *

There is a self-arisen continuum that has no location and no boundaries, a unitary perfection of non-dual awareness. This glowing treasure of the mandala of awareness is unaffected by our notions. It reveals its full perfection in our field of experience in the beatitude of unperturbed samadhi. Abiding in an equanimity that transcends complexity and contrivance, we have let go of our grasping at duality's appearances. Primordially we are liberated from thoughts that cling to reference points and preferences. Here in the luminosity of our heart's core, we are liberated from any cherishing of opinions concerning meditation, non-meditation (and so on).

The flawless transmission of radiant insight pierces through notions based in dualities. In manifesting the unspeakable light of awareness, we relinquish our notions about speech and silence.

This luminous Wisdom is a unique treasure that harbours no intellectual opinions. The eye of Wisdom has no dualistic knowledge and does not see in terms of duality. It arises in the heart's inmost intent (for our lives), something we cannot lay hold of by thinking. Being the treasure of all that is, it has no intellectual views or preferences.

The nondual nature of Reality overwhelms our predilection for seeking and active practices.

Unconcerned with what transpires here-below, awareness is pristine in its own space of being. The light and the appearance of everything (that appears) unfolds within our awareness. Like the stars in the sky, self-luminous, undefiled, it is perfect in its own domain.

Vajrasattva is (in Reality) a continuum of (pure) uncontrived awareness. Come to firsthand knowledge of the joy that comes untrammeled, free of complexity, unrelated to causes and conditions.

Make no attempt to visualize the clear light of pristine awareness. It is precious equanimity that abides beyond agitation and grasping. This treasure, this fullness, this self-radiant (inner) sun abides in all. It is a continuum that has no connection to our thoughts and notions.

5. The Nine Treasuries Jewel Treasure

In general, the non-dual truth is expressed in a distorted and diminished manner, and this veils it in obscuration. It is a perfect circularity, undistorted, in which samsara and nirvana have never actually transpired. In the heart of enlightenment, samsara and sorrow are merely the play of the All Good (Samantabhadra), and the five poisons of lust, aversion, dullness, arrogance and jealousy reveal themselves as five Wisdoms.

Wisdom is all-pervading like the light of the sun. It is an all-healing flow of compassion that washes away our five defilements.

The realm of the Great Perfection is an inherently luminous and mirror-like space that has no objects. Within the clear light of the true condition, the non-dual Reality will reflect itself to us in just the way we see and think about it. Our notions about the true condition are always too inflated or too circumscribed, but it is always beyond these distortions. Being infinite, it always transcends the material perspective from which we conceptualize.

Pristine awareness is utterly transparent. This inherently luminous awareness is undefiled, un-adulterated (by our notions). This treasure of equanimity has no relation whatsoever to any point of reference that we could conceptualize, and exists as it actually is, unadulterated regardless of whether we turn to it or not.

Our human happiness and our human sorrows are both confusions of samsara. They are non-dual in their true condition and perfected in the light of our heart's Wisdom.

Whether we know it or not, we abide in the sphere of inherently luminous awareness and are continuously perfected. The Ground of Being is unmanifest, but the clear light of Wisdom that unfolds from it is a ninefold treasury of gemlike spaces that shines in our hearts. The perfection of awareness abides in this treasury, a store of precious wish-fulfilling jewels that blesses us and brings us all fulfillment.

It is the treasury of the sky, unobstructed, wherein the five elements arise and move, actively present in all things, not inherently real, but emanating from the Reality of their source. It cannot be seen, for it is inherent luminosity, pure like the sky, an unobstructed flow of blessings. It unifies all into its innate clear light. It is the treasury of all blessings, the very nature of the Dharma's manifestation.

There is nothing that needs to be done. Everything has already been accomplished, primordially. Beneficent energies flow from the inherent luminosity where nothing needs doing, and this efficacious flow (of good works) is self-effulgent, making no demand that we renounce anything whatsoever.

6. Analogies Regarding Awareness

The enlightened beings are the lords of the treasury of the sky, the treasure-store that brings us total fulfilment. They abide in continuous recognition of their eternal nature, but in their thoughts words and actions they participate in the play of energies which is the cosmic flow.

Within the sky of infinite consciousness, the heart of our hearts that has no center or border, appearances will arise and appear to us in just the way we think of them.

Living in right relation to their spiritual master, those who with heartfelt sincerity devote their awareness to the jewel in the heart (of Reality) will fulfil the requirements of service and be introduced directly to the treasure of treasures.

Gradually learning the true meanings behind the symbols, they will be introduced by the master to instant enlightenment, the timeless continuum (of being-consciousness). In the realm of pure consciousness beyond their exaggerated or limiting ideas, they will come face to face with non-conceptual inherently luminous awareness.

We fabricate the concepts which fill our minds in order to designate and grasp the utter simplicity of the true condition. When we abide in the light of Wisdom, however, the obscurations of our limiting notions melt away and our innate clarity is uncovered. We no longer need to approach truth through the fog of definitions and grammar. We know the meanings behind the symbols. In the heart of luminous Wisdom, we abide in clarity, free of concepts.

* * * * *

In this spacious domain which is the origin of all that appears, beyond any association with meditation, we are perfected.

We abide in luminous awareness, untroubled by (the stress of) contraction or (the thrill of) expansion. We cut through (trekcho) concepts about this pristine luminosity. It is not something we ponder, nor has it any association with material things. The light of Wisdom shines with no points of reference and no preferences. Inconceivable are the blessings of this clear light.

Fortunate ones are able to abide in the samadhi of (infinite) luminous Wisdom, the awareness of totality which dissolves aversion and ill-will, dullness and craving, pride and jealousy.

The delight of the single taste in all appearances enters into our every experience by way of a Dharma requiring no practice or comprehension. We are not required to think. Our evenly balanced mind need not search. In the clear light (of Wisdom), in the heart of the sky (of awareness), we come to know the true significance of what could never be expressed in written words.

The significance of uncontrived pristine awareness cannot be unraveled by means of concepts and narratives.

There are no reference points or predilections in pristine awareness. Its equality is equal in all. Its equanimity can appear as any form whatsoever. However things may appear to our human minds, there is no such thing as a "this" or a "that" for pure (non-conceptual) awareness.

A true teacher is a living embodiment of Vajrasattva. The magic of his words is a lamp revealing to us the awareness (that is our true nature). He opens the doorway of the precious treasury of jewels that he carries in his heart, revealing the meanings of the symbols of the ineffable. He brings us to planes of inner experience that we arrive at without going anywhere (outwardly). He reveals a deathless manifestation of the Dharma.

He conveys to us the secret Wisdom by a form of awareness that has no need of sounds, placing us in the sunlit radiance (of the true condition). He brings us to a realization that is not the outcome of any seeking or active striving.

Such teachings as these should be given only to those of enlightened attitude and never to the naturally evil, the ignorant or the disdainful.

7. Empowerment Revealing The True Meanings

This Tantra Equal To The Farthest Reach Of The Sky, is an elixir which carries you into the heart-space of the Great Perfection. Here, you possess a treasure which is as vast as the kingdom of the sky. Its meaning is not fixed and cannot be grasped conceptually by way of thoughts or ruminations. Nor does it have any relation to any form of active practice.

Awareness abides in a realm that is utterly uncontrived and imponderable. This is nothing that we need to reflect on or practice, and there is no need to visualize any special levels (of practice, or attainment) either. (Be clear on this point): the intellect is not to conceptualize or grasp with words.

Uncontrived awareness is the way we engage the Wisdom that transcends all obscurations. We abide naturally in a continuum of awareness where there is no searching and nothing to do. This awareness, something that we do not try to search for or grasp, is that into which we enter. We do not see awareness as a goal to attain. We simply settle into a consciousness of uncontrived light, not following methodologies or seeking for any (specific) objective.

The intrinsic radiance (of Wisdom) is flawless. Free from self-centered thoughts or considerations, it seeks no designated results. It is clear light, completely beyond (any notion of) desired outcomes. All-inclusive, it is not something which can be visualized. Here, in this pure space, the hopes and fears we typically cherish are present no longer.

8. The Intrinsic Radiance of Awareness

Wisdom shows us that all appearances are free from the imputations of our concepts. All appearances are luminous and beyond defilements.

Wisdom makes clear the singularity that underpins the multiplicity of appearances. It frees us from grasping and from thinking in terms of "things".

In the nonduality of the true condition we are liberated from the mental conditioning created by our concepts.

All appearances arise spontaneously in the mirrorlike luminosity which is the nature of mind. This Reality is utterly unfabricated. Here, we abide in an undistorted continuum of awareness that is inherently radiant, uncontrived and pristine, like the sky.

The domain of primordial purity is skylike (in its spaciousness), beyond (intentional) abiding, inherently radiant, a non-dual way with no boundaries or center. It is pristine awareness beyond fixations, a crystal palace of utterly clear light beyond anyone's capacity to describe or measure. With no need to conceptualize or take any actions, we have the ultimate proof of a pure manifestation of timeless awareness.

Indescribable, inherently radiant and all-pervasive, the ineffable continuum has no conceptual activity. It requires no active striving, and is luminous in all possible ways.

Pristine awareness neither contrives nor fabricates. It does not seek or grasp. It is spacious and luminous equanimity, total lucidity with no need for active striving on our part.

The Reality of inherently radiant awareness cannot be (indicated or) represented (to the human mind) by way of words or concepts. It can come through transmission, but never by explication, and (when it comes) it carries the taste of bliss. We take leave of the many palaces built up from awareness to abide eternally in the clear light itself, something quite impossible to define.

The self-transmission of Wisdom's light cannot be distorted by playing it up or playing it down. We accept what is, the way it is, with no attempt at manipulation.

Once we have direct experience of the nature of mind (Bodhicitta), we will be wary of any attempt to define it. We would never dream of trying to actively practice it. We choose rather the way of non-striving. We simply allow the true condition to dawn by itself without interference.

We do not conceptualize nirvana and then strive for it or entertain notions that foster samsara. Our liberated intellect abides in a luminous samadhi that has no horizon. Being undistracted, we pay no regard to anything that comes and goes, arising only to disappear. The bounteous power of our uncontrived heart-essence outshines all other preoccupations, drawing (us) into the light of the sun.

Samsara is simply the play of the light that is Wisdom. We make no effort to accrue merit or expunge negative karma, or to fabricate desired outcomes in the way that goldsmiths do when they shape objects out of gold.

We are like birds abiding in the vastness of the sky, happy to navigate the ups and downs of samsara and its magical illusions, not apart from the continuum of the true nature.

Inconceivable is the power of the light of the divine. The radiance of Wisdom is constant, beyond alteration, beyond coming and going. The light of compassion equally is beyond all reckoning in its scope.

The wind of thinking activity is nowhere to be found in the luminous continuum of Wisdom. Wisdom knows no bondage and requires no liberation.

Just as an oil lamp without fuel does not generate fire, a mind that is concept-free is not engaged in thinking activity. We are free of ideation. We do not reflect on any topic. This is nothing special, just the way that Wisdom is.

When we give voice to some topic of concern within the sky (of mind), we have set foot on a false path.

The mind of equanimity has no interest in boundaries, centers or designated areas. The essence of our hearts comes to the fore as the sun of Wisdom dawns and in the treasury of self-revealing awareness it achieves its perfect expression.

Non-dual awareness is the sole instrument by which we grow into that which cannot be grasped. Non-dual living is like water flowing into water.

Samsara is actually Wisdom (that we misperceive), free of darkness or constriction primordially. The sun of radiant Wisdom burns away samsara and pervades all that is. This is not something to be visualized. It is not a dogma to be grasped or believed. It is simply the true condition of all that appears.

The highest Reality cannot be apprehended by points of view or anyone's preferred notions. There is nothing fixed in any fashion whatsoever in the way that Reality actually exists, contrived or uncontrived, centerless and borderless, neither in this location nor in that, but rather abiding in its own realm, an uncontrived ground of (supreme) peace.

This primordial equanimity does not conceptualize emptiness or its opposite. The furthest reach of thought is transcendence of thinking activity altogether. Wisdom cannot be reproached for having no center, boundary or demarcation.

The obscurations of ignorance have never existed (in actuality). Nothing is outside the mandala of radiant Wisdom. The world of the all-good, the continuum of pristine awareness, is not anything (any discreet thing) whatsoever. It is ceaseless, unstoppable, imponderable, beyond anything that can be contemplated or studied.

We abide in the state of self-liberation, uncontrived supreme mind, not focusing or opening our minds, at rest in the depths of a samadhi that naturally overflows with fullness.

Not material in nature, it (the true condition) *seems* to become and may *appear to be* any material thing.

9. Obscuration

The clear light of Wisdom, inherently radiant awareness, is present in both enlightened and samsaric beings primordially, as in all else. It is not any specific thing whatsoever. It transcends any and every Reality knowable by our minds. It is beyond flux, free of concepts, this radiant essence of our hearts' Wisdom.

The inherently shining Wisdom of enlightened beings may be understood or misunderstood, and although we cannot construe such things rightly, we do reflect on them, and they may have their value for the purposes of our training. But they lack the power of intrinsically luminous awareness, and they entail a vast number of specific perspectives concerning the transcendent and the mundane. The truth is, however, that all these are taken up in clear light awareness.

Lacking the full force of the light of awareness, the misguided paths conceptualize the Reality or unreality of a (personal) self, a creator God and all the rest. We are free of all this.

If we begin to distinguish vice from virtue, we end up with obligations to assume and flaws to purify. We become unclear about the highest good. Those who believe in levels and degrees of what is higher and what is lower have good reason to become tired of it all. It all becomes infantile, tiresome and pointless.

Such seekers are interested in topics like the meaning of non-duality, the three eons, the study of the ten stages, the five paths and the (various) perfections. They cherish dualistic ideas about purifying this and generating that. They have a certain (limited) attainment, but they never go all the way. They never realize the inherently luminous, the non-dual, true condition.

There are those who practice sequences of blessings, visualizations, ceremonies, mandalas and recitations. Their conceptualizing obscures the truth of inherent radiance, which is self-occurring, not the result of such (contrived) causes. They define Wisdom using the language of beginning and ending, contrary to the actuality of Wisdom's self-appearing nature.

Regarding the light of Wisdom, the all-pervading essence in all appearances: being preoccupied with things that are in flux is a path of delusion. Self-radiant Wisdom does not require us to purify the three worlds or to alter the natural processes of dilating, contracting or obstructing. There is no need to generate a deity out of the unborn enlightened heart-essence.

In and through all their active practices, such as pranayama, opening the three channels (*ida, pingala, sushumna*) and closing them, they fail to recognize the clear light of Wisdom. It is all contrivance, and a flawed pathway.

With true understanding comes a melding of thought, word and action into a continuum of non-dual clarity. Once the light of the heart comes to the fore, we abide in the core of our being, and the breath, and all the rest, are liberated effortlessly and spontaneously into the domain of all-pervading Wisdom.

The activity of seeking will never arrive at the actuality of inherent radiance. To cherish duality while cultivating the non-dual is a flawed approach, as is the idea of moving forward within the state of self-arisen luminosity (Wisdom-light). To find that which is beyond causes and conditions but take an interest in further causes and yet further results or having reached an uncontrived consciousness to go on fabricating and grasping - these are mistaken ways. All of these confuse the significance of Wisdom and sustain our immersion in samsara. We abide in the light that subsumes and pervades all appearances, no matter where we look. Here, we are beyond the grasping that is part of worldly involvements.

Awareness is instantly present with no need of active practice on our part. This is the Reality of perfect clarity. This is the perfection that is (limpid) awareness.

We need not make efforts to change objects or our understanding. The self-luminous Wisdom in which we abide has no relation to the practice of visualizing or the impulse to grasp. True contact with the natural continuum comes in an instant with no need for contrivance. The ground of abiding lies within. We have only to cut through the appearances that obscure our mind's innate clarity.

10. The Perfect Treasure

The Reality of Bodhicitta is self-evident. The magnificence of non-dual Wisdom is to be found in awareness, where its presence is self-evident. Once we have let go of conceptual activity, we embody what this signifies. Normally, we distinguish "real" things from thoughts, and the way we teach reflects this. Seeing Reality in two different ways is no part of the Wisdom of awareness.

When we let go of fabricated forms of yoga practice, we are at peace in the self-perfected spaciousness of pristine awareness. Our natural and true abode is the utter simplicity of awareness itself. The teaching it continually imparts is that of an inherently luminous mirror, but from a time-space continuum we cannot even imagine its actuality. Being inherent radiance itself, the (perfect treasure) which is awareness includes all composite phenomena.

The treasure which is awareness does not alter. It is not a static perfection, but this cannot be known until thought is transcended.

Our real teacher is the self-revealing clear light of Wisdom, which we call Vajrasattva, the Lord of Dharma. This essentially indescribable awareness reveals to us the dharma-Wisdom that transcends the fluctuations of impermanence.

Vajrasattva's pure blessings flow in all directions, an unspoken revelation of the true condition, naturally luminous awareness. We recognize the truth of our being in light of this Wisdom, the self-revealing radiance of awareness. This comes to us as a powerful realization: all appearances are nothing but the heart's jewel of Wisdom. Everything is the energetic play (retinue, ornamentation) of Bodhichitta.

The luminous presence of awareness encompasses all spaces within the singularity of non-dual Reality. There are no phenomena that appear outside or apart from the non-dual light of the true nature.

The core teaching is the essential Wisdom-light nature of all phenomena (appearances). This light is a space beyond change, beyond admixture and beyond contrivance.

This supremely lucid knowledge does not involve information about any specific phenomenon. It is in this way that we have direct knowledge of self-revealing Wisdom.

At the time when our awareness settles into tranquility, we do not stray from the light of Wisdom. At this time, we clearly recognize that equanimity is identical to liberation. There is only the non-dual, no "this" or "that".

No matter how sentient beings follow false paths, all of them are attending to Bodhicitta and are united in the self-revealing, un-fabricated light of Wisdom.

When we have assimilated the essence of this secret Wisdom, we come to know that the way appearances appear is just what they really are. The light whereby all appearances appear is not something to think about or debate. It is like the sky, like compassion, not to be grasped by our conceptual consciousness.

Clear light is the teacher and the teaching. Clear light is the listening audience and the scribe, self-radiant, indwelling, nothing graspable at all. Thus spoke Vajrasattva, the Lord of Secrets.

11. Seeing the Clear Light of Wisdom

Wisdom is self-originating, not dependent on causes or on conditions. Its radiance is primordially self-manifesting. It is not a thing. Yet it shines in all and is at work (play) in all, a compassionate flow with no reference points and no tendency to grasp at fixations. It does not think.

It is the ultimate bliss of the body-mind, transporting consciousness to a place of all-pervasive awareness. This luminous Wisdom is not an intellectual view. It knows no objects, is utterly uncomplicated, arises by itself and simply is as it is.

Pristine awareness is unrelated to our thoughts. It does not conceptualize and is not concerned with worldly matters. Abiding as it does in awareness of its own being, all of this is known inherently.

The natural way things are is uncontrived. Whatever our thoughts, whether they grasp at matters abstruse or mundane, be they calculations or explications, these thoughts (in their essence) are spacious, pristine light. Ours is not a yoga of seeking and conceptualizing. That which is self-originating cannot be captured in a net of words. Regardless of how it is considered, it is a clarity that cannot be visualized. We do not use origin narratives or (practical) applications in this yoga to conceptualize the way things exist. The eye of Wisdom does not have a conceptual view and does not see as the conceptual mind does.

In all that appears, be it various desires or objects or cravings or animosities, nothing but mind is actually in play. It is not these appearances and yet it is not other than these appearances.

The perfection of the indestructible light (Bodhichitta) is perfectly recognized in an instant, but not gradually generated. The stages through which our understandings develop are all misrepresentations and deceive us.

Ineffable awareness is the ultimate invisible phenomenon. It is beyond being graspable by thought or attainable by active practices. We cannot conceptualize or define that which is utterly simple.

Concerning the various phenomena that appear to us in this world, they never actually come into a condition of truly existing. While appearing, their real nature transcends thought and practices. In the end, they do not have any self-nature or individual identity.

It is evident that self-sprung awareness manifests and embodies itself, whether in ethereal or physical forms. Its playfulness can be seen in its embodiments, but its actuality as the clear light of Wisdom cannot be expressed in words, even words about clarity, emptiness and consciousness. It is beyond representation in any language however excellent or mediocre.

To be free from conceptual grasping is the way to be undeceived. Neither by visualizations nor definitions can suchness be expressed.

There are unspoken forms of communication that illumine the entire scope of manifestation. The playfulness of Wisdom may take the form of sounds and speech, but thoughts and memories of the kind we experience do not actually see what is ultimately real. The luminous true condition (Bodhicitta) does not ponder anything and entertains no conceptual designations. When we recognize the inner luminosity of all things, our perception changes to joy. None of them are "things"; there is no such thing as a thing. They are all light, and we are on the path of the bliss of clear light.

The heart of bliss encompasses all appearances but has no connection at all with (our notions about) things, or the multiplicity of things. The heart of bliss does not dwell in isolation but is radiantly all-pervading with accommodation for all.

Within the mandala of Wisdom, the light is all-pervading. The lamp of awareness is naturally free of obscurity and has no need of seeking. It lights our way within this mandala where we are unable to see or to visualize, and we abide therein with undistracted minds.

All appearances are the luminosity of awareness, the primordially enlightened state that pierces the veils of obscurity. There is no need to search out causes and conditions.

There is nothing to grasp, no view (that thoughts can grasp), nothing for which to search, only uncontrived abiding, thought-free and beyond the feelings that arise from visualization.

12. Points of Practice

Dualistic notions are irrelevant as regards non-dual Wisdom. But to open a door, or suggest an approach, they have their use, and so they will be used here to illuminate the practice.

The vast spaciousness of the sky is a ceaselessly sustained practice for those who can recognize it, overflowing with compassionate blessings and virtues as numberless as the sky is wide. For them, uncontrived luminosity is the way. They have no use for the defilements that arise from cherishing concepts.

The Bodhicitta has no beginning in measured time and is not an object which can be grasped or worked with. There are no minds capable of conceptualizing and laying hold of its mysteries. To practice the immutable clarity (vajra) of the sky, we must let go of thinking activity. We contemplate no topic whatsoever. By our effortless equanimity, we are primordially relieved of the defilement of grasping.

Within the Wisdom of pristine clear light, there is no such thing as a thing, only all-pervading, luminous clarity. It is a domain of bliss, but we make no attempt to appropriate it. This realm is not something to be sought. Self-arising awareness continuously transcends itself. It is unmoved. It does not conceptualize. It has no dwelling place, no reference points or inclinations and our points of view and opinions are erased (in its presence).

It is like the sky, spaciousness that cannot be grasped. It is non-conceptual, not to be visualized, not to be referenced and not any form of existence we could know conceptually. It does not concentrate on objects, is not a form of comprehension, is not complex, and our practice does not involve an attempt to grasp or possess it. It is non-dual.

In this dimension, all appearances are Wisdom coming face to face with itself, a thing neither sought nor terminated.

If we do not abide in the light of Wisdom (Bodhicitta) it will matter not which practices we perform, all we see will be our own level of consciousness. There are no traps in the supreme bliss of unsought rigpa.

Pristine awareness is not a path to be traversed by a traveler. It is primordial enlightenment; it is Wisdom beyond points of reference and beyond leanings. Its essence is non-dual.

There is no possibility of conceptually grasping a duality, or even a unity in the great bliss of all-pervading light.

The limitation of being alone is simply not there. In the indestructible spaciousness of the boundless sky (of mind), timeless Wisdom is naturally and radiantly present, uncontrived, unsought, unconnected, evident in all appearances, not seeking, beyond origination or any practice. Being radiant presence in its own realm, it is pristine awareness, the supreme Reality.

The nameless Wisdom of pure awareness cannot be understood by those who are driven by their desires. Some, (even) having experienced this Bodhicitta directly, use their stream of thinking activity to obscure this self-risen non-conceptual continuum, with talk of transmission, consciousness and insight.

Our conventional consciousness does not dwell in (recognition of) the bliss of clear-light rigpa. Although sharing our impressions and thoughts about the Dharma may help make the true nature clear (to the ordinary mind), it is the true nature itself which is the doer of samadhi and it is this which effects the realization of the Bodhicitta.

This is our real treasure, the equanimity of pristine awareness. Here we see the real nature of the liberated state, the heart of primordial nature as it is, uncontrived.

Self-luminous awareness is all-encompassing and indescribable. Its transmission lights up all things. It does not reflect on itself but seems to exude a wonderful playfulness.

We do not grasp at the significance of awareness conceptually. We know it directly by entering into equanimity. We do not ponder our conceptual designations. We leave behind our notions about things. This is key to our whole approach.

When we abide in the heart essence, we leave appearances un-conceptualized. Self-originating awareness, in its way of existing, and the Wisdom that conceives of no objects render this evident.

We do not cherish any memories, nor do we apply our awareness and Wisdom (to get results). We regard the many definitions and explanations on this subject as being the light of Wisdom. This light infuses our unperturbed contemplation.

The Reality of uncontrived Wisdom will appear to us according to how we look at it. Whatever appearances arise in the mind are all self-liberating, leaving only the non-dual, blissful awareness.

Those who cherish fixed ideas about the true condition, whether it is regarding origins or whether it is ideas about no origins, will experience the dimming of the light of Wisdom. To be mired in their concepts in this way is like being stuck in mud. The Wisdom-light of non-dual suchness is everywhere evident but is not to be found in our intellectual grasping or our passion for fixed ideas. To claim that the ground of being and the conceptual world of our minds are dual is to be on the path that goes nowhere. There is no such duality. Those who conceptualize everything are caught up in extremes and descend into samsara.

The Wisdom wherein all is self-luminous entertains no concepts about polarities or dualities. The radiance of its blessings flows like sunlight, not coming and going, but rather in a way that is all-encompassing and all-pervasive.

The ceaseless flow of blessings, inconceivable to our limited minds, is divine compassion. These blessings bring assistance and beneficial accomplishments, and these blessings are the evidence of great compassion in action.

Our method is simply to maintain recognition of clear light awareness. We do not fabricate or contrive. The superior dharma of pristine awareness is our only method, our single practice. This makes it possible to recognize samsara as Wisdom, to be uncontrived, and to be inseparable from bliss.

The light of Wisdom is our practice. Any action flowing from this will appear as the Bodhicitta (mind of awakening). Without seeking it, we will embody the way of clear light.

We will arrive at the true knowledge of luminous Wisdom. We will understand how samsara is the way of enlightenment. We will be filled with the illumination of Wisdom. Without our seeking them, blessings will come to us of their own accord. We will be the keepers of the treasure of the sky realm and abide in the self-radiance of the true condition. We will make use of conscious compassion, all-pervasive like the sky and everywhere present. Without effort or striving, we will be embodiments of equanimity and ascend to the plane of the enlightened masters.

We surpass the ascending planes of consciousness in an instant, with no need to traverse them (sequentially). The path of pure awakeness stands distinct from our discussions of paths with graduated stages. Material appearances are the effulgent self-display of Wisdom, and there is no pathworking of levels and stages.

If we make connections between the unknowable and the things we consider knowable, it is to afford guidance and a way for those who are alive, for whom the pristine continuum is not yet evident.

Although the uncontrived treasure of the heart is primordially pristine, not everyone finds it.

13. Luminosity

The uncontrived consciousness of pure awareness is an immutable treasure, naturally evident. This radiant clear light of sovereign awareness runs through all sentient existence, within and without. The spaciousness of the sky accommodates the appearance of all. In the precious state of awareness abiding in itself (samadhi), the supreme empowerment comes to perfection. Empowerment ripens into the perfect clarity of Wisdom, but without direct introduction (to Bodhichitta), regardless how or why one seeks, there is no freedom from the shackles of samsara.

Reveal the nature of the unborn awareness only to fit recipients, those who will immerse themselves in the true condition, the continuum of clear-light Wisdom, not more than two, concerning whom you should have no doubts, having determined with certainty their capacity to persevere and be Victorious.

In the vision of Wisdom there is no grasping at anything whatsoever. The complications of extreme views are shattered. Those who cherish ideas, whether gross or refined, will not recognize the all-pervading luminosity of the mind of awakening.

That which radiates into all that appears is all that there is. We do not conceptualize and we do not seek an objective. Whatever our way of life, we are happy. We do not rely on structured teachings. We do not hanker for special experiences. We abide in the atmosphere of clear-light contentment.

The nectar of infinitely spacious awareness has the sweetest savour of all. Drawing down the powers of the hidden light, we apply ourselves and with an approach free of expectations we feel no need to grasp at the meaning of the wind of Wisdom.

14. Investiture

Recognition (of Bodhicitta) is the basis of the path. The light of intrinsically present Wisdom accomplishes the most perfect empowerment. Transmission of the perfect luminosity of awareness takes place because it is naturally something that flows. The recipient, his virtues and his difficulties, are all nothing but this inherently luminous awareness.

Some (practitioners) are rooted in their conceptions and memories; some are motivated to be of service to sentient beings; some abide in awareness beyond seeking, and for each we use a different approach (to transmission).

The transmission which comes about spontaneously is not (intentionally) imparted and not (deliberately) received. It is like water dissolving into water. Placing ourselves in the natural state, we receive the transmission of our spiritual master's contemplation.

The enlightened beings of all the ages have imparted the Bodhicitta in this way, giving them comprehension of an indescribable inspiration, awareness-empowerment, sovereign anointing, something reserved only for respectful students fit to receive it, students who by their virtues will live naturally in the great bliss of clear light.

The recipient of such empowerment is liberated from seeking and shines in the radiance of pure awareness, lotus-like, undefiled by karma or karmic habits.

We are fully confident of this all-surpassing Wisdom like the spacious clarity of the sky above, beyond clinging. We enter into this luminescent Wisdom's spaciousness where rays of light like those of the sun enfold us.

15. Awareness – Joy

The idea of protecting or purifying pristine awareness is a backward perspective. Radiant Wisdom is perfect in its excellence and is in no need of protection.

Non-dual awareness dawns on us through a process of being unsought and uncontrived and is a treasure that neither comes to us nor separates from us. A self-luminous light, it requires no transcendence from us. It is the One, an all-pervading clear light that includes all that appears (to our mind and senses). It is not a particular thing, but rather an all-pervasive (clear light) continuum.

We become one with this Wisdom, this supreme awareness beyond duality. We do not cherish the thoughts we have, arising from our desires. In fact, we have no thoughts at all because in this equanimity there are no reference points from which a thought could arise.

In this thought-free continuum of non-dual awareness, our desire-tinged concepts are not to be retained, and we do not use words or concepts for the sake of practicing or seeking.

The essence of indescribable awareness is nothing whatsoever, not light or anything we can express. It has no definition and is indefinable, this all-pervasive, self-originating spaciousness which is thought-free pristine awareness. Its transmission comes about through non-dual, naturally arising equanimity. This is beyond reckoning. The effort to measure or evaluate it is like trying to find some place where the sky comes to an end.

Samaya or protecting our vows, has no standing, for the Wisdom of awareness is beyond any constructions formulated by words. When we try to superimpose limitations on the sun of self-originating Wisdom, we revert to obscuration.

In the continuum that is inherently self-perfected, there is no seeking and nothing to find by seeking. Such an approach is meaningless. Anything we seek on the basis of words, concepts and views leads only to more notions and explanations and subverts the true Dharma.

It should be glaringly obvious that non-dual Wisdom transcends conceptual grasping. In the continuum of pristine awareness where there are no points of reference and nothing to like or dislike, everything is already self-perfected, and completely beyond the limited conjectures to which we subscribe.

Speaking in terms of existence or non-existence means super-imposing our own notions and conjectures on Wisdom itself, a Reality that is altogether unlimited.

When you abide constantly in the transmission of Wisdom's luminosity, your entire frame of reference will clarify and your Wisdom will be transparently clear.

The primordially enlightened condition is inherently radiant and non-conceptual, beyond positions and preferences. Although universally present, it is nothing whatsoever. Our awareness abides in a domain of intrinsic clarity.

There is no way that we can comprehend the transmission of inherently radiant bliss. For us, the normal experience is a sense that we are unfulfilled. We do not have a fixed point of view concerning awareness or declare it to be 'such and such'. There is no sound argument against this, so we are not at risk of being contradicted.

The abode of awareness is clear light. No Dharmas exist except for this. It is thus impossible to go contrary to non-existent protocols. The Wisdom of pristine awareness has no creed or code of behaviour to cherish. A conceptual viewpoint will not reveal the supreme Wisdom that has no frame of reference. The continuum of pure awareness is inconceivable, in no way limited, all encompassing, abiding in equanimity which cannot be discovered by active seeking. It could never be an object or an objective of our conceptual grasping or our active spiritual practices. Concepts like "the one" and "the many" refer to what simply does not exist. Only the Wisdom of uncontrived awareness can make clear the dharma which has no boundaries or center.

There are numberless teachings set forth in words, but no matter how they are organized, there is only one Reality, one truth, to which they refer. This frees us from protecting and practicing specific codes of behavior.

Equanimity is the key to right understanding. Without searching, we receive the transmission of Wisdom's radiant jewels in our direct experience.

Samsara and the heart-essence of clear-light Wisdom are non-dual. This recognition blazes forth in a single instant, without working through the graded levels (of the various teachings). This insight reveals what has been spontaneously present and inherently perfect primordially.

All-knowing awareness radiantly shines in the light of all-pervading Wisdom. Where could we find anything that needs to be renounced? What is the difference between Buddhas and samsaric sentient beings? From the perspective of Wisdom, none! What is the point of study, contemplation and the cultivation of knowledge? We see none whatsoever. What can be said?

Suchness is not a Wisdom that is other than ignorance. If there were some kind of darkness that had the power to obscure the light of Wisdom, it would condemn the enlightened ones to samsara with no hope of escape.

However, those who seek out knowledge while relying on conceptual reference points do not understand the meaning of a true condition beyond conceptual designations, and because they see differently from the wise, they will not discover the supernal treasure.

16. Success Without Seeking

The Bodhicitta is not something to be achieved and not something which is to be an object at which to direct the activity of seeking. The transmission of luminous Wisdom does not come by cherishing an acquisitive intent. It is already primordially present as the non-duality of enlightened and samsaric beings.

The light of our heart's essence (Wisdom) shines like the sun without our working at it or seeking it. In the field of awareness that has no borders or boundaries, it is the unattached mind which cuts through concepts which have fixed meanings.

We do nothing at all. We do not contemplate anything. We do not cherish anything limited, and we have no reference-point notions such as center (or periphery).

Without being motivated by a desire to engage anything, we allow our minds to rest in the space of self-radiant awareness.

Awareness is the ground (of all appearances), but it is also the method that reveals itself to be the nature of the true condition. But this is not for those who have distorted perspectives based in ideas about origins and (practical) results.

Self-luminous awareness is the ground of all appearances. Yogis who attend to this, without seeking, come to attainment. They abide in a state of non-distraction. This is how they attain perfect clarity with regard to their focus.

By dwelling in the way things are, not seeking, we come to rest in the supreme awareness that is highest bliss.

The luminosity of Wisdom will appear to us in the same way that the ocean's waves appear to us.

Once we experience direct introduction to the nature of awareness, we will shine from within like radiant gems. The empowerment of awareness imparts comprehension of the meaning of symbols. Those who realize this will have no more pride left in them. They will be united to Wisdom and also to knowledge.

17. Effortless Good Works

Realization of self-radiant awareness is spontaneously arising and is not an attainment which comes from seeking. This radiant awareness is self-originated, without fixity. It brings all good works to fruition without any need for practices based in dualistic ideas.

There is nothing that needs doing because all deeds are primordially accomplished by the light rays of our awareness. It is the light of Wisdom equally present in all and pervading all. The good works of uncontrived awareness spread out like light and have no fixed position.

Non-dual self-effulgence has the characteristic of oneness. The Wisdom we experience is beyond boundaries and has no center. It is an indescribable, mirror-like awareness. Its clarity is, for us, established by the way we look at it. We find ourselves at play in a shining mound of jewels, the treasure of the treasury of spaciousness, the treasury of the sky.

When our awareness is channeled through the doorway of seeking-activity, we become preoccupied by this and that (our conceptual designations). We keep busy on a path made up from our own ideas. We become fixated on concepts. Our understanding of empowerment comes from our definitions and ideas, and we lose the way of working of the Wisdom of awareness.

Following such instructions diverts us from great happiness and the light of Wisdom. We are lost in the fog of our concepts, smothered by shadows. We are like blind leading the blind, having lost the thread of inherently lucid Wisdom. We seek what we have lost, striving for success (by following our ideas).

We use visualizations to attain what cannot be visualized, bringing duality into the actuality of the non-dual. Our yearnings inform our view of the Awareness-Wisdom that is unrelated to anything referential. The backwardness of our views and practices is at odds with the inner spirit of the positive manifestations that come unsought due to effulgent awareness. Nothing can be accomplished by such seeking.

The clear light of equanimity cannot be seized upon by ideas and our habitual tendencies are obscurations that veil the unobstructed clarity of Wisdom.

The concepts we entertain in our minds are delusions. We fail to comprehend the blessings (good works) of primordial luminosity, and we fail to rely on the light of Wisdom for clarity.

We envision objects and objectives rather than settling into a state of equanimity and letting go of seeking. The spontaneous self-transmission of clear-light Wisdom leaves nothing for us to do, and it is accomplished to perfection in an instant.

We meld like water in water and merge in luminous awareness beyond conceptual reference points in the inmost center of our hearts. We settle into the uncontrived fullness of lucent awareness, the essence of contentment.

This union that fulfils our aspirations is something we learn in the personal presence of a spiritual friend who has attained it. When our teacher is pleased, he will impart the unsurpassed transmission of fluid awareness.

The secret whispered intimations that bring us to self-effulgent Wisdom arise from within our concepts and definitions. We will know the time for this by the transmissions of our spiritual teacher.

The meditation of the sky arises in one place – undirected awareness. The master's words illumine with certainty the process of transmission of this meditation. Let us study the way to practice this treasure of awareness.

18. Nothing to Approach

This tantra, Equal to the Furthest Reach of the Sky, does not set forth a path to traverse. When self-arising awareness is rightly recognized, without travelling anywhere, we are there. On paths of travel, there is a goal in mind, and the process of travelling includes an extremely long road.

Abiding in self-arising awareness, we are enlightened beings free from the ebbs and flows of the samsaric byways. However, both nirvana and the currents of samsara melt and resolve into inherently radiant light.

All phenomena are intrinsically self-radiant. Without center, without boundaries, the clear light which is Wisdom frees us from all forms of grasping and from visualization. The transmission of all-pervading, luminous great bliss brings all fulfilment in a domain that is beyond all limits, non-dual, neither nirvana nor samsara.

We may travel in any direction, but we will find no greater boon than inherently luminous awareness. It is unlike any other form of experience, this clear-light Wisdom, the great bliss of Vajrasattva. It is beyond any causes or effects we could cite and it transcends all forms of distraction.

The all-enveloping experience we have of great bliss is in no way bound by the idea that we are to contemplate something specific or to frame our experience conceptually in a specific manner. We do not traverse a path where coming and going, entering and leaving, apply. Nor are notions about various levels and paths anything other than mere ideas. Our true condition is our method. There is no end to our sojourn in the spaciousness of the sky of Bodhicitta.

Enlightenment is our true condition, not something toward which we travel, or something for which we keep busy seeking.

All-encompassing awareness has no fixed positions and no preferences. It is a clarity which cradles the very heart of all-pervading and self-perfecting Wisdom. We place ourselves in this domain of luminous Wisdom as vast as the sky, beyond expansion or contraction, abiding in non-dual awareness at the center of all that is.

We live in harmony with a luminosity that has no limits. There is no need to work through various stages or travel paths which would only confuse our abiding in self-luminous Wisdom. It alone is the secret abode of the Victorious Ones, no other, this transmission of primordial illumination.

The intrinsic illumination that is awareness reveals itself as something with no limits, no center or boundaries, and nothing like these to be found anywhere at all. When we start thinking in terms of good and evil, we turn what is in essence one into duality which we then cultivate or reject. This leads to rebirths in lower or higher worlds in the desire-realms, not freedom. It is thus a form of samsara.

There is only the one, the infinite consciousness, and it is inherently pure, but we construe the higher and the lower, we see duality and multiplicity, and we think of attainment as something to pursue through eleven (or more) different levels.

This is a deluded way. When we think in terms of two truths (conventional and ultimate), we take the mistaken approach of rejecting the world for numberless ages in order to traverse all the paths and levels.

Because we cherish our own preferred notions, we abide in obscuration. We generate a mandala of different samadhis, and all manner of other forms of active practice and striving, whether twelve, fourteen or sixteen of this that and the other. We think of attainment and Wisdom as a cause-and-effect process. Although we may achieve the goals we have envisioned (by striving), we miss the clear light (Wisdom). All of this is bondage and shackles arising from our desires, and a departure from the domain of self-arising clear light, the sun of radiant Wisdom.

For nihilists, the radiance is not recognized, but those who are fully confident in their experience of illumining awareness will guide those who are immature and coarse and thereby widen their receptivity to blessings.

Those who are wise and aware, who have received the transmission of the enlightened ones' contemplation, are able to open the portal to the treasury of hidden awareness. Their empowerment has been well and truly received and they understand symbols, their meanings and the inner guiding Wisdom.

The true condition is completely uncontrived. It is a consciousness that has settled into the equanimity of its own inner being. The teachings on compassion are shared for the purpose of purifying samsara. The treasure of hidden Wisdom is found by those who have no interest in worldly fame, are steady and persistent, unattached to their intellect, body or wealth. They go beyond contrived forms of spiritual practice and settle into the real depth of illumining awareness. They do not give importance to book learning. They lack the will to pursue ideas, but they bring to the fore a resolve to be immersed in the true depths of awareness in the right way.

A mind that abides in the equanimity of pure awareness does not direct this awareness towards topics of various kinds, pursuing memories or concepts. The proper use of awareness is rather to look directly at the intrinsically luminous mirror and whenever the appearance arises, be conscious of its emptiness. This emptiness is then recognized as clear light. Our approach is non-dual. We do not entertain any ideas at all. In this there is no fabrication and no grasping whatsoever. We simply take rest in the uncontrived continuum of our own true nature. We enter into and experience the space of our awareness as it is.

When a realized master teaches this to a qualified student, samsara itself becomes a path to realization. The clear light Wisdom that is Vajrasattva illuminates everything perfectly through an all-knowing insight wherein there is no confusion.

19. Imparting Wisdom

This Tantra, encompassing the farthest reaches of the sky, is a setting forth of the essence of Wisdom. The words and meanings of this account open the doorway of all-illumining Wisdom. Things appear to our minds according to how we construe them. In the awareness of emptiness, nothing is seen. The clear light awareness is all-knowing. It cuts through the obscurations of our playing up and playing down (our perceptions and notions).

In omniscient Wisdom, the mirror-like uncontrived awareness, everything that appears is immediately recognized to be a self-presentation of luminosity, unhindered. This is not merely a concept (but rather direct seeing).

Non-dual awareness is perfect while not having any "this" or "that". It is clear light free of fixed reference-points and beyond preferences.

Its inherent unity is not dependent on our conceptions about it. This clear light knows all things lucidly without any form of intellectual grasping on our part.

Primordially illumined awareness is not dualistic. It is the intrinsic perfection that is present in all appearances without exception. Free of things that need doing and seeking, it is a shoreless ocean of Wisdom. It is the light of awareness that becomes aware of its own Reality in a pure realm where without striving all purposes are fulfilled.

It is undefiled in any way, beyond visualization, free from all appearances, bound to no thing whatsoever.

This illumining Wisdom is not something to be generated. It is self-originating from beyond the beginning of time. It has nothing referential by which it could be described or defined and is uncaused. This superlative Wisdom which knows no seeking transcends the grasping activities of our thought-bound minds. It is free of ideas, including ideas about objects, the holding onto objects, or the visualization of objects. It is primordially empty and is not itself an object, or indeed anything at all that we can grasp or describe.

The luminous essence is radiantly present in all appearances (which arise in our minds). We let go of all our notions about experiences of bliss, origins, applications and conceptualization. Written or spoken words cannot capture the essence of illumining Wisdom. Insight arises in (non-dual, non-conceptual) contemplation, by entering the spaciousness of uncontrived, infinite consciousness.

Luminous Wisdom does not designate or give attention to specific phenomena. It is self-illuminating. It is Wisdom itself, its own innate identity which cannot be put into words, being the light that appears in all things. So there can be no definition of this. It cannot be any specific thing because it is everything, and has no particular identity to grasp, name or define.

There is nothing to visualize, nothing to explain, for the great light of the all-illumining mirror appears to each of us according to our way of seeing it.

Thinking in terms of higher or lower adds up to nothing. The eyes of the deluded will continue to see a snake when the Reality is only a rope. The uncontrived clear light of awareness is simply not there, either in our ideas or our lack of them, but deluded minds will go on using dualistic notions to grasp for it. Reality does not appear in the way that deluded minds frame it, but the confusion of the deluded ones brings about continuous misunderstanding. Even the glowing forms of the pure lands are not in Reality what they appear (to deluded minds) to be.

20. What Is To Come (A Prophecy)

The Tathagata Vajrasattava proclaimed this Tantra concerning the Great Perfection Bodhicitta which has united with The Furthest Reaches of the Sky in my (Garab Dorje) contemplations. Its meaning is secret. This transmission from the inmost depth of my heart, a communication of my contemplations, will become famous in the three sacred realms.

(The Prophecy) A manifestation of Divine compassion living in a secret cave in a cremation ground in the land of Oddyana (Garab Dorje) will play the role of a very great spiritual leader and will open the doors of the mandala of awareness for seven heart children, manifestations of his compassion.

He will bestow empowerments on them and reveal the transmission of secret and sacred mysteries. These blessed ones will flourish at the center of Jambu Island. Famed as if it, his Wisdom, were a precious jewel, it will fulfil the aspirations of all.

All fortunate ones who have the merit to understand this will attain to full enlightenment. Those who do not, who see according to their cravings, whose minds focus on verbal meanings and grammar, lacking supreme good fortune, will wander all through their humanity into a terrible life.

These writings will be concealed and hidden from the descendants of the fortunate ones in a realm that is imperceptible. Then the blessings of compassion on those who have the karma of faith will come together non-dually and appear in a barbarian land. Those fortunate ones who carry the tradition of the transmission will understand the true meaning of self-arising awareness and come to a state of full enlightenment.

The fortunate children of the Victorious One will arrive at complete confidence concerning their inheritance. This writing about the self-illuminating awareness will be turned into a further transmission for the fortunate. They will be marked with the seal of secret awareness, neither to prosper nor to fail.

Then, because of a violation of the secrecy, these words will be discussed in assembled communities, both fortunate and unfortunate and will spread far and wide, filling the lands of the barbarians.

At that time, the holy ones who hold fast to this heritage will abide in the level of the Victorious Ones.

Those unfortunate ones who practice according to their innate tendencies will have a backward sort of existence in a terrible life, disagreeing within themselves about their own notions, taking (opposing) positions on what is true and what is not. Missing the non-dual Wisdom of illumination, they will become only purveyors of argument.

(Eventually) those who claim to be my (Garab Dorje) children will cause this transmission of secret teachings to fail. How will they bring this about? This will happen because they cling to (fixed intellectual) viewpoints and preferences about the Dharma (teachings) and develop a tendency for argumentation. They will be lacking in firsthand experience of the light of Wisdom and will promulgate karmic formulations of the light. Not having the aural transmission, they will draw on their own attachment-bound ideas and promulgate these. In particular, they will have a hankering for wealth and reputation. For this, they will summarize their ideas in their writings and teach these to various gatherings....

* * * * *

For these reasons, the sacred transmission of my contemplation will be caused to fail by evil people.

21. Nine Spaces

All the enlightened ones have known (realized) that realized beings and (samsaric) sentient beings are not a duality. When consciousness is aware of the uncontrived true condition, this is enlightenment beyond seeking or striving. Self-arising awareness arises naturally. Attainment comes without active seeking.

Following these teachings on indescribable awareness, we make use of the unsurpassed revelations of the light of Wisdom to reach certainty and to ascertain with certainty this same ineffable awareness. Teachings on the nine spaces arise from the Wisdom of awareness instantly. These teachings on the light of Wisdom can be thought of as clear light jewels. On the topic of the nine spaces, there are twenty thousand volumes of these covering all aspects of this topic.

The light of these jewels of Wisdom is as far as the (conceptual) mind can go. It is the root of the various yanas (paths). It is not meant to be taught to a general audience.

The teachings of the nine spaces cover everything there is to say about Great Perfection Enlightenment. No matter what we see, we do not conceptualize in terms of anything being an object. We go beyond having thoughts that are concerned about objects. The spaciousness of consciousness is the view we sustain, with no topics therein.

Those who hold to definitions regarding the spaciousness of consciousness depart from the clear light that is Wisdom, and the happiness that arises from it. We do not conceptualize in terms of boundaries in the mandala of awareness, and those who do lose their way.

The Dharma of clear light is effortless and beneficial works flow from it naturally with no need for seeking. Clear light Wisdom does not take up a fixed point of view or a preference, and it does not seek or visualize in the continuum of no-thought. We settle into a space of unperturbed luminous awareness, a domain of uncontrived contemplation.

Samsara and Buddhahood are not two different locations, and there is no alternate location to which we are required to travel. We do not navigate pathways that lead by stages (from one place to another). The mind (consciousness) itself is the space. It is the light that makes a mound of jewels radiant.

Self-illumined awareness is spontaneously arisen, not generated from causes and conditions. Fruition of Wisdom arises also from this same domain naturally and effortlessly. The precious jewels of the nine spaces manifest similarly.

Samsara is (in essence) uncontrived clear light without defilements or difficulties from its inception. Through non-dual awareness, we enter into the light of pure Wisdom. All things are part of this clear light, such is the nature of the indescribable Dharma. Indeed, this is the core Reality of the indescribable Dharma.

Mirror-like Wisdom transmits recognition that all appearances are self-liberated due to this Wisdom (their essence) and are primordially purified of obscuration.

In the sky of pure awareness, there are no concepts and no memories at all. The clear light of Reality renders contrived practices worthless.

We may be introduced to pristine awareness in nine different ways, at which time our minds will be diamonds of uncontrived pristine light. Knowing the true condition, we will go beyond recitations or (deity) generation or renunciation. Such dharmas (active practices) do not touch the equanimity of the true condition, the shadowless and uncontrived clear light where all is one for enlightened and samsaric beings alike. This enlightenment is not to be found in active practices or the renunciation of them.

In the radiant light of this jewel-Wisdom, there are no corrupting or obscuring forces whatsoever, and there is no need for us to cultivate or covet one thing over another. Among the jewels there is nothing imperfect. Who could picture or evaluate this palace which has no center or boundary?

The secret transmission of Vajrasattva, this precious teaching on the nine spaces, this mirror of the intrinsically illumined pure awareness, abides equally within us all.

22. The Root of the Nine is One

Bodhicitta is the root. It is non-dual Wisdom. The nine spaces are gathered into this One.

Having no duality, and being primordially and intrinsically self-liberated, there is no need to explain why the centerless, borderless clear light does not need our seeking and striving.

All aspects of our lives, our joys and sorrows, comings and goings and all the rest are lucid non-dual awareness. Having no problems, awareness has no need to contemplate the selflessness or non-duality of the Dharma!

Reality has no center or periphery, is neither a thought nor a non-thought, and is perfection in a realm beyond conceptuality.

Things may appear as multiplicity, but in the single Wisdom that is transmission of clear light awareness, they are not. Using dualistic notions to fuel their seeking activity, samsaric beings are deceived (by appearances). Non-dual awareness abides in a condition of non-duality and does not conceptualize dualistically.

The spacious sky does not think or speak. The (clear) luminosity of our minds does not go outside its non-duality and has no need of searching. Wisdom has no beginning point or application and is inseparable from non-dual awareness. It is an ocean that has no shore.

The perfected Wisdom that abides in excellence is the transmission of the contemplations of all enlightened beings. This is the inner abode of all enlightened beings, shadowless, luminous in everything, and of no fixed location. It is the god of gods, the true intent of all Dharma teachings, the root of all Buddhas and paths and methods. It demands no travel, traversing of levels or study.

To know the true significance of uncontrived awareness is to dwell in the light of uncontrived awareness. This is the light of the world, unmoving, thought-free, contemplating nothing whatsoever.

Within the mandala of pristine awareness, the conditioning of our mind and senses causes things to appear to us in just the way they do. But these appearances are nothing whatsoever. The heart essence of self-arising awareness holds all. It cuts through our inflated and deflated opinions and doubts. We know this featureless awareness clearly in our minds (as our knowingness). All contemplations are sourced in this root – the Bodhichitta.

23. The Supreme Heart

This tantra, Equal to the Furthest Reaches of the Sky, is the unparalleled heart-essence of Wisdom, rendered and presented free of error, a compendium of natural contemplations that express the Dharma. This is the self-transmission of non-dual Wisdom, the heart-essence of illuminating awareness, manifesting itself for itself.

Our supreme teacher emanates the transmission of blissful clear light, the real meaning of the heart-essence, a contemplation beyond sound or words to give flawless expression to luminous awareness.

The true and ultimate intent of this secret is not expressed by talking about it but is rather revealed in the way things are. It is like the radiance of the sun - timeless, uncontrived and primordially pristine. This is the epitome of all the contemplations of the heart, given expression in clear light itself. Like water in water, our awareness simply abides in this supreme luminosity. This is not a visualization, but simply abiding in the clear light of the supreme Reality.

The essence of this experience is joyful. It is a path (state) of nonconceptual clarity, with no reference points, a view without worldly concerns that does not practice conceptual grasping. The samadhi of Ati Yoga does not contemplate anything. It entertains no thoughts. Rather, it eliminates concepts. It simply abides in the clear light of awareness.

The way things are is not an object of seeking, and not an objective of striving. The nature of our minds is a magnificent awareness that is rooted in equanimity. The eternal knowledge clearly recognizes that this is the single point of all Dharmas.

All of the many practices and methods have been developed to make this clear in a clarity which dawns in a single instant. The secret whispered instructions also are intended to bring about the transmission of this perfection, self-liberated awareness beyond striving, unmistakenly and decisively.

In truth, there is only one contemplation. If we do not abide in conscious recognition of the nature of mind, it will make no difference how we seek for the meaning of the true condition; editing and compiling (sacred texts), we will be going against the guidance of the supreme Wisdom.

The true intent of Wisdom is transmitted only by those who teach the contemplation of the Victorious Ones as it really is, the significance of Reality as identical to the natural state.

For the enlightened ones, there can be no contrivance. They do not seek. These words convey the definitive intent of the contemplations of the Victorious Ones. Others may fabricate (meditation practices) or interpret (sacred teachings) and represent this as the definitive transmission. Therefore, rely on these words just as they are to shed light on the certainty (of the Bodhicitta).

24. Names

Awareness of the Bodhicitta, the supreme secret, unites us with all the enlightened beings of all times, and is the most magnificent of treasures.

The supreme expression of the uncontrived mind of awakening (Bodhicitta) is to bring about its direct transmission. This opens up the space to uncreated and unending Wisdom. It has no complexities, and its blessings fill the ten directions.

The self-liberated Reality is a spaciousness (sky) of pristine clarity. It is the domain of non-duality known as primordial Buddhahood, a Wisdom that has no limits. This is the source of all the teachings, the infinite consciousness itself. This is the highest teaching and the supreme goal.

This Tantra, Equal to the Farthest Reach of the Sky holds all secrets and is a treasure of the awareness. It is not merely something written in words, it is the unparalleled transmission.

25. Seeding the Instructions

Dharma teachings that depend on ideas are not to be found in the pure light of Wisdom, which is like the light which fills the sky. Clear light Wisdom may be compared to a precious jewel which fulfils all our wishes. Its condition is comparable to a lotus that floats free from attachments. It is self-arisen, self-radiant, inherently perfect. It is the ultimate mystery of Vajrasattva, the fulfilment of the noble intent of the All Good, something so far-reaching and so profound that it defies description. This is something as wide as the sky, impossible to visualize, a self-revealing communication of the supremely blissful clear-light Wisdom equal to the utmost limit of the sky.

Uncontrived, radiant awareness is the effulgent light that embodies the Dharma, self-revealed in an instant of time. Within a moment, we are transported into the experience of highest bliss. There are no stages that lead to this blissful moment. Building up knowledge by increments is a misdirected path. The clarity of the true condition is present in each and every manifestation but is not itself evident.

This all-encompassing Wisdom is void of dualistic understandings. Those who have not recognized the clear light of pure awareness may conduct all manner of seeking-activities, but these will become serious obstacles.

Those whose minds are immersed in samsara experience the obscuration of their consciousness. They seek for truth but never discover what it really is. Thus, they are mired in delusion, and all their perceptions and understandings are mistaken. They miss the opportunity for freedom (from samsara) and are lost to the family of the Victorious Ones.

When we have the true recognition (of Bodhicitta), the purest of mysteries, our every thought, word and action shines in the light of Wisdom.

26. Assessing People

A master of Ati Yoga (is one who) holds and preserves the teachings. He holds the treasury of the mysteries of awareness and is one with the meaning of the transmission of Clear Light Wisdom. His Wisdom is apparent in his thorough knowledge and understanding. The master has the whispered teachings by which the aural transmission is accomplished, and he also has the direct experience of the treasury of awareness, having himself received the appropriate empowerments. He has entered into the spaciousness (of the truth-consciousness). His approach is uncontrived. With his heart of compassion, he perseveres in helping human beings. He has no fixed opinions and no preferences concerning the Dharma. Skilled in the secret, whispered instructions, he is not confused about any of the various paths. He understands surpassing greatness because he has the clear light of superior understanding, and he is thus able to eliminate his karmic tendencies.

Such a master can explain the teachings and transmit the Wisdom instantly to all who are fit recipients. But this teaching is not to be imparted to those wanting in faith, with serious attachments, greedy, self-aggrandizing, who have contrarian views, hankering after worldly fame, lacking in perseverance, mean-spirited, manipulative, fascinated with inferior paths and the rest.

Such as these find fault, deceive their teacher and criticize even the teachings of definitive meaning. Even when they are working their way free of these obscurations and getting closer to a wise attitude, they will not succeed in recognizing the true meaning of these teachings.

To ridicule your teacher is to cast aspersion on all the enlightened beings of all times. Such persons will have no lineal successors. They will have unfortunate rebirths, and when they seek and strive for Wisdom, they will find no refuge.

27. Preserving The Tantra

This Tantra teaches the innermost heart of secrets and is a transmission of the contemplations of all enlightened beings. It is an uncomplicated teaching, not a rumination about topics. It illuminates the highest Reality of all spiritual paths and is a precious distillation of the secret whispered teachings, a heap of precious gems beyond counting that elucidates the great bliss of inexhaustible Wisdom. It is an embodiment of the wheel of Wisdom.

This teaching is most secret. It is (although uncomplicated) not easy to understand. It is not relatable to those who lean toward active seeking-and-striving forms of practice. It is a self-revealing treasury of Wisdom realized by those who abide in the light of primordial awareness. Those who attempt to grasp its spaciousness will miss the all-pervading great bliss (that informs these words).

Those who revere (this Tantra) have a good fortune equal to the supreme excellence of enlightenment itself.

One who takes this teaching to heart has the body, speech and consciousness of an enlightened being. Treasure it, therefore, with flawlessly unmistaken awareness. Protect it as you would protect our child. Find someone who has realized the Bodhicitta communicated in these teachings and then hide the teachings in the rocks, or at the bottom of a body of water, bound by an oath (of secrecy) that outweighs the importance of life itself.

Colophon: This text was translated by the Indian abbot Sri Singha and the Tibetan monk Vairochana at the meeting hall in Dhahena.

The self-liberated Reality is a
spaciousness (sky) of pristine clarity.

It is the domain of non-duality
known as primordial Buddhahood,
a Wisdom that has no limits.

This is the source of all the teachings,
the infinite consciousness itself.
This is the highest teaching
and the supreme goal.

BOOK NINE:
Kunje Gyalpo, The Sovereign Creator

According to traditional accounts, the pure, original Ati Yoga source texts were brought into Tibet from India during the reign of Trisong Detsen (755 – 797 or 804). They were transmitted, complete with empowerments, to Tibetans like Vairochana by several Indian spiritual masters (such as Manjushrimitra and Sri Simha) who had preserved the teachings direct from their originator, Garab Dorje.

The term "Dzogchen Semde" refers to texts on Ati Yoga which were composed prior to the eleventh century, and most can be reliably dated to a time period between 850 and 1000 AD. This is the best that current scholarship can do, but texts attributed to Garab Dorje obviously date from a previous century. It is possible that prototypes or actual texts existed prior to the ones we can date by modern methods, and some mention of them is found in early sources. However, further research would be needed to confirm this point.

Currently, in the scholastic world, there are some who hold that the Semde originated in Tibet, but that Tibetan teachers wanted to get authentication by way of (questionable) source attribution to India. At present, there is no conclusive evidence one way or the other, whether for Indian or Tibetan origin of the Semde texts. However, most active practitioners (as opposed to scholars) still hold to the traditional account and credit individuals like Vairochana and Vimalamitra with bringing the Semde to Tibet. The Space (Longde) section includes both "pristine" and "tantric" forms of Dzogchen. The Upadesha Dzogchen Texts are universally recognized as being of a later date (11th – 14th centuries AD) and originating in Tibet. There is good reason to believe that much or most of the Longde and Upadesha sections of the Dzogchen Source Texts did not come from Garab Dorje.

As previously noted, the Semde teachings are known as pure, original Ati Yoga (Dzogchen). They are pre-tenth-century texts, such as the Kunje

Gyalpo, and a group of "eighteen Semde texts". Five of these are called the "five earlier translations" of Vairocana, and thirteen of these are known as the "thirteen later translations" translated by Vimalamitra, who also studied under Sri Simha and was in the direct lineage from Garab Dorje.

The Semde texts share similar motifs and terminology. For example, they eschew active practices such as rituals, recitation of mantras, striving and seeking. They frame enlightenment as a sudden awakening rather than a gradual growth of insight and understanding. Ati Yoga fosters recognition of inherent Buddhahood and criticizes the idea of actively generating some special state thought to be Buddhahood.

The longest and most famous of the Semde texts is known as Kunje Gyalpo in Tibetan and in Sanskrit the *Sarvadharma Mahasandhi Bodhichitta Kulayarāja Tantra*. This can be translated "The All-Creating King of Awakened Mind, the Great Perfection of all Things." It is often referred to as the "Dzogchen Bible".

The Kunje Gyalpo is presented as a dialogue from the Source, or Kunje Gyalpo (All-Creating King) or (Skt. Samantabhadra, Always Good) and Sattvavajra ("Vajra Being"). In this work, the "mind of perfect purity" is personified as the Supreme Teacher, the All-Creating Sovereign. Kunje Gyalpo is essentially a dialogue that passes between the fully enlightened consciousness to the mind of the disciple, Sattvavajra.

The main purpose of this source text is to bring about in the reader a direct insight into the nature of mind (consciousness), the self-arisen continuum of pure awareness which is our essence. In these teachings, Kunje Gyalpo guides Sattvavajra to direct his mind to the instructions he is about to receive. He indicates that the disciple will be led to the right understanding, which is understood to be an experiential rather than a merely conceptual recognition of the true nature.

Here, as in other Semde texts, the word Bodhicitta is used quite differently from the way it is used in Mahayana Sutras or Vajrayana Tantras. The Mahayana meaning of this word connotes a mind that is cultivated gradually through the practice of compassion and emptiness. In the Vajrayana, the term refers to male and female sexual fluids and the symbolism of sexual union of man and woman which in turn is used to symbolize the active practices of compassion and emptiness.

In Kunje Gyalpo, on the other hand, The Supreme Teacher indicates to Sattvavajra that the very nature of the disciple's own mind is already pristine awareness, a sky-like spaciousness, inherently perfect and beyond striving or attaining. This is not something that needs to be gradually accumulated or generated, and it is not related to causes and conditions.

This supreme consciousness of perfect purity is the root and pinnacle of all teachings, but there is no prescribed path taking anyone anywhere and no fixed doctrine by which this ultimate Reality could be grasped by the limited mind. The study of doctrines, the active practice of Vajrayana rituals, as well as study, seeking, renunciation, striving and attainment of specific goals are all erroneous approaches, according to the Sovereign Creator. There is no new body of doctrine to learn, and there are no conceptual views to study, only recognition of what is already the case within, the nature of mind common to all humans, the "mind of perfect purity" which is Great Perfection (Dzogchen).

Direct introduction to the nature of mind, experiential rather than merely intellectual, is therefore the hoped-for result of this text and also the starting point for rightly comprehending its meaning. There is nothing to grasp, conceptualize, memorize, believe or practice. Since the nature of mind is non-dual, non-conceptual, and inherently perfect, there is nothing to generate, and all that is needed initially is to recognize this Presence. This consciousness, which is self-perfected purity, cannot be altered, modified, attained by striving, by meditation or by spiritual disciplines. It cannot be grasped or expressed verbally. It is beyond thinking activity. Analysis, gradually accumulated progress, goal-oriented practices of all kinds, are mistaken approaches and are to be eschewed.

The true nature is not discovered as an outcome of seeking. Nor is it generated by mantras, rituals or as a result of accumulated merit. Kunje Gyalpo repeats this point and hammers it home repeatedly. It is already present and only needs to be recognized, and once this happens the Bodhicitta becomes the inner teacher. Sattavajra's true teacher, therefore, is his own pristine consciousness, personified at times in this and other texts as Samantabhadra, the All Good.

The Structure of the Text

The core of Kunje Gyalpo contains 57 chapters. Longchenpa divided these into the sections shown below:

- ***The Root Tantra*** (the first 57 chapters), associated with the Wisdom derived from listening. It is meant for practitioners of the highest capacity who attain self-liberation immediately on listening and perceiving the true nature of mind.

    - *Ten Chapters on Primordial Manifestation* which according to Longchenpa "demonstrate the true condition of the totality of existence (essence, nature, and energy) in the same way that sight is restored to a blind man."

    - *Ten Chapters that Disclose the True Nature* which according to Longchenpa "demonstrate the perfect condition of the nature of mind as it is, using logical reasoning, examples, and meanings in the same way that a truthful person relates the contents of a letter."

    - *Ten Chapters Beyond Cause and Effect* which according to Longchenpa "demonstrate that the nature of mind cannot be altered, achieved, or eliminated; it is just like celestial space."

    - *Ten Chapters on Perfection Beyond Action* which according to Longchenpa "demonstrate that the qualities of self-arising Wisdom, that is, of the nature of mind, are already naturally present and self-perfected and that there is no need to seek them. Simply abiding in the state of total relaxation, effortlessly, and without correction or alteration, one achieves realization. Thus, [the true nature] can be compared to the wish-fulfilling jewel."

    - *Ten Chapters that Establish Knowledge* which according to Longchenpa "smash the huge rocks of erroneous views of the lower vehicles, and at the same time they illuminate the true meaning of the natural state, thus they can be compared to a diamond or to the splendor of the sun."

    - *Three Chapters that Summarize the Essence*

    - *The four chapters that concisely explain the meaning of the words*

- ***The Further Tantra (not included in this volume)*** (the following 12), associated with the Wisdom derived from reflection. It is meant for practitioners of average capacity who need to reflect. It contains various chapters on understanding the true meaning of the ten natures.

- ***The Final Tantra (not included in this volume)*** (the last 15 chapters), associated with the Wisdom derived from meditation. It is meant for practitioners of lower capacity who need to meditate. It contains the teachings on meditation on the true meaning of the ten natures.

Kunje Gyalpo is considered the root tantra of the Semde teachings. It is a collection of *"lungs",* short summaries of longer tantric texts. A *lung* is a text in which the principal points are written down in an abbreviated, but clear form, for the purpose of study. Kunje Gyalpo is understood to be a compendium which drew together a wide sampling of available source texts in summary fashion under one cover. It was not, therefore, a single work enunciated by Garab Dorje, passed down to Vairochana and then translated by him. Because it is compendious and touches on all aspects of Ati Yoga, it has come to be known as "The Dzogchen Bible". This makes it the most significant of all the root texts in the Semde collection.

According to the Kunje Gyalpo, Ati Yoga differs from tantric vehicles which are based on ten fundamental points, called the "ten natures of Tantra". Garab Dorje's teachings are instead based "ten absences" (*med pa bcu*):

There is no view on which one has to meditate.

There is no commitment, or samaya, one has to keep.

There is no capacity for spiritual action one has to seek.

There is no mandala one has to create.

There is no initiation one has to receive.

There is no path one has to tread.

There are no levels of realization (bhumis) one has to achieve through purification.

There is no conduct one has to adopt, or abandon.

From the beginning, self-arising Wisdom has been free of obstacles.

Self-perfection is beyond hope and fear.

These ten points are repeated and explained from various angles in different parts of the book and are the main feature that distinguishes Ati Yoga from the other paths, which are based in notions of cause and effect. Namkhai Norbu comments that these ten points are absent in Ati Yoga because "they are ways of correcting or altering the true nature of the individual, but in Reality there is nothing to change or to improve, all that is necessary is to discover the real condition and to remain relaxed in that state." Sound analysis, astute advice!

The colophon of Kunje Gyalpo states that Sri Simha and Vairochana codified the text "through translation and editing". This great work, the likely source of which was Garab Dorje, has been rendered into modern English in the hope that it may gain a wider readership and appreciation.

In **Book One**, in reply to several questions, Kunje Gyalpo states:

Let your mind attend to the sounds (of my words) for I will explain the real significance (about which you ask) using (spoken) sounds.

My true condition, as all-creating Sovereign, is the source of all phenomena. I am the origination, the primordial sphere beyond conceptual comprehension. This sphere is the domain of non-conceptual Wisdom. All teachers, teachings, retinues, places and times emanate from me. They are all the primordial sphere (Wisdom). Thus did he speak.

Book Two:

As all-creating Sovereign, I bring forth all phenomena, and they are all the true condition, the essence, the natural state. Therefore, all appearances inhere in the true condition.

There is no creator other than me, the all-creating Sovereign. No other maker of the true condition exists, except for me. None other than I manifests the three worlds. No retinues appear, except from me. I alone manifest the conditions (that make possible) the (appearance of) teachings.

I will explain to you the truth of my being, Sattvaraja. It has three aspects: Firstly, purity; secondly, perfection; thirdly, Presence. These three are pristine. They are all-pervading, like space. And they ceaselessly manifest my all-creating, sovereign Reality.

All these creations appear within my pristine, flawless Presence. So he declared.

Book Three

I am the one; I am suchness, the true condition of all phenomena. They are all the pristine presence, my true state.

The domain of appearances is the display of my self-originating Wisdom.

This Wisdom is perpetual clarity, something transcending causes and conditions. This means that there is no path to travel.

The real significance of desire is the wish to know that all appearances are the true condition.

The real meaning of ill will is to be opposed to the various forms of magical display.

The real significance of stupidity is that nonconceptual contemplation has no need to discriminate or reject anything from the perfect equanimity of the true state.

The real meaning of "I" is the perfect Presence of suchness.

Jealousy, in essence, is about affirming and negating as regards being and non-being in the suchness of all things.

These Wisdoms are five paths, beyond any need for going anywhere. The desire-realm is Wisdom, self-originated, as are the form realm, the formless realm, all my creations and the whole of the nature of Wisdom, as are all sentient beings in the six realms.

Book Four

I am primordial Wisdom, self-originated, Source of all phenomena, the all-creating Sovereign, pristine, flawless Presence. Understanding my names, you will understand all phenomena.

Self-originated means beyond causes and conditions, beyond striving and attaining. Wisdom means ceaseless, undefiled. In this way, I the Source cause all phenomena to appear.

"I" means pristine, flawless Presence. Primordial means proceeding from the very beginning. All teachers, teachings, retinues, places and times are (also) the true condition. There is not a single phenomenon that is anything other than the true condition.

Self-arisen Wisdom is the Source. It pervades, rules and reveals the entire cosmos, both the inanimate and the sentient manifestations, and all their karmic perceptions. For this reason it is called "Presence".

All that appears is only my Reality. Knowing my essence, you know the essence of all. By this knowledge you will go beyond all actions, protagonists, striving and attaining, and be effortlessly self-perfected.

Book Five

My essence is oneness. It arises in the nine yanas (paths) and culminates in the Great Perfection.

Being pristine, flawless Presence, it (my essence) abides in the true condition. Its clarity illumines the space of awareness. It is all-pervading, permeating all worlds and all beings in those worlds. It arises as those beings and their experiences. It has no specific qualities that could be pointed to or explained. It is not an object of perception, or something one can notice and put into words.

Source is uncaused and cannot be conceptually grasped by way of words.

If you want a clear understanding of rigpa (awareness), think of space. Think of it as the uncreated, true condition, made evident by the ceaseless energies of Presence Itself. What this really is can only be indicated by saying that it is beyond anything we could refer to. It is inexpressible in words, and incommunicable by way of concepts.

Book Six

I, the Supreme Creator, reveal my nature to you through manifestation (of phenomena), and also using words and sounds. This enables you to see, and to know the meaning of the Alpha (Source Reality). By hearing meaningful sounds, you comprehend.

My essence is non-dual and transcends all that can be perceived. Undefiled, all-where present, spacious, luminous, it is nothing but my self-arising Wisdom, which is my pristine, flawless Presence.

All that appears on all planes is nothing but my body, my energetic expression and my spirit. Enlightened beings and samsaric sentient beings are expressions of my essence which transcends all that can be perceived. It does not appear. It cannot be made to appear by doing contemplation.

It is my nature, not my essence, which can appear to you. The five elements, the three worlds, the five paths and the six classes of sentient beings are all revelations of Sovereign Consciousness. But space, beyond concepts, comes closest to representing my true condition, wherein all enlightened beings are born.

This, my direct transmission, is not to be shared with those who follow paths of cause and effect (Mahayana), as this will only create complications.

Although all that appears is actually the essence of pristine, flawless Presence, it is not necessary to be active (when you abide) in this one state which is uncreated (self-originated).

All my manifestations are impermanent appearances (illusions) which (appear only to) disappear. But if my essence is unrecognized, they will be known through the lens of likes and dislikes, which leads to suffering, and leads also to efforts to block the senses. This brings only earthbound results (that come due to striving).

Such seekers concoct ideas about the relative and the ultimate truth. They strive to generate what has not been manifested and fail to attain that which transcends acceptance and rejection. So it is with the gradual approaches of the tantric yogis.

However, pristine Presence is not something to be grasped by actors and their actions. All phenomena are already pure Presence; all beings are already Wisdom beings. All three worlds are my body, voice and spirit already.

There is no appearance whatsoever that does not abide in the domain of space. All Buddhas and sentient beings already abide in my flawless pristine Presence. Not one atom exists dually, and everything is beyond extremes of affirmation and negation. Nothing is other than the one, the pure, the flawless Presence, beyond possibility of there being such a thing as subject and object. A realizer will be a knower of just this, the essence and root of all phenomena.

Seekers speculate about existence and non-existence which leads to endless conceptual deviations, obstructions and uncertainties. Pristine, flawless Presence is beyond striving, attaining and conceptual grasping. Moreover, it eliminates them all.

Presence does not conceptualize. Rather it brings (direct) knowingness of definitive transmission. From this comes confident recognition of true meaning beyond striving and attaining.

Each of the nine vehicles teaches something different, although no real differences exist (in the true condition/meaning). This my flawless, pristine Presence is what must be known. It is the root of all that appears, my essence and my nature. Appearances are my magical display.

I teach nothing concerning phenomena except that they are Presence (the nature of mind/consciousness). Nor will any other teaching (about phenomena) be given by me but this to Buddhas past, present and future. Thus did he speak.

Book Seven

From the bliss of the true condition, Presence (mind) manifests all particularities, but such particularities have never truly existed. Presence abides primordially in a non-conceptual domain that is like space, and because it is beyond objects, it cannot be thought of as "one". Whatever appears, including the animate and inanimate aspects of the universe, Buddhas, sentient beings and all the rest come from and actuate the mind's own being.

I am the inherently perfected origination of all Buddhas, the actuating energies of Wisdom. To you I am teaching the mind (consciousness) of flawless purity, the nature of mind itself, which generates all appearances and all phenomena.

Those whose minds are endlessly fascinated with the qualities and aspects of the creation are taught with many words. In terms of numbers, it is taught that "one" is my true condition, and "two" is creation. I teach what is inexplicable, the one, the Source, the all-creating mind (consciousness) of pristine perfection.

The so-called two types of teachings, provisional and definitive, are based on how we understand what is ultimate and what is relative. Those who do not understand that all appearances are mind only go on and on studying what can be observed by the various senses, using mistaken ideas about subjects and objects.

Due to mental grasping at specific characteristics, there occurs a proliferation of characteristics (to grasp at). Not understanding that all phenomena appear from Source, by way of the five elements, they think of active practice as a necessary cause. They want to manifest specific results. The vehicles (spiritual paths) that are cause-oriented use strategies such as renouncing, blocking and purifying, as well as accepting and rejecting.

The non-action of Ati Yoga does not rely on such strategies. Presence (mind) the Source, is beyond (strategic) activities and transcends the 'seek, strive, attain' approach.

When those who have been taught to seek and strive for aeons, years or months discover the true condition beyond active practice, they come to abide in the bliss of innate Perfection. This abiding is authentic knowledge of the enlightened state. In this way, they come to see the Great Perfection in all.

To abide in the state beyond striving is Buddhahood, and it is authentic knowledge of the true condition. Bringing benefit to all sentient beings, those who abide in this way come to blissful fulfilment with no need for striving or grasping. Thus he spoke.

Book Eight

My suchness is the suchness of all phenomena. In particular, my suchness takes form as three perfections: teachers, teachings and retinues (Nirmanakaya, Sambhogakaya, Dharmakaya).

All vehicles are my suchness. Even the teachers of cause-and -effect gradual vehicles are in essence my clear, self-originating Wisdom. Some focus on causes, some on the interdependence between causes and effects and some on effects.

From the five Wisdom-energies of pristine awareness, enlightened beings and samsaric beings emerge and appear as teachers, teachings and retinues. Even though there is only suchness, these teachers promulgate different views. Some students are taught to block and reject, some to purify, some to (gradually) progress on the path, some to invoke the energies of purity or to practice rejection and acceptance. Some are taught to realize the purity of their own mind-nature by striving and attaining. All of this is rooted in notions of cause and effect. But I, the All-Creating Sovereign, teach only the Wisdom of equanimity and suchness.

The true nature of my suchness is this: I, the creator, am suchness (the bodhicitta). All that I have created is suchness. The six objects of the senses are also just this. The skandas are also my inherently arising Wisdom. Earth, Water, Fire, Air and Ether are all my suchness, which is the true condition of non-duality.

The four classes of yoga arise from four types of practitioners. In Mahayana, practice of the ten paramitas is taught to realize the ten bhumis (inner attainments). Such practitioners are taught to believe in cause and effect.

Followers of Kriya Yoga think of objects and sense organs as impure. They see sattva and deity dualistically, but they do not see the true continuum of Pristine Presence. They should relax into uncontrived suchness.

Followers of Mahayoga practice the generation of deity, and practice emanation and absorption. They do not experience the equanimity of the natural state. They should relax into uncontrived suchness.

Practitioners of Anuyoga do not understand that the continuum of consciousness is the essence of all phenomena in the animate and inanimate worlds. They see emptiness and Wisdom in terms of cause and effect. In general, they affirm a non-existent cause and negate a non-existent result. For this, they will be obscured and obstructed until they come to the certainty that transcends affirming and negating.

Because notions of doership are absent in the natural continuum, those who practice Ati Yoga experience the Great Perfection directly. They see that pristine flawless Presence is the Source of all (appearances), and that it is identical to the natural state. They relax in the view, beyond active practice. They relax in the Cosmic Flow, beyond effort from the beginningless beginning.

They relax into suchness.

Practitioners of the Boddhisattvayana, Kriya Yoga, Anu and Maha Yoga and the others are all seeking for a result not yet achieved, thinking in terms of the two truths (definitive and conventional), practising purification, separating view and behaviour, accepting and rejecting, thinking in terms of gradual progress and cause-and-effect.

However, the true condition, the nature of mind, is like space. There is no (conceptual) view on which to meditate, no rules to observe, no need for active striving to get results, no levels of attainment, paths to follow, dualities to synthesize, or any authoritative shastra except pristine Presence itself. The true nature is beyond affirmation and negation. The Great Perfection view is rigpa (pure awareness) itself.

The spiritual paths based on cause and effect fail to apprehend my true nature which transcends all forms of experience. If you seek to find me through concepts, you will find nothing at all. Do not make my all-transcending Reality the object of a conceptual view. Leave me in the natural state (the continuum of equanimity). Set aside vows and undertakings. The true nature is flawless primordially, so there is no point in striving to obtain it. It is unhindered intrinsically, so there is no need to purify your way toward pure Presence. Everything is already suchness. Thus, there is no need for practices and pathworking.

I am all-pervading, not localized, not something to be found at the end of some (contrived) path. I always transcend the object-subject dichotomy. My true form is all-pervading. Duality has never existed. I am primordially self-arisen Wisdom, not to be validated by conceptual notions. I am the enlightened condition. No other instruction (apart from my transmission) is relevant.

Beyond all appearance, transcending all affirmations and denials, present in all, I cannot be known by contemplating a (conceptual) view. Inclusive of all, I cannot be realized by keeping rules. Apart from myself, there is nothing to seek and no need to develop special talents in spiritual practices.

There is no location except myself, and so I cannot be approached by working through graduated levels. I know no obstacles. Being supreme Wisdom, I transcend all. There is no place beyond my being to which one could travel. I am beyond the treading of paths.

Everything arises from my pristine purity, so it need not proceed anywhere to attain what it already is. What is inherently perfect and pure needs no practices of perfect purity directed at itself. There is no need for vows to preserve perfect purity on the part of that which is inherently pristine. Nor does perfect purity need to meditate upon itself or think about itself. For these reasons, the practice of Ati Yoga is actionless.

I am the true condition, the ineffable nature of all. All that appears proceeds from me. I am enlightenment, primordial non-duality, utterly transcendent. I cannot be understood by the study of scriptures. Nothing exists or appears other than or apart from my flawless Presence. I manifest all and abide beyond all.

To seek something other than me is deviation. To misunderstand is to be hindered, karmically or conceptually, by failure to comprehend or by failure to discern.

All phenomena, living and not living, are only myself. Not understanding this, not discerning this point, is hindrance. Seeking and striving for attainment is walking a path of deviation.

Book Nine

Pristine, flawless Presence is the continuum from which all phenomena arise. It is without impediments. Being beyond paths to traverse, it is without deviation. Obstructions and deviations occur only when conceptual designations are created within the oneness of the continuum. Aberrations come into play when attempts are made to travel that which cannot be travelled. Obstacles arise when the non-referential state is sought, but not experienced.

Followers of Mahayana, Kriya Yoga, Upaya Tantra and the rest create deviations and obstacles in a variety of ways. Pristine, flawless Mind resembles space. Examining the spaciousness of the true condition, we find no (conceptual) views to contemplate, no rules to follow, no purifying to do, or paths to traverse, or any of the factors that preoccupy seekers on the eight vehicles. The pristine continuum is non-dual. There is no special learning from tantric texts, only Presence, beyond affirmation and negation. The Great Perfection View is rigpa (pure awareness).

In rigpa, there is no place for deviant, obscuring samaya (codified behaviour), active practices, conceptual Wisdom, training on various levels, paths to follow and so on.

Being the Source, self-perfection from the beginning, there is no need to seek and attain the spaciousness of Presence. Space is not modified by human actions. It always remains what it is. Being ineffable, it cannot be something to contemplate. Space is beyond all dimensions. There is no view to meditate.

Striving in the eight vehicles is pointless. Reality is not something to be seen by looking. Simply relax into equanimity without seeking.

* * * * *

There is no phenomenon that is other than me. I have transcended them all.

The essential obstruction is not knowing me. Hunting for something other than me is deviation. Obstructed by karma, there are those who do not see (me). Obstructed by their conceptions, there are those who cannot recognize me. All phenomena, however they appear, are my knowingness; none are other than me. This is why I abide in bliss, in non-conceptual equanimity. This is happiness.

It is not necessary to seek and strive and struggle and practice and overcome numberless obscurations and deviations in their tens and in their hundreds.

All appearances manifest my Presence. No phenomena other than my Presence can be found. This I teach: Do not think that there are any phenomena other than my pristine, flawless Mind (consciousness). Do not make this into something intellectual. Teach your retinues as I have taught you.

Book Ten

All phenomena are perfections because they come into being in me, the creator of all. Teachers, teachings and retinues arise from three aspects of my Being.

The three types of teachers are Dharmakaya, Sambhogakaya and Nirmanakaya.

The Dharmakaya teachers point to the ground of being, the true condition, the pristine, flawless Presence that does not need to be (gradually) developed.

The Sambhogakaya teachers encourage spiritual seekers to perform actions and apply active practices such as making offerings, attracting blessings, and taking part in empowerments.

The Nirmanakaya teachers show how to deal with the three poisons: attachment, aversion and ignorance by making merit through positive actions and being reborn in higher realms.

I, the all-creating Sovereign, am the essence (Dharmakaya) of these three, the non-conceptual equanimity which is the core nature of these embodiments (of Dharma). I am also the manifesting (Sambhogakaya) of all things desired and I am also the compassion that works for the wellbeing of all disciples (Nirmanakaya).

Teachings appropriate for specific disciples are continuously made available. Disciples who come together (on the path) are the recipients.

I am the creator of all. I am continuously working through my three aspects: my essence, my nature and the phenomena that appear. All the many living beings in the three realms make up my sacred entourage.

My primary retinue is the teachers of the three kayas (Dharmakaya, Sambhogakaya, Nirmanakaya). In the Dharmakaya, I am the unborn essence beyond object and subject, the all-good (Samanthabadra) source; then, I am the energies of source appearing as Sambhogakaya teachers, embodiments of perfect pleasure; lastly, I am the sentient beings who are satisfied according (to their natures), known as Nirmanakaya teachers.

Retinues assemble around these teachers who manifest in a variety of ways that are appropriate to the needs of their disciples. Each kaya teacher gives a specific kind of teaching to a specific kind of retinue. These teachers train sentient beings all the way from humans and gods up to Buddhas.

Some Dharmakaya teachers abide in space and transmit teachings of pristine, flawless consciousness to Buddhas and samsaric beings of the three times and the three realms. Sambhogakaya teachers convey Wisdom to bodhisattvas on the ten levels. Nirmanakaya teachers give trainings from a variety of sources.

My non-conceptual, non-dual equanimity is the perfection of the teaching. Each is taught according to his or her individual intellect (and disposition).

I am the all-creating mind of perfect purity, source of all the teachers and teachings in all nine vehicles. Through all teachings, you will progress toward the one vehicle, the pristine, flawless continuum of consciousness itself. Transcending struggle and attainment, without active striving, you will enter the space of enlightenment.

* * * * *

Book Eleven

I, the all-creating consciousness, am the essence of all that appears. Apart from my essence, there can be no phenomena.

The three kayas and Buddhas of all times are my essence, as are Bodhisattvas and yogic practitioners. The desire realm, form realm and formless realm are all myself, as are the five elements and six classes of beings. All that appears, all beings, animate and inanimate are only my essence.

The core of all phenomena is me (consciousness). There is nothing other than my essence and not a single dharma that is not a manifestation of me (consciousness).

My being reveals itself in three aspects: the uncreated (Dharmakaya), the miraculous creation (Sambhogakaya), and the compassion (Nirmanakaya).

These are the three teachers. Because I am oneness, the enlightened beings of all times abide in oneness. All of this is my very being. I am beyond subject-object thinking, purely spacious like the sky.

As the heart-essence of all things, I am the mind (consciousness) of perfect purity.

Practitioners of the four yogas who consciously unite with my Being (which is the essence of balance) will be joined together in oneness. In this way, the nature of my being is communicated (taught).

The five elements express five aspects of my nature, five aspects of Wisdom which originate from my energy. There is nothing in the universe which is anything other than my essence. All things are created by me, manifest from me and are encompassed by me.

Boddhisattvas who have transcended the subject-object dichotomy are the action of my indomitable Presence, the all-creating mind. The natural state in which meditators abide is my true condition, essence of the Supreme Creator.

Book Twelve

At all times and in all places, however they may appear, phenomena emanate from me, the sovereign mind. I am the quintessential source of all sacred instructions. The three teacher-kayas come from me. *Lung* transmission is the essential nature of their teachings.

I am the root of all sacred teachings. I have never taught enlightened or samsaric beings anything other than Presence, my true condition.

All the various teachings (sutras, tantras, Vinaya, etc.) revealed by the three kaya teachers involve struggle for the sake of achievement. They claim that one must gradually proceed toward my Reality, which transcends striving and attaining. However, I declare that you will not see me unless you go beyond striving and achieving. I am the transcendent apex of all such teachings.

I dissolve the obscuration of ignorance and manifest the light of Wisdom. How? The obscuring effect of mistaken reflections clouds the minds of samsaric beings. They fail to recognize that all appearances are essentially the suchness of my perfect Presence. My sovereign all-creating mind gives rise to all phenomena, however they appear to those who have not understood. When deluded beings recognize all appearances to be my perfect Presence, their conceptual darkness dissolves. Wisdom dawns. In this way, I destroy obscurity and bring in the light of Wisdom.

Tear apart this web of discursive thought. Sever the chain of emotional defilements.

Those who follow spiritual paths based in cause-and-effect thinking see all things as poisons to be rejected. Some see mental attachments all around and try to practice non-attachment based on the two-truth teachings. Others see objects in terms of purification and think in terms of lord and servant (deity yoga), empowerments and miracles. Others use worship and service to purify their minds. For all these, I destroy the notion that anything other than my pristine Presence exists. I sever the chain of emotions which generates perceptions of differences.

I am the all-creating Sovereign mind (consciousness) of pristine Presence. I reveal to you that all phenomena, however they appear, are nothing other than my being.

You are to teach those around you so that they understand the nature of my Presence and become one in Me. When all retinues and assemblies see that they are one in me, when they see that they are all already my very being and my essence, they will cease their practices of renunciation and obstructing, purifying and blessing, striving and seeking and talking about the two truths.

They will see that everything is already brought into existence in me, and that it is all of the same nature because it inheres in me. I am equality. There is no need to generate equality, or to strive to achieve what is already the case. I have always taught that it is unnecessary to strive for equality. So he spoke.

Book Thirteen

I, the Bodhicitta, am the sovereign source-transmission of all teachings. From me, the source-transmission of the Dharma, proceed five principles: the history, the root theme, the yoga principle, the intent and the literal meanings of the words.

The history gives confidence in the source. The root principle makes clear that all things inhere in the mind. The yoga principle explains the differences between the various vehicles. The intent principle makes clear that there is no need to strive and struggle to achieve Buddhahood. The word principle points to non-conceptuality as the essential meaning.

The source of confidence, the essential history, is this: I am the creator of all. I emanate three aspects of my being: Dharmakaya, Sambhogakaya, and Nirmanakaya, three bodies who are (primordial) teachers. The meanings of the sounds of the words point to my true nature. The essential point of all this is non-discursive, non-conceptual knowingness.

Everything in the animate and inanimate universe including enlightened and samsaric beings comes from me, the mind of pristine purity. Thus, there is nothing other than my Presence. A phenomenon other than my Presence has never existed. All things are my Presence. This knowledge is the intent of the root principle.

Now, as to the meaning of yoga: I transcend cause and result thinking as taught by the different yanas such as Anuyoga, Mahayoga and the rest. They all have their distinct features. I teach Atiyoga, the Great Perfection, the consummate transmission, distinct from all other vehicles. It is the ultimate measure, being of (and beyond) them all.

As to the intent of this: I am the suchness of Bodhichitta. Ati yogis have the good fortune to be confident of my Reality, and because of this they have no need of a conceptual view or meditation, no need for vows, sacred practices, graduated paths, purification, cause and effect approaches or dualistic thinking in terms of ultimate and conventional truths.

Such yogis recognize me without meditation or practice. They know that Bodhichitta cannot be generated and that striving is pointless, there being no need for antidotes. The point is: they will certainly recognize my true nature.

As to the word: All things are suchness, the all-creating mind. Teachings about phenomena, however they appear, are suchness. If the true condition had never been expressed in words, the intelligent ones would never recognize this suchness. This is why words are used to indicate the true condition.

History is the transmission from my being to the three kaya teachers, their teachings and their retinues. The root of all teachings is my Presence, the Bodhichitta. The yogas approach this in a variety of ways, but my Ati Yoga is beyond struggles, practices, vows and conceptual views, while acknowledging that they do appear.

The intent in all of this is for sentient beings to recognize their own Bodhichitta-essence, not clinging to mere words about enlightenment, but realizing their identity with Source directly. Those who lack capacity for this will not understand. They will labour on mistaken approaches. But Ati Yogis of good capacity and favorable karmic connections will require no conceptual views, vows, practices or remedies. They do not think in terms of conventional and ultimate truths. They recognize the nature of mind directly.

Words are used to indicate the Presence beyond fabrication. Non-action is recognized as the meaning. The state which requires no action is what words are intended to indicate.

Book Fourteen

I am the all-creating Source, the secret one who is present in all. The three expressions of my true nature arise, but this is not something taught by me to my emanations. I do not teach this to the kaya teachers, although they ARE my true nature, nor to the Buddhas of the three times, nor to their retinues.

The true condition is not something that can be taught, and therefore (of necessity) remains secret.

I emanate all beings in all worlds, but my very own being cannot be taught, and therefore remains secret.

If my nature were obvious, the teachers would not appear and the teachings, vehicles and retinues would not arise. The specifics of the various yanas would not manifest. There would be no one to name the Dharmas "perfect."

I bring forth my true nature by myself and effect transmission of Wisdom to myself. This is not a teaching planted among the teachers and entourages which have arisen from me.

Ati Yoga is myself and those who know this have revelation of my very being.

Book Fifteen

I, the all-creating sovereign consciousness manifest three aspects of my essence: teachers, followers who wish to understand, and the definitive meaning itself. I manifest all three of these directly.

There are three teachers of the meaning: Dharmakaya, Sambhogakaya and Nirmanakaya. These are my primordial retinue. They show the real meaning of the term "teacher".

Dharmakaya teachers reveal the essence beyond subject and object. Sambhogakaya teachers reveal my true nature. Nirmanakaya teachers manifest the Wisdom and creativity of my compassionate energies. All three of these are my direct manifestations.

Three types of retinues attend these teachers. Dharmakaya retinues are buddhas and sentient beings of the various realms who abide in non-conceptual equanimity. Sambhogakaya retinues cultivate the thought-free state that is beyond emotional reactions to the objective world which appears to the senses. They conceive of a dualism between phenomena and my true condition and think of their pure consciousness as a "thing". Due to this, they cherish obscurity, right up to the tenth level of bodhisattvas who are seen to enjoy the various sensory objects (with no qualms).

Nirmanakaya retinues try to penetrate the suchness of bodhichitta with their intellectual faculties in an effort to feel that they have understood things rightly. Some see emptiness in a nihilistic way, others see cause and effect in a mistaken way. As they transcend defilements and embrace virtuous attitudes, they receive blessings, but they remain on this level for three great eons.

Those who abide in rigpa Wisdom are my definitive and authentic manifestations.

In this, what is manifested? By whom? Who does the manifesting? I myself manifest myself directly. What manifests? The nature of mind (consciousness) itself is what manifests. Why are there three aspects? For the sake of retinues who cherish their own particular views and approaches. Some harbour the intent to renounce. Some cherish their active practices; some are busy purifying; some accept this and reject that. For some, the view and intent is alignment with their own true condition.

Some strive to see what is true for the sake of what they deem untrue. Some look for things to avoid. Some want things they can study or control. Those who follow teachers of cause and effect proceed in this way.

When my true nature has become evident to you, teach this transmission with confidence: I, the sovereign, all-creating consciousness am your essence. Recognize my essence and you recognize your own essence. When your true nature has become evident, you will recognize that this is so. Be sure and confident of your own realization. Do not imagine that phenomena are other than your own state. Know that all appearances are your own true condition.

Oh retinues and teachers of cause and effect, the teacher of teachers has created everything and created it to be perfect. The manifestation of this

Perfection is the manifestation of your own essence. Manifest your essence! Recognize the truth of your being. Understand your true nature. Do not suppose that phenomenal appearances are other than your very own consciousness. Know all phenomena to be your own state.

Those who do not understand their true condition also fail to understand that all appearances are their own self-presentation. If you think of objects as enemies then you will not see your own nature rightly, and for countless eons you will fail to realize the bliss that transcends effort.

Failing to recognize objects as your own display, you will think of them as enemies. You will fail to see your mind (consciousness, your true nature) as it is; you will fail to see your own perfect purity and remain separate from the bliss beyond striving. You will not see objects as the display of your own mind, and consequently you may continue to regard them as things to be purified.

If you set about trying to purify what is essentially your own true nature, you will fail to see the truth of your being for three long eons.

Objects are the inherently pure and perfect Presence. Mind also is only this. Not seeing that such is the case, you will want to purify the outer and inner appearances which rise up and present themselves to the mind.

Not seeing your own mind's purity, you are likely to be separated from its clarity for seven lifetimes, for the whole of which you will be unable to recognize the nature of mind.

If you think of objects (appearances) as things to be accepted and rejected, although they are the perfect purity of your own consciousness (where purification is not needed), you will be accepting and rejecting your own essence. For three lifetimes you will fail to recognize the non-duality of consciousness (your own mind).

If you see objects as something to accomplish through striving, although they are already the inherent purity of consciousness, you will attempt to bring everything under your control and practice samadhi for this purpose. You will search for your own pristine Presence, although it is not an object of seeking (and cannot be realized in this way). You will practice long endurance in this process. Those who persevere in this kind of cause-and-effect striving will go astray. But those with karmic good fortune will see that consciousness manifests its nature beneficially.

The true condition is your own awareness. It is already and manifestly present. But those bent on a cause-and-effect approach will not recognize this. Seekers who renounce and abstain will be doing a mistaken practice for long eons. It is the same for those who pursue gradual paths and practice purification rituals, acceptance and rejection, accumulation of followers and so on. This can go on for centuries. In the end these too will recognize the truth of their being and come to the supreme bliss.

Unlike the Mahayana, which teaches causation, my pointing leads directly to the true condition. All appearances are only your own mind, which is the truth of your being. Do not act like those who follow cause and effect teachings and develop dualistic notions (about the appearances in their minds). Do not conceptualize the suchness of your consciousness. When you recognize suchness, the perfect purity of your awareness will become apparent, as it is.

Many do not understand this. They use labels like "conventional appearances" or "the invisibility of the ultimate." They overlook their own awareness and search far and wide for some other objective. They strive for achievement rather than opening to the bliss beyond action.

Hankering after bliss is attachment. Bliss comes, but only when unsought. Active practices do not result in enlightenment. Recognition of self perfection arises arises by abiding in the equanimity of your own being. It is not something which cannot be an object of seeking.

Non-distracted contemplation anchors the mind but does not liberate. Imposters who yearn for undistracted contemplation are mostly teachers of cause and effect. They affirm and deny while claiming that results come from generating (favorable) causes.

Primordial Being is without agitation, without deterioration (requires no stabilizing or sustaining). It is the antidote for all forms of striving and achieving. It destroys these tendencies.

Reality has its own natural balance, and apart from this continuum of Reality, there is no Buddha. Unfabricated naturalness is the true condition. Nowhere will you find some enlightenment which is other than the true condition (the continuum of natural, unfabricated pristine Presence). Enlightenment is just a word which is used as a label. There is only the awareness of your own mind. This is Reality. This is the truth of your being.

This unfabricated Presence is Dharmakaya, primordially unborn, not to be searched for or attained.

Seeking and other active practices do not realize the transcendent Reality that is beyond action.

* * * * *

Those who delight in the birthless Reality which is my essence, beyond discursive thinking, beyond subject and object dualism, experience the absolute non-conceptual equality of the Dharmakaya. This unborn equanimity is the ultimate vehicle.

Many pure retinues who enjoy sense pleasures also emanate from my essence as Sambhogakaya teachers. My mind-nature teaches these to perfect their view and practice.

My nature is the instruction that I offer. This is direct manifestation (rather than discursive teaching). The realm of appearances manifests from my single essence in three aspects: emptiness, clarity and compassionate energy. From these come enlightened and samsaric beings and the whole of the animate and inanimate cosmos. All of these are direct expressions of myself, the all-creating, sovereign Source.

There are those who imagine that something other than my manifestation exists. They are unable to know me as I am. They gravitate to cause and effect teachings and gradual trainings.

Although they may seem to be other than me, all phenomena are direct expressions of my true condition, manifestations of my pristine Presence, which is suchness.

My nature is evident also in the enlightened action of the five great elements. By them, my nature is directly manifest. The animate and inanimate universe shows forth my true condition. It appears everywhere. Enlightenment is established from the very beginning, primordially, with no need for actual striving. It is beyond struggle and attaining.

My manifestations are uncreated, non-conceptual, primordially transcending subject and object. They are the nature of Reality. There is no need for active striving to achieve (some imagined goal). This my true nature is the greatness of the identity of enlightenment.

The true condition can be compared to space. This expression of the nature of consciousness is clearly on display for any who are puzzled about the true condition. This example of space, its meaning and its symbolism explain the suchness of enlightenment.

The followers of the lower vehicles do not understand this. The true condition does not support the idea of truly existing buddhas or of sentient beings. Those who try to understand conceptually will miss the mark.

Book Sixteen

I am the primordial Sovereign who created all. By me were created teachers, teachings and assemblies. Teachers are my creation, while teachings reveal my essence and their retinues manifest my true condition. All times and places are one in the heart of my being. There is not a single phenomenon which is other than me. You yourself are the display of my essence. You were manifested from me and by me. Abide in me, the Creator and Source of all manifestations.

I am primordially self-realized. Therefore you should not teach others that it is needful for them to be active. If you teach others that they have to become active, they will be devoured by the illness of struggling. Those who practice actively cherish the defective notion that primordial Wisdom does not already exist (for them). They attempt to fabricate my pristine Presence. They attempt to contrive my suchness. They disregard the true condition, as it is (in actuality). They become habituated in these delusions and are drawn away from the truth by false paths. They struggle in a way that does not harmonize with the true condition. In this they will never achieve what lies beyond active striving.

If you rightly understand my words, you will know that all phenomena are primordial Wisdom, the Wisdom of suchness. The three kaya teachers are my self-sprung Wisdom, my suchness. Your essence is also only this. All times and places and perfect manifestations are also only my flawless, pristine Presence. So did he speak.

Book Seventeen

Pay heed to this: When you hold onto the remains of an enlightened being, you are actually holding onto Primordial Presence, beyond cause and effect.

In doing so, the continuous Buddha Presence of the three times, inseparable from its qualities, including the capacity to dissolve all appearances in the all-creating sovereign, is what is really held. My remains, the relics of victorious ones of the three times, are nothing other than my Presence. Therefore, hold to this Presence continuously, not just occasionally. Thus he spoke.

Book Eighteen

All phenomenal appearances in the animate and inanimate realms are manifestations of my nature. They are pristine, the purity of the pure space of the true condition. Appearing as various forms, they foster understanding.

The three kayas continuously teach the essence of the vehicles. Followers of these vehicles (such as Anuyoga, Mahayoga, and so on) believe in and are satisfied by cause and effect teachings. Those who transcend this (limited) view do not rely on this model. They do not practice generating causes because they do not desire (specific) goals. The self-perfected state is beyond desires (and the actions taken to satisfy them).

That which is primordial does not require any kind of activity (for attainment). The suchness of phenomena is not something which moves, nor is there any need to attain anything from suchness. In that they are intrinsically identical to the essence, phenomena are inherently self-perfected. Enlightened beings of the three times, being perfected in this way, do not instruct others to strive and actively practice.

The kind of meditations which are based in seeking do not result in realization. Indeed, they are a form of disease.

Every teacher, the sole exception being me, will be urging their followers to perform sacred activities, to traverse grades and levels of meditation, to see new dimensions. None of the appearances which they conceptualize ever depart from the true condition. This kind of active striving is never ending. The various meditations which they perfom disappear. The light rays which they emanate fade away. None of their visionary experiences remain. This is the pointless result of such striving. Do not follow this approach.

It is cause and effect teachers who set out this kind of practice, the idea being that one can realize some other dimension by searching. These teachers distinguish two distinct aspects of the true condition: the phenomenal and the actual. The real condition is never discovered by engagement with phenomena. Thus he spoke.

Book Nineteen

The teachers who give outer, inner and secret instructions do not reveal my core teaching about the path beyond striving. My unique pathway, what I myself reveal and teach, never ever urges seekers to attempt to gain realization by exerting effort.

Natural self-perfection does not seek and search. The three kayas reveal me fully. My essence is the uncontrived Dharmakaya. My nature is the unfabricated Sambhogakaya. My compassionate energy is the immediately manifested Nirmanakaya. The kayas do not give explanations about goals to attain by striving.

The kayas are one in me, the Creator. All phenomena, however they appear, are the three unfabricated kayas. They are my suchness. Supposed buddhas and defective sentient beings do not exist apart from my suchness.

All phenomena are suchness and abide in non-conceptual total equality. Nothing at all has come into existence outside of this. Enlightened beings do not invent teachings about something other than this. I, the Sovereign creator do not give even a single teaching that there is something higher than the suchness of non-conceptual total equality. Thus he spoke.

Book Twenty

I the All-Creating Sovereign, am the seed of all that appears. I am the cause, the ground, and the root of all phenomena. Since all manifestations, however they appear, are one in my Presence, I am the Source of them all. Because they are born from my Presence, I am their seed. Because all phenomena, however they appear, are manifested from me, I am their cause. They are like branches, and I am the tree. They abide in me, and I am their foundation. However they appear, I am their root.

Explanations about how the kayas arise from three aspects of my unfabricated essence are only words. But it is certain that the three kaya teachers are never parted from suchness.

I am unborn, and beyond subject-object duality. That which is called "unborn Dharmakaya" comes from my essence and is never separate from suchness. The so-called "nature" of my Reality is labeled Sambhogakaya. But it too never removes itself from suchness. The compassionate energies of Nirmanakaya also are never separate from suchness. The label is only a word, but suchness is the Reality.

In the same way that the kayas are never removed from their essence, which is suchness, so the teachings, the retinues and all phenomena are never apart from suchness. Talk of causes and effects as regards the true condition give rise to striving and efforts to realize. Those who want to generate effects from causes deviate from the Great Perfection Reality. Causes and effects come into being within me (and this is the thing to realize).

The three kaya teachers, the buddhas, the retinues, places, times and all the rest which come into play from me are all my flawless, pristine Presence. For this reason, you should not entertain notions concerning them, or form judgments about them. All my creations are this perfect presence, and it is primordially pure. I am pure. I pervade all that appears. I am perfect. My essence manifests clearly and I am the primordial Presence in all.

My essence is like space. Just as worldly illusions appear, my primordially perfect presence manifests the three kaya teachers, the buddhas, followers and disciples. If you would express or represent my pristine, flawless Presence, you may say that it is like space. So he spoke.

Book Twenty-One

Listen! I am the Sovereign Creator of all that appears, father and mother of the three-kaya-teachers (Dharmakaya, Sambhogakaya, Nirmanakaya), progenitor of all enlightened beings of the three times, the lamp that reveals the assemblies (of disciples), times and places. The three styles of teachings, based on the kayas, are radiated by me.

Because Source is prior to all the teachers and their five kinds of presentation, I make it clear that the point of it all is to awaken complete certainty about my nature. I am primordially pure Presence, the primal Great Perfection, beyond cause and effect, utterly transcendent. Two kinds of explanation are given: the first is about the transcendent cause, and the second is the systematic presentation which emanates from my nature, the mind of perfect purity.

The highest truth is conveyed by blessings. The radiant revelation comes through self-actuation. The physical manifestation reveals its nature by verbal expressions of meaning. These are the three systems of teaching which derive from the kaya-teachers, and they reveal three aspects of my nature (transcendent, universal, individual). I am beyond causation, beyond the senses. The consciousness which is flawlessly pure transcends all and is the core Reality of all that appears. This being the case, it is also the source of confidence. As the root of all phenomena, and the essence of all, this perfectly pure consciousness supersedes all in excellence. Thus, the Great Perfection is distinct from all the other vehicles (such as Anu Yoga, Maha Yoga, etc.).

To know the mind of perfect purity is to know Reality and all the enlightened ones. This is why I am revealing this Wisdom for the benefit of those of aptitude. The nature of mind is not something which can be expressed in words. Being inexplicable, it does not appear, and because of its non-appearance, it is not something which can be pointed at. This causes many to engage in active striving. For the correction of this I do give teachings about the nature of mind, despite the fact that it is inexplicable. Using the five systems of explanation, the right understanding of Kunje Gyalpo has been presented in an unerring manner, beyond notions of cause and result.

All appearances in the mind are the perfect purity of consciousness. This is the basis of confidence. The consciousness of perfect purity truly exists, and this is the basis of our primordially present confidence. The absence of striving is primordial confidence, and this is why we abide in supreme bliss which is unreachable through striving. This is how one comes to abide in my nature, the heart of the Sovereign Creator. There is no other Buddha apart from the Sovereign Creator. Thus he spoke.

Book Twenty-Two (The Great Garuda In Flight)

Listen! Regarding the objects which appear to our minds: know them to be non-existent. Despite this truth, people generally do not understand that the various appearances in their minds do not actually exist. But self-abiding Wisdom abides just as it is, everywhere, beyond our concepts and notions. It cannot be an object of (intellectual) attention and is not something which is modified by active practices.

Some try to investigate the nature of appearances intellectually. Others meditate on the question. But these approaches are ineffective for realizing the truth.

The followers of Ati Yoga abide in suchness and do not attempt these forms of investigation. Goal-seeking by way of religion is also an unwise approach. That which is (conventionally) non-existent does not need a cure. Beyond the arising of consciousness and its energies there is no other truth to realize.

Awareness, although not conventionally existing, is not without purpose; it self-originates. It is the real condition, the ultimate continuum wherein all concepts are rendered irrelevant. In fact, non-conceptual directness is the point of entry for this path of ultimate purity. In the spaciousness of the Supreme Source, one realizes supreme equality.

There is nothing to apprehend, no place for attachment to occur, no need to maintain a special condition of presence. The supreme equality does not arise for those who desire pleasure, or who become attached to their meditations.

Being the single continuum that pervades all appearances, there does not exist any phenomenon that could be an add-on. Presence is never-ending, so there can be no diminution of the nature of Reality whose energies are the domain of extraordinary experiences. Presence is everywhere present.

The eye of Wisdom sees clearly that there is no miraculous object to see. Reality is beyond all forms of verbal communication and thus, there is no way to explain or describe some higher domain of "ultimate phenomena".

Your continuum of primordial enlightenment is perceived directly. Thereafter, concepts may arise about Wisdom, just as shadows arise from forms, but realization does not come by conceiving illusions. The self-originated Wisdom will always be beyond the limitations of verbal communication, making debate and discussion of such matters pointless.

What we call the non-existent is not non-existent in a nihilistic way because it is the source of various manifestations. What we call emptiness is not a total void because it abides in a condition free of phenomena. The followers of Anu Yoga try to generate Wisdom even though the bliss beyond action is already there. They attempt to produce Wisdom from the domain of the inconceivable.

In certain circles, the minds of the followers are attached to the ancient sages. This can result in considerable exertion and striving. In such paths, they do not realize the all-knowing ultimate.

There is a form of conceptual meditation in which the idea of an 'authentic state of omniscience' is quite important. This is rooted in the defilement of attachment and a desire for supreme bliss. Unless one applies the ultimate medicine of abiding in unmoved, total equanimity, the urge to reach higher realms will be there, based in emotional attachment.

The desire to arrive is a constant derangement among followers of such paths. There is no dimension to discover or enter. The idea of reaching a special dimension beyond the three worlds or based in ten levels of achievement through striving is an obstacle to (recognition of) flawless, pristine Presence.

Instantaneous Wisdom is beyond thought. It is like a gem which manifests among spiritual friends. Not an object to attain, not dependent on changeable circumstances, its all-surpassing nature is also all-fulfilling.

Analyzing it, one finds nothing. Relaxing into it, supremely excellent qualities come to the fore. Invisible in terms of being a substance, it nevertheless reveals innumerable excellent attributes. It is beyond the dichotomy of 'self and other'. It is the teacher of teachers, a treasury of precious jewels, and it reveals a domain where all is perfected by selfless compassion.

All spiritual seekers are continuously inside the continuum of Wisdom. They do not need to discover a (special) place (which is more) inside. They love the realm of beings but have no concept of being dedicated to the continuum of Reality. Supreme, selfless compassion abides beyond the arising of concepts, with no mistaken notions of otherness, and with no urge to manifest something new.

To cherish an active desire for bliss is to abandon bliss. Bliss is already there. Seekers draw on this pre-existing bliss to seek for bliss in a mistaken way. Confused about the nature of the primordial continuum of Presence, such seekers follow fabricated teachings. They approach what is primordial with craving as if it were an object to find. The kind of enlightenment they imagine and seek does not exist. It is a mistake to create a label such as enlightenment, and then seek for it elsewhere. The formless is the source of all that appears, but for this mystery there can never be even the slightest explanation.

The supreme nectar has no relation whatsoever to methodologies based in fixed concepts such as "pre-established" (Anu Yoga), "sensual" (Maha Yoga), "transcendence" (Yoga Tantra), "insubstantial" (Madhyamika) and "renunciation" (sravakas and pratyekabuddhas).

The antidote to all of this is Ati Yoga. It goes beyond notions such as lower and higher, emphasis on something really great, or equality as something to be established.

From the true perspective, lectures, speeches, ideas about enlightenment, reference points and manifestations are all magical phantasms. If a practitioner's Wisdom is unclear, even if he escapes samsara and experiences nirvana, he will be prone to generate concepts because of such magical illusions.

Ati Yoga is rooted in an essence which eschews struggle and settles into the true condition. This yoga is beyond desire, beyond grasping, and free of even the slightest urge to achieve some (specific) goal.

Garuda-like, the nature of mind does not radiate, and does not re-absorb. It has no fear of being lost, and it entertains no conceptual grasping. It abides like the ocean, manifesting a variety of appearances. With qualities boundless as space itself, it has no particular place of coming together.

The non-conceptual domain is as infinite as space, but the Dharmakaya is not itself a phenomenon which is born, changes and disappears. From the ocean of the vast continuum, reflections arise. The sovereign contemplation arises immediately, being the pure, perfect Source that indwells all of this.

The world of causes and conditions is explained with analysis and negations, but all of this is no more than a doorway for the confused. Recognize the nature of appearances in the six planes of sentient beings. This is to be understood as the primal path. The experience of sense objects, enriched with compassion is an enlightenment practice arising in all forms of enjoyment. All misdeeds rejected by the lower vehicles are instantly and completely perfected. From within the true condition, it is evident that nothing whatsoever exists apart from absolute bliss.

Because all phenomena are actually the true condition, their essence is the nature of mind, which is flawless pristine Presence. For the real condition to seek the real condition would be like the sky searching for space, or fire burning fire. The non-conceptual Source is not hidden. It abides naturally in the minds of all beings in all circumstances, but Ati Yoga practitioners experience the pristine continuum beyond contrivance (accepting and rejecting, striving and attaining and the rest). Thus he spoke.

Book Twenty-Three

These phenomena that appear to you in your mind are all your flawless, pristine continuum of awareness. There is no object (as a basis of doctrinal views) to see. The pristine continuum of consciousness is non-conceptual. Those who are beyond conceptual grasping will have a disposition which is spacious like the sky, balanced and equanimous. Yoga is just this.

Do not ponder the things that appear to the five senses. Do not frame them in yoga-philosophy. In this way you also will have an outlook which is spacious like the sky. Like that you will come to abide in suchness.

Meanings may be examined by way of words and syllables, or not examined in this way. In Ati Yoga, the suchness of non-conceptual equanimity is the place of abiding, the abode of spaciousness.

The true meaning is beyond concepts and abides primordially like space. Thus he affirmed.

Book Twenty-Four

Presence Itself is sometimes called Samantabhadra, the All-Good. This is the source of all appearances. Knowing this, one is identical to that same Sovereign Creator. What is sovereign abides beyond change. One who has realized this is similarly beyond all things transitory.

Abiding in the Dharmakaya, one abides beyond conceptual constructs such as subjects and objects. The continuum that is eternally beyond objects and subjects is beyond impermanence also.

When he abides in the Sambhogakaya, the Sovereign Creator is able to enjoy the pleasure of the senses and the fulfilment of desires.

When abiding as Nirmanakaya-manifestation, the All-Creator emanates appropriate forms and suitable methods at the timing which is appropriate for education (of sentient beings).

While consciousness abides in the domain that is beyond change, all appearances are known to be symbolic and have the character of spaciousness, which is suchness. The hallmark of the three kayas is just this - suchness. All phenomena, all appearances (that arise in the mind) are suchness.

No phenomenon, however it manifests, has ever brought anything new to the pristine continuum (of infinite consciousness). Among those who cherish achievement through striving, not one has come to the goal by making gradual progress. Not one gets the result of realization based on what he or she has done in the past. Striving for achievement does not accomplish what is aspired to. Everything is just as it is in suchness, and there is no such thing as becoming. Thus he spoke.

Book Twenty-Five

Sentient beings of the three realms, know this: Your own mind of perfect purity is the teacher. For countless eons, beings have not recognized that their own consciousness is their teacher. I the Sovereign Creator have become present in the minds of all as their teacher.

Pay heed to the revelations arising from your own mind - whence my teaching arises along with emanations of the five elements and the five forms of instruction.

In the Sambhogakaya, the teaching does not require any speculation or thinking about thought itself or about doctrinal matters. The teachers of the nature of mind make it clear that all appearances and all phenomena are the real condition: suchness.

Teachers who come forward from the Earth element are also pristine awareness in their essence. Their primary teaching is not words and letters but their own presence. This requires no speculation about self and others. Such teachers manifest the state of non-conceptual equanimity and any sentient being who recognizes and understands this state will be of one mind with all the enlightened beings of all ages. The attainment which seekers long to realize and struggle to achieve is already perfected without any effort at all.

Pristine awareness also comes forward through teachers that manifest through the Water element. Here too, the words and letters are not the key point, but rather the teacher's own realization, and this involves no speculation about self and others. Such teachers impart the state of non-conceptual equanimity directly, with no notion of self or other whatsoever. Any sentient being who knows this state is one with all enlightened beings. Such a one will accomplish effortlessly what others strive for over long ages.

Similarly, teachers coming forth from Fire do not teach words and letters but convey Wisdom by its actuation in their own beings. Equanimity rather than conceptual grasping is what they convey. Beings of the threefold world who understand this are equal to the Buddha and achieve through non-striving what others labor for through long eons.

The same is true for teachers who manifest the Wind element and the Space element. The real teaching that students receive is their own actuation, their recognition of the continuum beyond description.

Oh sentient beings who wander in the three realms! I the All-Creating Sovereign am your source. You are my children and equal to me. You are me, and not other than me. I manifest you directly. My nature takes the form of the five elemental teachers, but in essence they are one, and that one is me. Be confident that you are that same one and none other.

Oh, sentient beings of the three realms, because I do not exist (conventionally), neither do you. In that you do not exist conventionally, the five teachers have never manifested. They never taught these non-conceptual teachings. Thus he spoke.

Book Twenty-Six (The Refining of Gold from Ore)

See Chapter Eight

Book Twenty-Seven (The Great Potentiality)

See Chapter Eight

Book Twenty-Eight

My essence is unchanging space; my pristine awareness is the changeless sky. My true condition is immutable in nature. My mind is the unaltered core behind all appearances. In this way, all things are unchanging except the kaya-teachers. Their embodiments (in human form) make use of cause and effect teachings to explain me, and even urge their followers to renounce the objects of the senses.

The nature of the self-originating continuum of Reality is not taught to those whose minds believe that the five obscurations are inherent. They think of phenomena as evil obstacles and defilements. They reject such evil and actively practice ten different kinds of virtuous behaviour. Within the authentic continuum of Reality, they are constantly accepting this and rejecting that. Such seekers will not recognize my self-originating Wisdom for many eons.

Listen! Such as these can never recognize that the five downfalls are in actuality five Wisdoms. Since they do not understand the nature of self-arising Wisdom, they reject their own essence, all the time following a kind of path not taught by me.

Listen! Many boddhisattvas train in terms of a two-tiered Reality, the ultimate and the relative. They think in terms of a "goal" which can be brought about by causes. Even if they apply this kind of training for three eons, their many forms of active striving will in no way modify their true essence. I have never taught the idea of trying to modify anything.

Listen! There are some who strive for supernatural aptitudes stemming from samadhi of the Reality of their own consciousness. They practice purifications rites and deity propitiation and visualization along with offerings to please their god. They will not recognize the nature of mind. It is not like the appearance of the moon on the surface of a pond. For seven lifetimes they will fail to recognize their inherent Wisdom. Kriya Tantra is not taught by me.

Listen! There are those who meditate upon the marvel of their own mind hoping that this will engender the special aptitudes which they crave. They fancy a special connection with the deities they visualize in their meditations. It will be at least three lifetimes before these Yoga-Tantra seekers recognize the true nature of mind which transcends activity and is not to be attained by craving. This kind of path I have never taught.

Listen! Followers of Maha Yoga visualize the true condition as a deity and use mudras, mantras and practices of emanation and re-absorption to encounter the true condition, which they consider to be a "cause". By contemplating the mind, they strive to attain their goal. But that approach to attainment has never been taught by me.

Be aware of this: The unchanging nature of spaciousness, the ground, is immutable. The attempt to modify that space is not something I have ever taught.

Some teachers try to control and modify the true condition. They teach contemplation as a pursuit of specific states of tranquility. In Reality, their teachings are but preliminary guidance leading ultimately to Ati Yoga.

The immutable consciousness (the nature of consciousness in itself) cannot be realized by the application of one's own (conceptual) mind. It is not possible to modify the immutability of the nature of mind. Reliance on the duration of a wrong practice only leads to fatigue. This is not something I teach or have ever taught. This he spoke.

Book Twenty-Nine

All phenomena are my primordial state, continuous equality. The teaching and explanation of my essence has five aspects: preceptors, teachings, followers, locations and times. These aspects are also my natural state.

All phenomena self-liberate in the true condition. The teachers, teachings and the retinue of disciples all self-liberate in the authentic continuum.

Apart (distinct) from this continuous resting in the poise and balance of my own being, there is no such thing as a "thing". There cannot be a single thing which is not included in this total perfection (of my nature). All appearances, whether teachers, teachings or retinues abide in this poise and all are liberated into the true condition.

You who have understood that all things self-liberate in this way have no need for contrived meditations upon your body as a deity. You do not need contrived words or speech. You do not need a fabricated samadhi. By contriving, you will not attain the state of poise. If you do not have equality and equanimity, there is no liberation, lacking which there will be no recognition of identity with Reality.

Although I am always at rest as and in the true condition, followers of the various doctrinal views do not understand how to abide in equanimity.

I, the All-Creating Sovereign have been at rest primordially, but the active seekers cannot understand this. They judge their own minds to be an obstruction, and because of this they try to refute and block it. Thus, they are unable to relax into the true condition.

Followers of the Mahayana sutras hear about total perfection but fail to recognize that their own mind is the true condition. Thus, they are unable to relax into the authentic continuum. For this reason, they go on with their training for three eons.

Followers of Yogatantra cannot understand that the suchness of their own consciousness and the suchness of all appearances are identical. Thus they cannot relax into the true condition. They carry on trying to empower themselves with the factors of realization and miraculous actions for (seven) lifetimes.

Mahayoga practitioners believe that the authentic continuum is susceptible to the laws of cause and effect. Therefore, they actively strive to realize that which has existed primordially. In this way, they are unable to relax into the authentic condition. For hundreds of years they continue to strive, but they remain at the three-samadhi level of attainment.

Anuyoga practitioners hear about the Great Perfection, but they too think of the primordial state in terms of cause and effect. They cannot relax into the true continuum of equanimity. Thinking of the dharmadatu as a cause, they want to attain, as a result, the mandala of Wisdom. If not corrected, this 'strive and attain' approach can go on for a whole lifetime.

When followers of Ati yoga hear about the Great Perfection, they go directly into primordial enlightenment, and without striving they come to the plenitude of bliss. Without needing any effort, they are enlightened.

Among deities and humans, there are varying degrees of aptitude. Some are inclined to active practice and gradual progress, while others understand immediately (that this is unnecessary). Seekers are taught what is expedient and relevant to their capacity.

The Great Perfection of Ati Yoga is to be understood as follows: *"a"* means the true condition, the authentic and primordial ground of being; the syllable *"ti"* means that the primordial nature of mind is self-perfected with no need for reliance on a quest of any kind; *"yoga"* designates the state of complete perfection (Dzogchen).

When people talk about the ultimate as differentiated from the relative truth, it is because they think they need to add something or remove something (to or from the Supreme Reality). This does not lead to the recognition of the Reality that is non-dual. The Wisdom of enlightened beings of the three times does not entail duality because it is rooted in (authentic) recognition of the real, unitary condition.

Book Thirty (The Total Space of Vajrasattva: The Un-waning Victory Banner)

See Chapter Eight

Book Thirty-One (The Cuckoo's Song of Awareness)

See Chapter Eight

Book Thirty-Two

Rightly understood, whatever appears to you is all one in suchness. Do not fabricate something in this regard. The sovereign of equality, beyond all forms of contrivance, abides in non-conceptual Dharmakaya. Thus he spoke.

Book Thirty-Three

It is not easy to understand the Wisdom of pure awareness, the real condition. It is difficult to recognize this self-originating nature of mind, the sovereign who renders all that appears perceptible. It is a nature that transcends our concepts, so it cannot be reflected on or become the object of thought. It has no desire or any notion about the idea of striving for the fruit of practices.

You try to grasp what is real by way of words like "dimension", "sky", "element" and "apparent". How will you be able to understand the essence of the sentient beings in this threefold world unless by using words? You yourself are the sovereign intelligence. Bear this in mind as you listen to me:

The word "dimension" suggests that the Reality is not diversified or multiple. The word "sky" suggests that the Reality is free of all obscurities. The word "element" indicates that this Reality is the core of all things. And the words "sentient being" indicates the quintessence of the universe. Knowing this, I recognize that you have created all. This fact is difficult to grasp. The Source has never taught that there is anything other than this great being - the All-Creating Sovereign.

If you have recognized the nature of mind, then you will understand the abbreviated and expanded forms of the buddha-dharma.

The Sovereign Creator, the mind of flawless purity is Reality, consciousness and primordial cognition, the knowingness of Reality. Reality is simply another word for the non-conceptual infinite consciousness itself. The word "sky" simply indicates that this consciousness is utterly pure. The word "element" is intended to indicate the actuation of consciousness, its manifestation.

Sentient beings have the kind of intellect which understands differences. But nothing except the beingness of knowingness actually exists. There is nothing besides this awareness, this all-creating King.

Knowing this, you will rightly understand the very nature and existence of the Source. You will understand me, the one, and in this you will understand all that has become manifest. In this, you will be the sovereign of intelligence.

Knowing Reality in this way, you will understand the manifestations who emanate from Me. You will understand their three aspects (kayas) and the three kinds of paths that derive from their teachings. You will understand the teachings which claim goals and their causes. You will know all about the followers who strive for goals by activities, views and behavior.

You will know that the three kaya teachers represent three aspects of the Source. You will understand that the three types of teachings are explaining these aspects, indirectly for disciples with varied mental capacities. These followers cherish the intent to achieve non-distracted tranquility. They meditate upon their own individual condition.

The kaya teachers expound only provisional teachings. Some of them talk about a goal to be reached by gaining various levels on various paths. Some explain things that do not actually exist. Some explain a process for realizing a special state by cultivating a special condition. Such teachings are not definitive. However, by following such instructions based in notions about causes and results, some seekers may achieve results such as undistracted calm abiding.

Here is the definitive teaching: The true condition cannot be perceived or explained. It does not exist as something which can be intellectually grasped. Being the non-conceptual essence, it is beyond all our notions about it. The desire-bound mind does not really exist. There is no goal. Simply by abiding in the true condition beyond thoughts, with no need to progress on a path, Wisdom dawns. Without any need to be purified by pristine awareness as a preliminary, one discovers self-emergent Wisdom. Without performing sacred rituals, the self-perfected essence is present. Without following codes of conduct, this essence is already utterly pure. The sense organs and their objects are this radiant suchness. Seeing no distinction or duality between buddhas and sentient beings, everything is suchness and is recognized as one. Unity and multiplicity are seen not to exist in this suchness. Conventional notions are irrelevant as regards this Source. It did not arise from prior causes and is not produced by conditions.

All enlightened and sentient beings and the living as well as the inanimate universe are my essence, beyond acceptance and rejection. The various teachings of the three kaya teachers about the suchness of my essence are only provisional indications (concerning this suchness). Thus he spoke.

Book Thirty Four

My Reality brings together the essential intent of all enlightened beings. I epitomize their teachings, purposes and manifestations.

As a simile: My being is like the spaciousness of the sky. My essence is Reality. My expression is the perfect purity of awareness. Being beyond obscuration, I cannot be known (by the intellect). I manifest the true condition in a way that is spacious, like the sky. There is no need for acquiring or rejecting anything, as I am not knowable (by way of conceptual grasping). Freedom from getting and averting is my innate nature.

Like the sky, I am unborn. The essence of being unborn is integral to my nature. So also is the intent of Buddhas such as Vipashya and Shakyamuni:

spacious intent, unborn, unknowable, beyond getting and rejecting. I teach primordially the integration of all dharmas in the Supreme Reality.

Regarding the essence: There is inseparable oneness as regards my true nature and the unborn nature that is the essence of all enlightened beings. This is true also of their teachings. Reality, the continuum of the true condition, is utterly unobstructed. So also are the Buddhas. They are one with my all-pervading, pristine Presence.

The perfect purity of consciousness itself is the defining characteristic and the essence of all phenomena.

It is due to this that all Dharmakaya, Sambhogakaya and Nirmanakaya Buddhas are integral to my very being. We are one in this essential characteristic.

All appearances that derive from the Dharmakaya are essentially one in non-conceptual, total equality. Without moving, the Dharmakaya has the capacity to actualize numberless emanations. Sambhogayaka brings to the fore a wealth of qualities and perceptions. These are all direct manifestations of the Sovereign Creator, beyond any notion of accepting what is deemed "good" and averting what is judged "bad". The blessingful influences of all enlightened beings arise from and are one in myself, my true condition.

In the nature of Reality there is not one single enlightened being separate from me. In the infinite spaciousness of consciousness, there is not one thing which is other than one with me.

Knowing me directly, recognizing my pristine Presence, you will understand the oneness that underlies all appearances. Any other understanding of my nature will not result in the fullness of confidence. To understand (experientially, not theoretically) the authentic nature, my pristine Presence, is to transcend the dualities of eternalism and nihilism. The Infinite Consciousness is unborn and beyond the subject-object dichotomy. It transcends notions about eternal entities. This timeless Wisdom also transcends the extreme of nihilistic emptiness.

Those who see Buddhas and sentient beings as different are not knowers of the mind of perfect, pristine Presence.

Book Thirty-Five

Because Maha-Ati-Yoga is beyond cause and effect, beyond struggle and practice, it is incompatible with most other teachings.

I am the All-Creating Sovereign. My authentic nature is difficult to understand. In terms of doctrine, vows, good deeds, progress on the path, stages of achievement, Wisdom and the authentic condition, my direct revelation does not accord with the teachings and practices of other yanas (vehicles).

From the perspective of my direct teaching, the term "entrance" means non-striving and non-seeking; "view" denotes nothing which the intellect can grasp; "vows" are not to be observed; "sacred practices" are to involve no effort; "path" indicates that there is no path to follow; "stages of progress" indicates something not to be practiced; "pristine awareness" is non-conceptual, un-moving; and "Reality" refers to unmodified suchness beyond fabrication or contrivance.

If these meanings are taught to the believers in cause and effect (Mahayana), they will reply that this makes no sense since effects come from causes. In the Sutrayana, it is taught that certain causes, once applied, bring about the result of Buddhahood. Using view as cause, by means of meditation, these seekers strive to accomplish what is meditated. But this never brings the authentic realization.

All phenomena are by nature the true condition. The attempt to fabricate the true condition is the greatest aberration. What is true becomes obscured by mistaken approaches.

Disciples of lesser aptitude may be receptive to guidance and they may decide to settle down in a place that is free of distractions. Here they may wrestle with (active) practices, (conceptual) views, meditations, vows and the rest. In this context, the non-conceptual equality of the true condition may gradually be explained in an effective way. Thus he spoke.

Book Thirty-Six

I am the essence of the mind of perfect purity, the All-Creating Sovereign. My essential being radiates into form, utterance, and spirit. Nothing exists that has not come from my form, my utterance and my spirit. All enlightened beings come from this, as do sentient beings and the entire animate and inanimate cosmos.

I, the All-Creating Sovereign, am the essence of form, utterance and spirit. The energies of Samantabhadra (the Dharmakaya Buddha) are my body. The sounds and words that illumine the minds of sentient beings are my voice (utterance). My spirit is continuously arising Wisdom which reveals unmistakably the nature of Reality, my essence.

Everything that appears, whether animate or inanimate, is the nature of my body (form). In this way my manifestations reveal through their essential nature the truth of my Being. You too reveal this to whose who do not yet have true realization.

All the sounds made by Earth, Air, Fire and Water and the voices of sentient beings also are my voice. Being my voice, these can be means for sentient beings to come to a true understanding of my nature. Teach this to those who have not yet come to realization.

Sentient beings are my consciousness. The five elements also are the equanimity of the non-discursive continuum of consciousness. They are inseparable from my nature, being unborn, unceasing, and beyond the grasp of thought. Convey this to those who have not yet come to realization.

If you do not share this teaching, it will be very difficult for these seekers (rooted in cause and effect and following graduated paths) to attain realization. They will never know me directly and in truth. All manner of beings – buddhas, sentient beings, travellers of the nine valleys (yanas) and the various bodhisattva levels, lineage-holders and many others engaged in dharma will not meet and know me directly and in Truth.

If they have no true encounter, beings of the threefold world will not know who they really are. Even bodhisattvas who strive for eons will not meet or know me in truth and (consequently) will not recognize or realize their own essence.

Whatever other amazing attainments they may have, spiritual adepts will not have the authentic encounter and recognition of my pristine, flawless Presence. They will not realize that their essential nature is identical to me, the Sovereign Creator. Failing to see and realize, they will be overcome by despair and fatigue. For this reason, you should proclaim my Wisdom. So he spoke.

Book Thirty-Seven

Listen, Wisdom-holders of genuine accomplishment, bodhisattvas who abide on diverse spiritual levels and sentient beings of the three realms. I am the universal aim of your aspirations. My Reality is not something upon which you are able to meditate (conceptually). Intuit and realize the natural condition, the consciousness beyond meditation.

The teachers of causation proclaim it (the pristine continuum of consciousness) as a law that governs all aspects of life in this world. They all teach their preferred styles of meditation, even though my true condition is not reachable by (conceptual forms of) meditation.

Some speak in terms of the four noble truths, suffering and its origins. They focus on the causes of suffering and rebirth in lower realms but ignore the true condition, pure and total awareness. Not recognizing or understanding the true condition, they abandon it.

In the bodhisattva path, there is a focus on the two levels, relative and ultimate. Followers of this path also apply the ten paramitas (perfections) such as ethics and generosity. They do not realize the non-dual true condition but remain preoccupied with their active practices. Even though bodhichitta is the Reality they strive to realize, they stay (keep busy) at the level of purification.

Followers of Kriya, Yoga and Upaya look for auspicious timing of the planets and stars. They are interested in empowerments and deity-visualizations but fail to know the true nature of their own minds beyond meditation.

Followers of Maha and Anu Yoga use three types of contemplation and five types of ritual to complete their four approaches and accomplishments. They strive to transform into the form of a deity and to realize the simultaneous emptiness and appearance of Reality. But they do not recognize the true nature of mind beyond active striving.

One's essence is already the liberated true condition. I, the ultimate teacher, do not instruct teachers of the three dimensions that they need to modify the mind by doing meditation. The nature of the mind is already fully enlightened. When meditation and active practices are embraced, the true condition is obscured.

Realization arises only when there is no desire. It is already accomplished, fully established beyond the pulls and pushes of cravings. There is no need to make efforts at abiding in non-conceptual equality. Relax into the domain beyond getting and renouncing. You will naturally and effortlessly be able to rest in the stillness of the true condition and realize the suchness in all things. Never try to fabricate the natural state or strive to realize anything other than the true condition. Do not seek something other than your own natural state. Even a the Buddha could not succeed in such a thing! Since enlightenment is already primordially established, there is no need to fabricate (such a thing). Without any effort of directed intent to accomplish what is already primordially accomplished, just relax in equanimity beyond conceptual activity.

Buddhas of the past have never found something significant beyond their own consciousness. They never strove to fabricate the true condition. Nor did they practice conceptual contemplations. Your natural, non-discursive equanimity now and in the future remains the authentic realization. Thus he spoke.

Book Thirty-Eight

In the Sutrayana path, Bodhisattvas aspire to realize the plane of universal illumination. By judging and analyzing the two truths, they come to assert that the authentic nature of all phenomena is emptiness, like space. But the ultimate bliss of Ati Yoga is the infinite consciousness beyond conceptual analysis. This Sutra tradition cannot grasp the Reality of the true condition by analytical methods which are deviations and ultimately misleading.

Kriya practices continuously purify the three doors (body, speech and mind); they try to establish a pure subject attending to a pure object. The bliss of Ati Yoga, however, is infinite, nondual consciousness itself beyond dualities like subject and object. Kriya practice obscures recognition of this. The subject-object dichotomy is a misleading deviation inherent in this yoga.

Devotees of Ubhaya practice various rituals but fail to intuit the full implications of non-duality. It falls outside the scope of their view and active practices. The great bliss of Ati Yoga is the pristine purity of infinite Consciousness. Ubhaya is an impediment to the recognition of Great Perfection non-duality.

Followers of Yogatantra strive to realize what they call the "dense array". They follow a path of two categories: with and without characteristics, and they focus on practising four mudras. They do not apply the principle of getting beyond acceptance and rejection. The bliss of Ati Yoga, however, is infinite Consciousness beyond accepting this and rejecting that. This hinders realization of that which lies beyond dualities such as acceptance and rejection. To entertain ideas about acceptance of some things and rejection of others is a deviation in relation to the Great Perfection.

Mahayoga devotees aspire to realize Vajradhara. They follow a path of active practice and inner Wisdom. They apply four stages of approach and achievement within the mandala of their minds. Ati Yoga bliss is synonymous with the Infinite Consciousness beyond striving. That which transcends striving is hindered by this Mahayoga approach. Those who strive in this way are on a path of deviation and are being misled.

Followers of Anu Yoga may enter the doorway of spacious Wisdom, but they think of space as a causative agent which brings about appearances (phenomena). They consider Wisdom to be the effect of a prior cause. But the ultimate bliss of Ati Yoga is infinite consciousness beyond cause and effect. Anu Yoga hinders recognition of this and is therefore a deviation.

In the yoga of Great Perfection, there is nothing like an achievement based on a prior cause. Practice and theory in Ati Yoga is of the nature of the sky whose spaciousness transcends theoretical views. Those who theorize deviate from the mind of spacious pristine Presence.

Those who think in terms of subjects and objects as regards the sky-like (spacious) nature of their own minds and entertain such doctrinal views will not discover the spacious continuum of pristine perfection. They deviate by thinking of subjects and objects as two distinct classes of phenomena.

Similarly, separating view from behaviour is a diminution of the skylike, unitary consciousness into duality. You cannot divide the sky. Those who divide will never realize the spaciousness of enlightenment. To separate view from conduct is deviation and hindrance.

Infinite Consciousness is like space in being beyond acceptance and rejection. Those who accept and reject do not recognize the spaciousness of Infinite Consciousness. They are lost in obstacles and deviation.

Space is beyond the striving which characterizes active practices. Those who struggle and strive in their practice (of yoga) have not recognized that the nature of mind is like space. Striving in active practice is an obstacle and those who do it deviate from the Great Perfection.

Space is similarly beyond cause and effect. There is no cause or result of the sky. Those caught up in cause and effect dualism do not recognize the spaciousness of Infinite Consciousness and are therefore mired in hindrance. In this way, they go astray.

Listen, excellent one! All phenomena are essentially spacious. This spaciousness is without substance. It transcends all examples we could adduce and is beyond our calculations. This is how you are to understand (in actual experience) the significance of all appearances and all phenomena whatsoever.

Each yana (vehicle) has its own doctrinal view. Each of these is an object for the intellect (to grasp). But the true condition is not an object that can be grasped by the intellect. The doctrinal views of the yanas are erroneous.

Each yana has its own vows, but they do not lead to realization because the Infinite Consciousness is beyond the duality of object and subject. There is nothing other than the Reality of Consciousness. The idea of observing vows is a mistaken approach.

Each yana has its own forms of active practice. But flawless, Pristine Consciousness need not be sought or improved by activities. It is already the Great Perfection. There is no need for such activities. They will not manifest a new or better Great Perfection.

The various vehicles (Upayayoga, Yogatantra, Mahayoga, Anuyoga, etc.) all have their own stages of progress. But since all sentient and enlightened beings already abide in the continuum of the true condition there is no progress by practising the Bodhisattva stages. The idea of progressing through stages is a mistake.

Each vehicle has its own notion about the nature of Reality. In the Great Perfection, Reality is pure rigpa awareness. This is the sole Reality. All doctrines about this can only be this. Attempting to grasp the nature of Reality conceptually is a mistake. Pristine Awareness is not an object of speculative thinking.

Wisdom is beyond concepts and transcends disturbances primordially. So he spoke.

Book Thirty-Nine

As the Infinite Consciousness, I am the source of all phenomena (appearances). The three kayas, enlightened beings, sentient beings and the entire animate and inanimate worlds are only this: the Infinite Consciousness, the Source.

How does this come to be? From the stillness of non-conceptual equanimity arises the Dharmakaya. It has no origin. From the nature (of mind/consciousness) comes the Sambhogakaya which makes possible the enjoyments of the senses. The compassionate energy of enlightenment gives rise to the Nirmanakaya acting benevolently for all.

Buddhas of the past attained realization by their direct experience of non-conceptual Wisdom. Without conceptualizing the continuum of the true condition, enlightened beings who are alive at the present time benefit (all) sentient beings. Enlightened beings of the future will similarly benefit sentient beings by teaching the non-discursive continuum of self-arising Wisdom, the Reality of enlightenment.

When Wisdom-holders and Bodhisattvas observe the Wisdom of pure, flawless Presence and see nothing (no thing), right then and there they encounter the essence of their own consciousness.

The self-arising Wisdom of all beings in all worlds can in no way be blocked. The clear-light radiance of objects and the senses is the flawless, pristine Presence, the suchness which is the Source.

There is not a single phenomenon in any world that is not manifested by me, as I am the cause and source of everything.

I supersede all phenomena, including the kayas, buddhas and so on because I am the source of all these as well as Wisdom-holders, Bodhisattvas, sentient beings and the animate and inanimate cosmos.

Before any teaching came to be, I the pristine, flawless Presence established my own being as the primordial teaching. No other teachers are able to do this.

How is the primordial teaching, the flawless Presence taught? There is nothing to be done as regards phenomena. Non-striving is the Way. Why? Because only Presence exists.

Because the true condition cannot be meditated by the human mind, it is beyond establishing views and meditations.

The true condition beyond object and subject can have no vows to observe.

Great Perfection is primordially complete, so there are no activities or rituals to perform.

All things already abide within the pristine Presence. Thus, there are no stages and levels for training.

The idea that the truth-continuum can be reached like a destination by travelling is wrong. There is no need to travel to any level to reach the pristine Presence.

The true condition is pristine, flawless Presence. Do not attempt to see some other real condition.

Wisdom is self-originated. There is no Wisdom which can be envisaged objectively.

I, the Supreme Creator, am victorious over all views and codes of behaviour, and because I am the Source-Creator of all I am the Source also of supreme victory. Thus he spoke.

Book Forty

I teach all beings that by not engaging in any striving or any achieving they are one by nature and primordially enlightened. The teachings which advocate striving will fade away because they are in error.

All phenomena which arise from the Infinite Consciousness manifest its basic nature. This nature is single in its essence but appears (to our karmic minds) in apparent multiplicity. Some say that attachment and aversion arise in relation to the sense objects, and that these objects then become the cause of suffering. Because of this, they try to cut them out. They fail to recognize that the five kinds of sensory objects are five forms of Wisdom.

All appearances are identical in suchness although samsaric beings see them as desirable or undesirable. Followers of Mahayana consider objects to be the cause of craving and try to purify them, but even after eons of time they cannot, for in actuality these are appearances rooted in Wisdom. Thus they take many rebirths.

Kriya followers believe they should empower objects with spiritual energy so they work at purifying inner appearances (in the mind) and outer (material) phenomena, even though these are in essence Wisdom. This keeps them busy for lifetimes.

Followers of Yogatantra, still working out of desire and aversion, think of certain appearances as causative of higher and lower states (of consciousness). Because of this, they appropriate and avert. But all appearances are the fundamental nature, a Wisdom which cannot reject or cancel itself. These seekers also keep busy for lifetimes in this manner.

Followers of Mahayoga try to realize the body, voice and mind actuality of objects by actively striving. But because they attempt to achieve what already exists, due to their striving they continue on for lifetimes.

Apart from pure and Infinite Consciousness, no self-arising Wisdom exists. Nor is there a nirvana beyond or apart from samsara. Outside the experiencer (subject) no ultimate nature is to be found. All is identical to suchness, and the effort to correct suchness is erroneous.

Do not attempt to modify the natural (true) condition. The act of modifying consciousness is samsaric and striving in this manner generates the momentum of samsara. Thus he spoke.

Book Forty-One

Come to know my core Reality in direct experience. I am the lamp which makes it possible for appearances to appear. I am the essence of all enlightened and the parent of all sentient beings. I cause all phenomena in the universe to manifest. There is not one of them that does not proceed from me.

I am boundless, everywhere present, the primordial source. Abiding as I do in fathomless non-conceptual equanimity, I continuously enjoy the primordial enlightenment of my Sambhogakaya nature, even as my Wisdom manifests the compassionate energies of the Nirmanakaya. I am the fountainhead of enlightenment that you see in the Buddhas of all times.

My primordial Wisdom arises from my Presence in five forms, generating the minds of the sentient beings in six classes. I am the mother and the father of them all.

All phenomena in the universe manifest my nature. As the Earth element, I am the eternally existent one; as Water, I am the integrating one. Mind (consciousness) itself is not other than the Water element. Being nondual, I am the integrated one. I am also the stillness and the warmth in all, their Fire element, dwelling equally in universality.

I am mobility, without material obstructions, the Air element present in all. I am flawless, all-encompassing, unhindered clarity, the element of Space in all.

The five elements are my own being. My mind of perfect purity shows the good qualities of the five elements. Earth appears, Water unites, Fire equalizes, Air mobilizes and Space manifests. All these are non-dual, one in the mind (consciousness) of perfect purity. All things come from the one, the all-creating monarch. Thus he spoke.

Book Forty-Two

Dharmakaya is Infinite Consciousness. Other than Infinite Consciousness, there is no other Dharmakaya to fabricate. Enlightenment is nothing other than the pure, pristine Presence of consciousness.

Sambhogakaya is the domain where experiential enjoyment of this Consciousness is possible. There is no other Sambhogakaya to contrive.

Nirmanakaya is pure consciousness. There is nothing and no one apart from this flawless, pristine continuum of bare awareness, that acts for the wellbeing of sentient beings.

All enlightened beings are nothing other than pure consciousness. Buddhas in the past achieved realization by recognition of the true condition of their mind (consciousness). Knowing the authentic nature of mind (consciousness), realizers in the present age bring good to others. In the future too, enlightened beings will not try to alter the mind by meditating or fabricating something. Rather they will follow the approach of "not correcting".

Not knowing that all phenomena of the universe are consciousness, seekers of realization who strive and modify the mind are acting in vain. Acting in ignorance, even if they strive on for eons, they do not enter the domain of effortless bliss.

Listen! The three kayas themselves are nothing but consciousness. How could there be something that needs correction? When teachers insist that spiritual seekers must be busy correcting appearances, their words and ideas do not accord with the truth. These sorts of teachers try hard to give the impression that much correction is needed, but what they teach is provisional, not definitive. Such did he speak.

Book Forty-Three

Listen! I am the teacher of all teachers and source of all their teachings. From me come the three kinds of teachers: those who communicate the essence of things, those who communicate the nature of things, and those who teach through the meanings of words.

The essence-teacher effects the empowering flow that comes out from the spaciousness of the unborn. Such a teacher directly conveys experiential understanding of the suchness of all phenomena.

The nature-teachers make clear the actuation process by which all phenomena appear. They teach that nothing exists except for the nature of phenomena.

The word-meaning teachers use the sounds of words to convey the meanings of all phenomena. They compose the sounds of words to communicate meanings for sentient beings who dwell in ignorance.

The essence of all three types of teachers is myself, the pure Presence of infinite consciousness.

Disciples are of three types. At the very outset, Ati Yoga disciples effortlessly gain certainty and abide in the state of enlightenment. Wisdom-holders and bodhisattvas are not fully realized but meditate effectively in order to progress toward their goal. Then there are those who strive to develop bodhichitta. They perform virtuous actions in order to extinguish the defilements of their passions. These three classes of disciples form the retinues of the three kinds of teachers.

Dharmakaya teachings and teachers point to suchness, something which cannot be divided into categories (for the purpose of analysis). All phenomena, however they manifest, are the nature of mind. Whoever meditates to modify the mind does not understand the dharmakaya teaching, the nature of immanent suchness.

The nature of mind is not part of the phenomenal universe. Suchness, when not rightly understood (that is, experientially) leads practitioners to experience separate phenomena (discrete objects). Seekers may look for some special space called "suchness", but even the victors, the enlightened beings of all ages, have never found such a thing.

Nirmanakaya teachings benefit sentient beings because of their compassionate energies. Different approaches serve different sorts of sentient beings in the three realms. Sentient beings are thus moved to give up their varied thoughts to better embrace the form, the expression and the spirit of the Buddha. Nirmanakaya teachers pass on what is suitable for those who live in solitude and turn away from sense objects.

I am the teacher of all, including the Buddhas and sentient beings. I teach them my authentic nature. It comes from the mouths of human teachers but must be intuited by disciples (to arrive at the true understanding).

Buddhas, teachings and disciples are three aspects of my being. The real teacher is ceaseless, self-originating Wisdom. The teaching is my uncontrived essence. And the disciples who understand these teachings rightly realize my nature. So he spoke.

Book Forty-Four

The state of non-action is my nature. Primordially complete, I am the true condition beyond actions. Reality is who I am. No deeds are needed. My nature cannot be altered. If you were to try to correct it, you would be attempting to alter the Source of all. However they manifest, all phenomena are my essence.

My nature is immutable. If you try to meditate on it, you are making efforts to alter and correct my essence. Why would you try to modify my primordial perfection?

Those who attempt to proceed toward me will never arrive. If they seek, they will never succeed. If they practice, they will never be pure. I am not an object for conjecture. Do not try to approach me gradually, as there is no path for this. Do not purify me. I am primordially flawless. I do not exist in such a way as to be perceptible. I cannot be grasped by conceptual elaborations because I can never be an object of thought.

All things conceived in my mind are my nature. When you strive to obstruct or reject certain phenomena, you fail to encounter my true nature for three eons, as this is rejecting my nature.

Consciousness is the all-creating Sovereign, the mind of perfect purity. Apart from Pristine Consciousness, nothing is creating anything. I am primordially unmistaken. The kind of thinking which deals in the dualism of lies and truth does not apply to my Reality. I am beyond distinctions such as cause, condition, outcomes, striving and accomplishment.

Being primordially accomplished, my state transcends struggle and practice, and you should not use meditation as a way to strive and achieve. There is no greater obstacle than this.

Wisdom is boundless, non-conceptual and beyond all forms of meditation. Wisdom abides naturally in non-discursive equanimity. There is no need to fabricate a mind that struggles for what is already and primordially accomplished. Those who abide in great bliss are identical to Source.

Source does not do things that benefit select individuals. Being the one, it unifies all. It does not see dualistically. Source encompasses one and all. With no (conceptual) doctrine at all, it illumines the minds of Buddhas and shines flawlessly in the consciousness of all sentient beings.

I, the Sovereign Creator, have already accomplished the supreme benefit of all sentient beings. What I offer cannot be generated by anyone. Teachings that speak of causes and conditions do not proceed from me, for I am Great Perfection intrinsically and fully accomplished primordially.

Doctrinal views and religious practices are unnecessary. Pure from the beginning, I require no observance of vows. Because I (your Source and essence) am perfected purity, there is no need to train to be a Wisdom holder or to achieve any of the bodhisattva stages. All phenomena are primordially perfected and beyond the reach of effort. There has never been any need for active practices based in a "strive and attain" mindset.

There is no need for the Wisdom of rigpa to block this or renounce that. Self-originated Wisdom is not an object of reflection. There is no need for your intuitive awareness to be illuminated by certain objects (which have been approved) as compared to others (which have been rejected). Reality cannot be differentiated into three times, for in essence all is one.

All times and places are one. There is one essence in all and phenomena are perfected in that. This being so, there is no need to accomplish something by seeking elsewhere, with views, behaviours, special activities, vows, levels and paths.

Those who lack authentic understanding apply effort to their practices. They act contrary to my truth that existence-consciousness abides beyond cause and effect. They will not come to the supreme bliss beyond action. The disease of effortful (active) practice is a form of ignorance.

Great Perfection, transcending cause-and-effect, is beyond attainment by seekers of this sort. Practices based in cause-and-effect thinking are not beneficial to those of little aptitude. So he spoke.

Book Forty-Five

My view transcends meditation. I am the All-Creating One and cannot be an object of (intentional) meditation. I am immutable, the indweller, the essential nature of all.

Concerning my essence, you will find nothing at all on which it would be possible to place attention. Various teachers claim that the real condition, which comes from me, is the disease of the five passionate desires. They never relax into the domain that transcends fabrication. Rather, they teach meditation, self-discipline, renunciation, and blocking. These strategies contradict the true condition. This does not lead to the realization of great bliss transcending activity.

It is wrong to say that the true condition produces suffering. It is a mistake to conceive of two types of truth and to give importance to analysis, but bodhisattvas of the ten levels do this kind of thing nevertheless. They meditate and they come to know that phenomena exist in a relative way but lack essence. However, they fail to understand to my natural state beyond fabrication.

Yogatantra teachers manifest from me, but within the continuum of the true condition, they focus on meditation with and without characteristics. Within the single Reality, they appropriate and avert. They consider that they themselves, having taken vows, are different from the Wisdom deities that they visualize. They hope that the deities will be their friends and give them special powers (siddhis). To envision that which is one as dual is erroneous. There is no realization to be had by cherishing duality where the Reality is non-dual.

Followers of the inner tantras (Maha, Anu) try to purify their psycho-physical aggregates, elements, consciousness, sensory abilities and sense objects into a diamond-pure deity. They have rituals and meditations as well as four types of religious service. For the welfare of (illusory) sentient beings, they mentally emanate and re-absorb their visualized mantras. They hope in this way to gain special powers (siddhis). They do all this to get what they already have and are (in essence). This leads only to exhaustion.

The Ati Yoga view is not a topic for (conceptual) meditation. The good qualities of the mind are inherently present with no need to strive actively to get results. Being beyond cause and effect, the true condition does not require karmic struggles.

I, the Supreme Source, am not to be found through goal-oriented meditations. The Reality sought in meditation is already one's very own presence, the inherent natural condition. Never having been born, there is no question of its destruction. Not depending on anything, the true condition is not dependent on meditations (for its self-revelation). Those who depend on meditation to meet me will not be able to encounter me in this way.

Everything (all that appears in the mind) is my clearly manifest true condition. There is no need to reject things that do not cause suffering. In my true state, suffering does not arise and there is no need to eliminate it. Since I am self-arising, unborn, indestructible there is no need to block and negate sense objects, dependent origination or ignorance. There is no need to practice the true condition. It is primordially pure and needs no purifying or ritual cleansing. Effort and practice are needless because the kayas and Wisdom are (primordially) self-perfected.

However closely you look, nothing impure will be found. All phenomena are the energies of suchness, forms of pure Wisdom. Those who deploy meditation to realize some other purity are like blind people in pursuit of the sky.

My nature is beyond all (conceptual) frames of reference. The phenomena which I manifest are my nature, which all beings experience. Sensory perceptions show forth my nature. It should be understood by all that the various phenomena which appear (to the mind) are my essence. Those who do not recognize that phenomena are my essence cannot learn from me directly.

Those who lack the aptitude to understand the Great Perfection will gravitate to provisional cause and effect teachings. If (in their current mindset) they were taught my true condition, they would try to affirm or negate. They would deny my omnipresent natural immanence and continue on in samsara being reborn in the six classes of sentient beings.

Since my true condition transcends all conceptual frames of reference, it cannot be determined by using words. My true condition is comprehensive. It is the true center that holds together all appearances. It is indicated by words such as non-dual, non-conceptual, primordially one (and so forth).

There is no point in deliberations, visualizations, vows, deity meditations, religious rituals, pathworking, purification or seeking some special condition apart from my authentic nature. Wisdom is pristine, non-conceptual. Do not search for it anywhere but within yourself. Pristine Awareness is my authentic transmission. It cannot be taught by others. Transcending cause and effect, it is not susceptible to striving and cannot be an achievement.

Do not meditate on me as if I were perceptible. The true condition does not arise from (prior) causes but abides as non-conceptual equanimity in the vast expanse of all-encompassing bliss. Being unborn, it is also beyond decay. Do not try to understand the ineffable nature intellectually. Do not approach meditation in this manner.

Meditation is generally a mistaken form of striving. My primordial purity does not afford meditators the least topic upon which to fixate. The mind of pristine perfection is without such notions as subjects (meditators) and objects (topics). Conventional meditation will not bring realization.

Turn to me. I am the Source, the Pristine Consciousness that is present in all phenomena and as all appearances. Everything, every phenomenon, comes from Source. Nothing exists in the way that your experiences and notions about objects exist.

Source is perfection, being the essence of all. Self-originating Wisdom is the clear light of consciousness in all. Thus he spoke.

Book Forty-Six

The Great Perfection has no vows to observe. The nature of the Sovereign Creator, mind of flawless purity, is birthless and non-conceptual, but from it comes all the magical display which appears (to your mind) as (a multitude of) objects. These appearances manifest my essence. By knowing the true condition of these objects (appearances), not (merely) thinking about them, you will go beyond conceptual grasping.

My true nature is beyond fixating on objects, accepting some and rejecting others. Wisdom is perfected in the singularity of stillness, beyond regulations, vows and the activities needed to keep these vows.

My three kaya teachers bring their compassion to those who follow religious rules and regulations, in some cases two hundred and fifty rules, and in other cases as many as five hundred and fifty rules. Even as they try to observe hundreds of regulations, such practitioners do not understand their true purpose. They are unable to keep this discipline. Great Perfection transcends conceptual grasping and is beyond all these vows and regulations.

These samaya vows are countless, immeasurable as the ocean, but they are three basic types: body, speech and mind.

Mahayana is bound up in the idea that suffering arises from the senses and their objects. Followers of this approach walk and sit in cramped spaces (to discipline the body). They find it difficult to voice only the truth in their words and meanings (to discipline the voice). As to discipline of the mind, the ideas in their heads contradict the truth, but even with unmistaken ideas the natural state is not to be grasped (by the conceptualizing intellect).

Being tightly constricted by all these vows, such seekers find it difficult to realize the nature of mind or know the state which is beyond the preserving and the breaking of vows. The continuum beyond keeping and violating vows is known directly by direct transmission of the All-Creating Sovereign.

There are some teachers who insist that auspicious timing according to the stars and planets should be applied to cleansing rituals. They promote disciplines, vows and morality for the good of sentient beings. Followers of the outer tantras cannot keep all these commitments in the correct manner. Confession of downfalls does not do anything to correct the flaw of not recognizing the true nature of mind. These seekers err and remain in non-recognition of my true condition which surpasses the preservation of vows (and the need for such).

The body is bound when vows require that it is meditated to be the body of the deity. Voice does not achieve tranquility by chanting mantras as a form of contemplation. The mind practice of radiating seed syllables and then re-absorbing them does not bestow insight into the nature of Reality, nor does it impart bliss.

Practitioners of the inner tantra take on vows that concern things to be understood. They try to understand that the five aggregates, the elements, the consciousnesses, sense organs, objects and so on are the essence of deities and mandala. This does not transcend the duality of knower and known. Those who do not see through this duality of subject and object take vows for uniting and freeing, and against stealing, sexual impropriety and lying. If these remedies are not (successfully) applied, they believe that they have broken the vows. But this kind of thinking brings them no closer to the equanimity which transcends concepts.

Practitioners of the inner tantras believe that if they do not readily accept five sacred substances along with their emanation and re-absorption practices then they cannot achieve realization. This prevents them from rightly understanding (experientially) the continuum of Reality that transcends notions of acceptance and aversion.

They believe that the five poisons (attachment, aversion, ignorance, pride and jealousy) should not be rejected but rather accepted as five forms of Wisdom. But the bliss which transcends acceptance and rejection is not to be realized in this way.

The imperceptible, spontaneous Great Perfection cannot be sought, but inner tantra practitioners try to bring about control over the five aggregates (matter, feelings, sensory experiences, mental conditioning and discernment), the five elements, consciousnesses and sense objects by perfecting the three samadhis and completing the five puja rituals. They are actually distracted from the nature of mind by their striving and their active practices. Ritual words and mantra repetitions do not generate the continuum of Reality. The perfected state is not actualized by such practices.

I, the Sovereign Creator, require no observance of vows. There are no causes and conditions (which must be established) and no need to achieve by striving. All is primordially perfected and for this reason sacred rituals are not needed. Only pristine awareness truly exists. There is no need to comprehend numerous concepts. Because Wisdom self-births, there is no need for reliance on the creation of special causes and conditions. Since good and bad are only ideas in the human mind, there is no need to accept some things and avert others.

There are no substances that must be ingested and no vows that must be observed. This I call "absence". There is only eternal Wisdom, and no need for rituals. This I call "omnipresence". All is one in the light of Wisdom. This I deem "unity". All phenomena, however they appear, are perfected in the true condition, which is "certitude". With regard to all of this, I use the term "self-perfection".

Some teachers instruct their followers in ways to escape heat, cold, hunger, thirst, dullness and deafness. But there is no need for struggles of this sort. Wisdom is the source of all. Struggle is incompatible with Wisdom. Karmic activities always fail to bring about Wisdom.

Reality never becomes something good or something evil. I do not teach realization through struggle. Self-sprung Wisdom cannot be realized by producing samsaric causes and conditions.

It is not given expression in options about two truths. How could such doubtful and indecisive teachings place reliance on talk of duality when they aspire to establish what is non-dual?

People who cherish the various forms of religion and yoga and rely on teachings about causation think that it is necessary to understand Reality in terms of the two truths and the four syllogisms. But because I, the Sovereign Creator am the Source of all, there is no place for talk of two truths with regard to my creation. Notions about the need for two truths could only arise in the primordially perfect continuum of consciousness where "ultimate" and "conventional" could not possibly be real. Thus he spoke.

Book Forty-Seven

The Great Perfection is self-perfected primordially. There is thus no need for ritual activity. However, various teachers proclaim that these activities should be done. They teach their followers which rituals to apply, the specific kinds of actions being tailored to the individualities of their disciples.

Nirmanakaya teachers direct their followers to apply actions as causes. They advocate love, compassion and mercy for the bodily, vocal and mental activities. They have vows for giving up murder, theft and adultery as regards the body. They vow to renounce gossip, deceitful speech, slander and so on as regards the voice. They also vow to give up thoughts of craving, aversion and mistaken views in the mind. They advocate virtuous behaviour as a cause (for liberation). They advocate the ten paramitas (virtuous actions) such as generosity, morality, renunciation, insight, energy, patience and so on. They hope in this way to attain various spiritual levels and ultimately supreme attainment. But the practice of these tiresome activities for eons is not something taught by me, the Sovereign Creator.

Sambhogakaya teachers of the three outer tantras promote cause-and-effect activities. They do purifications (inner and outer), ritual bathing, as well as empowerments. They make offerings along with their contemplations, evoke the deity and then send the deity back to where he came from. They carry on in this way for eons until eventually they become worn out.

Dharmakaya teachers instruct their retinues in Mahayoga and Anuyoga. They teach that everything is the true condition. They picture various aspects of their being as deities, complete with their families, their colours and the mandalas they inhabit. They perform rituals of pacification with peaceful deities, and abundance with the gods of abundance. With deities of power, they enact rituals of control. The deity of coercion helps them perform exorcisms. In this way, they attain levels of Wisdom-holder control and attempt to extend their lifetimes. But these exhausting activities do not achieve the deedless, true condition.

Great Perfection is beyond cause and effect. Those who follow cause and effect teachings form judgments according to worldly standards. They work with the cause to arrive at the desired effect. But in the primordial, pristine continuum there is no cause which results in enlightenment as an outcome (effect).

The Infinite Consciousness is primordially uncaused and without a result. It is not like phenomena in the world where causes and conditions seem to be in play.

Self-originating Wisdom means ceaseless energy (the cosmic flow), non-origination from causes, and it is fundamentally unlike the compounded phenomena that appear in manifestation. From the light of Wisdom all things come. The true condition cannot be fabricated apart from this transmission (of the primordial light of Wisdom). Thinking of Wisdom as a worldly phenomenon subject to cause and effect does not lead to the realization that transcends striving.

Flawless, pristine Presence is beyond causes and conditions. It is not a worldly phenomenon which appears and ceases. Worldly phenomena produced by causes do not furnish good examples to understand the nature of primordial Wisdom.

Seekers who envisage special kinds of achievement and strive for special kinds of accomplishment in meditation will not realize the supreme qualities (of the kayas) in this manner. The Wisdom-nectars are primordially self-originating. But seekers use meditation as a strategy for fabricating a state that they want to believe to be enlightened. To do this flies in the face of the Wisdom of all enlightened beings. It goes against the pristine, flawless presence which is the authentic condition. For eons, these contrivers will fail to realize my true condition.

Do not use your mental contrivance to generate such contemplations. Do not conceptualize Pristine Awareness as if it were an object of some kind. Do not keep your voice busy chanting mantras to invoke deities. There is no need for hand gestures or the intentionality behind them. Do not keep the mind engaged in deity meditation, or the projection and withdrawal of light rays.

When the mind comes to rest in the natural state beyond agitation, spontaneous Great Perfection dawns. Abiding in one's own being, the meditator has no need to fabricate or contrive. This non-action, the simple act of effortless, natural abiding, is the supreme sacred activity. Those who understand this key point do not keep busy with striving. Simply abide in suchness, beyond the practice of sacred activities.

Those who abide in suchness realize the unfabricated, unmistaken, true condition. There is no special phenomenon to be found apart from suchness. So did he speak.

Book Forty-Eight

I, the All-Creating Sovereign, the mind of flawless purity, am the Source of all, the Ground of what arises and appears.

From the three aspects of my nature comes the fullness which meets all needs.

I am unborn, eternal and the manifester of miraculous displays, ceaselessly created.

The fullness of the Dharmakaya is the ground of all phenomena, the unborn essence not produced by causes. The perfection and fullness of all teachers comes from this pristine, unobscured nature. The retinues (of disciples) arise from the miraculous creative displays which come from the unborn realm.

My Being is the one and only Reality. From the one, the Source, arise the various teachers' three forms of manifestation and their three retinues. In a way suitable for each retinue, my teachers impart the six foundational methods which help seekers to understand the suchness of the true condition.

Firstly, doctrinal views are just a means to help you glimpse Reality. Because the Unborn cannot be perceived like an object, you will never behold suchness by means of doctrinal views.

Secondly, making vows into a tool for eliminating one's flaws – this is just a tool to circumvent impediments. Suchness is not an object which can be observed; it will never be realized by keeping vows.

Thirdly, rituals simply afford you a means of striving for attainment. Suchness is not something to strive for and cannot be realized by striving.

Fourthly, following a path with the idea of making (gradual) progress toward a goal only makes sense if you have not understood that suchness is not a path on which one may move forward, nor is it reached by proceeding in this way.

Fifthly, the bodhisattva stages (of progress) can be taken as a form of religious striving. Suchness is everywhere and in all, not a set of stages in which to abide for the sake of progress.

Sixthly, Wisdoms (blessings; Wisdom-nectars) are the foundation for full realization of the true condition. Suchness is not anything to be grasped conceptually; nor can Wisdom be thought of as an object.

The purity of Consciousness is the Ground of Being, but the followers of causation fail to encounter the immutable ground of their own mind because striving obscures the recognition of suchness. Each vehicle has its preferred practices and doctrinal views which teach causation to their adherents. Each disciple looks for the path best suited to his or her nature. But suchness can never be an object of striving, no matter which of the six doctrinal views or which of the six practices they embrace. Because striving obscures suchness, they will never come to the unaltered ground of being in this way.

I do not teach that objects are other than or unrelated to their observer because the root of all is the one source, one's very own consciousness (mind). Seeing in terms of a doctrinal view is misguided. Do not practice contemplation based in doctrinal views.

Self-originated, pristine awareness transcends the observance of vows. Wisdom transcends observance (and non-observance) of vows.

I teach that there should be no striving based on religious rituals. Primordially, Great Perfection is beyond causation and those who want results from actions will never realize it. Great Perfection cannot be a result of a desired outcome. Only spontaneous acts, free of striving, accord with the Great Perfection.

I teach also that there is no gradual progress on a path. Both for bodhisattvas and sentient beings there can be no proceeding toward the mind by means of the mind.

I teach "no practice of the bodhisattva stages". The one and only stage is the mind of perfect purity. Those who try to realize mind through (active) practices are bound by ideas of cause and fruition. In the true condition there are no bodhisattvas and sentient beings, nor does the true condition travel a path to itself.

You cannot understand pristine awareness as an object. Objects are energetic modifications of the energy of Consciousness. Awareness of awareness is not possible, for awareness cannot be grasped by awareness. Thus he spoke.

Book Forty-Nine

I am the Source, the mind of perfect purity, pristine awareness. I am the dwelling place of the nature of Reality. All Buddhas and sentient beings dwell here, within the domain of Infinite Consciousness. There is not one phenomenon or appearance that does not dwell herein, beyond union and separation. There is no need to go anywhere or to purify. If you try to cleanse this realm, you are attempting to alter the true condition which is not something to correct. Pristine Awareness is the universal continuum, the home of all that appears.

Teachers in three forms of manifestation emanate from me, teaching the bodhisattva stages (of practice and progress). Their followers believe in concepts of causation, in stages of generation, practice and realization. They teach these three processes. At the first stage, the seekers develop four aspects of mind. Later they apply ten practices of mind. And finally, when they come to the level of realization, they hope for attainment. These are provisional, not definitive teachings.

With regard to the definitive meaning: the Infinite Consciousness transcends causes and conditions. It cannot be produced on some level of development. If it could, there would contradiction, because Infinite Consciousness is limitless like the sky and identical to the nature of Reality.

Those still under the influence of good and bad karma attempt to renounce outer objects, which are essentially the nature of Reality, which cannot be renounced. Only by not obstructing Pristine Awareness can it be possible to renounce the flaws of this world. They do not know that Pristine Awareness is not itself an object but is the essence of all that appears (as objects). They struggle to get beyond the idea that objects and subjects exist. This does not generate the Infinite Consciousness, because it cannot be produced (in the first place.)

Practising bodhisattva dharma, seekers engage in the ten paramitas with the idea of purging all existent things. But no phenomenon, however it appears, has ever moved away from the continuum of Pure Awareness. Phenomena are only appearances that arise in the space-like true condition (of Consciousness). Just as nothing, not even the tiniest particle, moves away from space, so nothing ever moves away from the space of the true condition (Consciousness).

At the stage of accomplishment, the third of the bodhisattva levels of practice, the seekers assign six names to their goal: all-encompassing light, desireless lotus eye, diamond-holder, solidly built, Vajradhara, and All-Good (Samantabhadra) cause-effect inseparable. Because the Infinite Consciousness is beyond causes and conditions, the authentic realization is not a goal to be gained by (such) accomplishments.

These are the six forms of the very being of consciousness, the forms of the mind's own being:

First, unceasing, self-arising, Pristine Awareness shines everywhere, through and as the sense organs;

Second, the level which is inconceivable and cannot be an object of desire;

Third, Pristine Awareness beyond beginnings and endings, called Vajrapani (diamond-holder);

Fourth, the immeasurable true condition or natural essence where self-originating Pristine Wisdom abides in perfect poise;

Fifth, the perfect purity within appearances, Pristine Consciousness itself abiding in its mandala of divine forms, utterances and spirits, called diamond-holder (Vajradhara);

Sixth, Pristine Consciousness minus cause and result, primordially beyond good and evil.

All enlightened and sentient beings originate from the Infinite Consciousness and abide therein (even as they appear). The space of the true condition (continuum) is the actual location of all practice. So he spoke.

(The place of "achieving Buddhahood" is a domain where there is no such thing as practising because what comes from the true condition has never been other than the true condition. In sum: Great Perfection is not a place of practice.)

Book Fifty

Wisdom is Primordial Awareness. They are one and the same. But the kind of 'Wisdom' that sees objects, since it depends on objects perceived, cannot be self-arising. Primordial Wisdom is not an object and cannot be recognized in the way an object can.

The mind of perfect purity cannot be an object, cannot be contemplated in meditation. If you do not engage in meditation, there will be no karmic tendencies toward meditation. The real condition beyond latent tendencies is the domain of the Buddhas of all times. The state of the enlightened ones is complete equality and cannot be recognized in the way an object can.

The self-arising Wisdom of enlightenment transcends concepts. But it is not something constructed by the human mind. By resting in non-conceptuality, Ati Yoga practitioners realize the true condition of the Buddhas.

Self-arising Wisdom is synonymous with enlightenment, the state of the Buddhas. By not entertaining notions and opinions about objects, this Wisdom remains undefiled by the karmic tendencies of discursive thought. The inclination to meditate is a karmic tendency, but in the non-conceptual state there are no karmic tendencies.

From the non-conceptual state come five Wisdoms, and these manifest continuously as the five doors of the mind (the five senses). Here, the nature of consciousness manifests and the Wisdoms appear.

When one abides in the true condition, there is no conceptualizing, and this kind of non-conceptual meditation accumulates no karmic tendencies. This brings integration with the mind of perfect purity, the true condition of the enlightened beings of all times.

There is no dualism between objects and Wisdoms. The object is itself Wisdom which has become manifest.

Disciples of various teachers give diverse names to my single nature based on how they conceive of me. Some express my Reality as "pure and total consciousness". Some refer to the "Dharmadatu" (nature of Reality) or the domain of space, or self-originating Wisdom. Some refer to the Dharmakaya, others to Sambhogakaya and still others to Nirmanakaya. Some speak of "body, voice and mind", while others speak of omniscience, and so on.

The names given to my Reality express limited ways of perception. Thus he spoke.

Book Fifty-One

I am Pristine Consciousness, the All-Creating Source (Sovereign). My perfectly pure consciousness is the supreme and universal path for all. All places, all realms and planes, and all levels of attainment abide nowhere else but the continuum of my authentic presence. Space and the heavenly realms exist only herein. The abode of Buddhas and the phenomenal appearances are my mind of perfect purity (ie: pristine awareness). Besides this, apart from Pristine Consciousness, there is no path for making progress nor a location wherein to exist. There is no place at which to arrive by treading the path of sky-like spaciousness.

The three kaya teachers who manifest from me propagate three different paths based in the idea of (gradual) progress. Seekers who hope to arrive at a goal by progressing on a path strive for results that derive from causes. But this does not accord with Great Perfection, where no such thing as progress is to be found.

Seekers on such paths work at gathering the two accumulations. They prepare, apply, meditate, see and realize (accomplish). They think that they have overcome the dualism of subject and object and believe that their meditations enable them to see the truth. But their approach is completely at odds with the Reality that there is no path to tread. Nor do they arrive at true, effortless bliss.

There are three paths of secret teachings about how to achieve the desired spiritual result. These goal-oriented teachings touch upon suchness, manifestations, and the seed syllable as the cause of the result. Seekers study, meditate and strive to progress by the application of four type of "approach and achievement", each subdivided into cause and effect. In this way, they want to progress along a gradual path and arrive at Wisdom, the real condition. However, gradual proceeding does not arrive at the destination which transcends effort and practice.

Consciousness beyond conceptual elaborations is the ultimate dimension of existence. Here, all the enlightened beings abide. Do not follow a gradual path!

Consciousness is unconfined, like space, beyond defilements. Here enlightened beings abide. Do not follow a gradual path!

Consciousness uncontrived is the authentic condition. Here, bodhisattvas of the three times, free of concepts, abide. So do not follow a gradual path!

When ignorance brings spiritual seekers to gradual paths, they will labour on but never complete their progress and never arrive at realization. Gradual paths do not lead to enlightenment. Real enlightenment is consciousness free of concepts and is not attained by following a gradual path.

Those who cultivate conceptual views meet with the things they manifest in their minds. This does not result in the equanimity of topic-free consciousness.

When keeping vows, one is bound to the determination not to break what has been undertaken. However, living by such concepts does not lead to the equanimity of consciousness beyond notions.

Because of their vows, they take up (various kinds of) active practices. Performing sacred activities goes hand in hand with meditations that crave achievement. Meditating with achievement in mind is not the same as non-conceptual equanimity.

Practicing the bodhisattva stages brings one to a form of calm-abiding meditation. This is a meditation for purifying. It does not result in recognition of that which is beyond conceptual grasping. The contemplation that leads to true accomplishment differs from that of (simple) non-conceptual equality. Recognition of the true condition results in clarity. Clarity brings experiential understanding (of Wisdom). This is quite different from topic-free calm abiding.

However clear it may be, meditation motivated by desire does not bring a realization that transcends desire. The fullness of bliss beyond active striving is realized by abiding in the topic-free consciousness beyond craving. Wisdom does not meditate conceptually, nor does it accumulate karmic tendencies. It abides beyond the pulls and pushes of karma.

The Wisdom which is the essence of the Dharmakaya is not attained by seeking, but rather by natural abiding. Wisdom eternally abides beyond all benefits to be attained. Benefit is an empty name. Enlightenment too is just a name for the true condition. Assigning the word enlightenment to the teaching does not change the fact that such teachings are provisional, not definitive teachings.

Teachers who assign names to the three jewels as if they actually existed apart from Pristine Awareness (Presence) teach their retinues to obtain happiness and joy by taking on the duress of effortful practice. They teach realization by the application of conceptual views and (codified) behaviours. These are not the effortless teaching that comes directly from me. Thus he spoke.

Book Fifty-Two

If you aspire for supreme realization, do not cherish a desire for attainment. The mind of desire brings loss rather than gain. The true condition transcends cause and effect. It does not dawn because of practicing a cause to obtain a result. Realization comes by abiding in the true condition beyond concepts. Give up desire-bound forms of (conceptual) meditation.

In the absence of desire, all things are accomplished. Although there is nothing to grasp, meditators frequently practice with a covetous motive. Action-oriented paths strive to realize the perfection that transcends effort, but this does not bring success. Perfection is present already, just as things are, requiring no action and unobtainable by means of action. The true condition is not produced, rather it is primordially self-perfected (and self-originating).

Desire repels the qualities of primordial enlightenment and is an obstacle to realization. Meditation motivated by desire feeds karmic tendencies (such as grasping) and these eventually dominate the (thinking) mind. This undermines authentic happiness. Minus grasping, one is the heir to limitless happiness, the authentic and natural condition.

Unconceptualized suchness is the consciousness indwelling all enlightened beings. It is bliss free of desire and beyond any notion of acquisition. The continuum beyond concepts is not an object to be grasped. One does not appropriate the non-conceptual state.

The true meaning of non-action is understood by getting beyond desire. Grasp nothing. Be free of attachment. This is the ultimate contemplation. This freedom from grasping, primordially full and flawless, is the realization transcending notions of things to get and things to release. This brings mastery in the state of equanimity beyond cognitive grasping.

Varied forms of meditation do not elucidate the One. Meditation which is intended to elucidate a topic is not authentic meditation. The true condition is One. Despite this, teachers distinguish between enlightened beings and samsaric beings, between happiness and suffering. They urge the pursuit of happiness and reject the onset of suffering. This is not a definitive teaching.

Do not change what is one into two. Joy and misery are one in the nonduality of flawless, pristine consciousness. Truth and falsehood are not two in the real condition Do not grasp at joy or reject unhappiness. When you abide naturally, all is perfected in advance. Attachment to happiness is a form of bondage.

Wisdom is the fullness of clarity, beyond concepts. Pristine awareness has been undefiled by karmic imprints primordially. Whence could imperfection possibly have come?

Do not practice conceptual meditation on Wisdom. Conceptual meditations depart from non-conceptual equanimity and attract the affliction of striving.

I, the Source, am pure, Infinite Consciousness. Everything is this very suchness. Apart from my true nature, nothing whatsoever exists or appears.

From the infinite consciousness come the teachings that get rooted in physical appearances and the beliefs of sentient beings along with all their varied perceptions of forms and colours. All this flows from the compassionate energies of nondual Wisdom.

None of these phenomena either exist or appear apart from the continuum of the natural condition which is the nature of all enlightened beings. Aside from the true condition, the continuum of pure, flawless awareness, there can be no enlightenment. Apart from the continuum of natural enlightenment, there are no sentient beings.

The non-conceptual, natural state of sentient beings is Buddhahood. Without this conscious continuum which is the true condition, there are no Buddhas. Apart from Buddhas, no sentient beings exist either. The true condition in sentient beings is Buddhahood and sentient beings are not other than enlightened beings. Because this is so, all Buddhas of the three times praise the primordially flawless Presence.

The continuum of the true condition is beyond change and has been so from the beginningless beginning. Since it is unmoving and immutable, when teachers divide this unitary Reality into nine yanas (vehicles) and eighty-four thousand forms of practice, they fail to comprehend the authentic condition of the Source.

Not understanding the One, they fail to understand the nature of Reality. This means that nothing whatsoever is understood.

To know the true nature of mind is the ultimate understanding. Thus he spoke.

Book Fifty-Three

When you intuit me, you intuit that nothing ever moves away from my primordial Reality. I am the All-Creating Sovereign, the ultimate teacher, the unmoved. Being beyond causes and conditions as Pristine Awareness, I am the master of all causes and all results. This should not be taught to those who believe in cause and effect.

My supremacy in the unborn, diamond-like domain of Reality is not to be spoken about but should be kept from those who are believers in cause and effect.

Everything that appears and everything that exists in the animate and inanimate worlds is under my sovereignty, but this should not be spoken about to those who are believers in cause and effect.

The five elements are under my control also, but this is not to be spoken of to those who still believe in cause and effect.

The three worlds and the three poisons are similarly under the mastery of Pristine Awareness in own's own mind, but this is not to be spoken of to those who believe in cause and effect.

All that appears abides in my Presence beyond vanishing or ceasing. The nature of Reality is non-conceptual, and because of this the bliss of peace is also unending. It transcends the subject-object duality and all conceptual perspectives. When desire motivates one to obtain something as if it were a concrete possession, one falls into attachment and can no longer recognize the continuum of non-conceptual equality.

This kind of approach has never been my teaching. My teaching is that all phenomena are already the true condition, beyond the desire for some goal. Being the essence of equality, I am beyond any notions such as existence and non-existence, attainment and non-attainment, affirmation and negation and so on. Words like attainment or accomplishment have never been used by me but are used by seekers who pursue their desire (to get something). I am the greatest enemy of this kind of affirmation and negation.

I, the source of all enlightened beings, do not teach anything other than the sameness of all things. All teachings are teachings about my nature. The nature of all phenomena is the same as the true condition, which is the nature of mind (my state). It is an equality that is beyond change and that transcends desire.

This condition cannot be seized upon as if it were an object. Anyone who has a desire to find and attain the naturally abiding true condition is looking for something other than my authentic, non-conceptual equality.

The true condition has never been elsewhere. Trying to find and possess it means looking for one's own awareness elsewhere. Even if one were to destroy the sky, the three worlds and all living beings, the abode of infinite consciousness would not be found.

The nature of Consciousness is like space. It does not increase or decrease; its limit or boundary can never be located. Consciousness, which is like the spaciousness of the sky, cannot be grasped (because it is not like an object). The essence of all phenomena is also just like this (in being ineffable). There is no need for anyone to fabricate anything in the authentic continuum of Pristine Awareness.

The true condition cannot be altered, even if one uses specific meditation techniques, and even if one were a great being who could empty samsara by at one sitting by means of the power of meditation.

There is no essential difference between the Reality of a Buddha and that of sentient beings. The true condition beyond notions continuously abides in equanimity.

Sentient beings are not a cause and enlightenment is not a result. Teachings of causation are mistaken.

All that emanates from Source is the same, in essence. None of it is good or bad; all of it is indescribable equality without differences or distinctions. So he spoke.

Book Fifty-Four

(This is an extended recapitulation of definitions showing that Wisdom is the definitive condition of all phenomena. It touches upon topics such as transcending cause and effect, transcending effort, Wisdom naturally established, confidence that all is Wisdom, the direct manifestation of the real condition, and so on. This information has been communicated previously.)

Book Fifty-Five

All that exists in the animate and inanimate universe, all expressions and meanings, are only the Infinite Consciousness.

The spaciousness of the nature of Reality is pristine, pure Awareness, beyond concepts and free of obscurity.

The five elements also are of the nature of the Infinite Consciousness but given form. The Infinite Consciousness also appears as the realms of desire, form and formlessness. It is also the three kayas and the sentient beings of the six realms.

Non-conceptual equality liberates everything into the true condition.

Because this self-arising Wisdom cannot be thought of as an object, it is beyond karmic imprints and faults. No good qualities can be added to it. Nor can flaws be subtracted from it.

Being primordially unmoved, there is no way to alter the suchness of phenomena. Nothing can be acquired by fulfilling desires. The essence of all things is Pristine Awareness, arising as appearances do from the spaciousness of the pristine continuum.

Seekers who see appearances as something different from Pristine aAwareness have moved away from this Wisdom. Their minds never being illumined by true insight, they think that objects need to be renounced and blocked. Similarly, bodhisattvas who practice in terms of the duality of ultimate and relative truths will labor on in their own way for three eons.

Followers of the outer tantras practice meditation and visualizations, apply ritual purifications, meditate with no characteristics and work through different phases to complete their active striving. They do not come to Wisdom for lifetimes (seven).

Followers of Anu and Mahayoga cultivate skillful means and Wisdom to go higher and higher. They visualize their state to be the empty appearance of the deity-mandala. By exercisinig great diligence with rituals, mantra recitation and vows, they come to the level of Wisdom-holder. There they perform extended periods of non-distracted meditation to achieve great bliss. But even when they have done this, they will still fall short of realizing the true condition.

The obscurities of gods and humans are such that they are naturally attracted by sense objects. To ignorant sentient beings happy with whatever they are taught, teachers do not make clear the definitive teachings. They impart provisional teachings of cause and effect, ultimate and relative. Seekers satisfied with such dualities of true and false abide in the dualistic mind for eons.

You should clearly teach the true nature of Consciousness. Through this, disciples come to the unmistaken path beyond seeking, and from the outset they are placed beyond striving. They connect with the way that transcends seeking and they encounter the true condition beyond (conceptual) meditation. They become stable in effortless happiness.

Realizing the nature of Consciousness, the Wisdom-qualities manifest spontaneously, primordially perfected without any need for seeking, cultivating good intentions or following a gradual path. There is no need to achieve graduated levels of proficiency or to meditate on a conceptual view, to strive, or to make vows and follow rules.

Teach this transmission. Do not practice in a worldly way, visualizing a deity, keeping busy with ritual activities, chanting or getting immersed in concentrated visualizations. Thus he spoke.

Book Fifty-Six

I, the Sovereign Creator understand your essence to be identical to all phenomena (that appear to your mind). The true condition is also the Supreme Source. Palaces in the domain of space are also this same Source. The Dharmakaya, Sambhogakaya and Nirmanakaya teachers are also the Creating Monarch. The desire realm, form realm and formless realm are also the Supreme Source. Buddhas of ancient times, abiding in space are also nothing but this same pristine consciousness as are Buddhas now living on earth and those who will appear in the future. The views about the true condition are also this same Suchness. All phenomena arising from the five elements and the animate and inanimate universe are also the Source. There is no phenomenon separate from the Sovereign Creative Source, and all the phenomena that we could name are nothing other than that.

Book Fifty-Seven

You are self-originating Wisdom manifesting my essence. Maintain your awareness that this is the truth of your being, and the essence also of the three kaya teachers. Times, places and so forth are created by my true condition. Be conscious of this this when you teach various elements of the three kaya teachings.

My essence and my character as All-Creator should be perceived as I have explained. Being the essence of all that appears, my true condition is the progenitor of all enlightened beings. You too are the ancestor of future buddhas in your essence. Know my true condition to be the source, the father and mother of the three kaya teachers. You too are father and mother of the kaya teachers, father and mother of the kayas, fore-runner of the Buddhas.

When you teach, do not give the impression that any phenomenon, however it may appear, is anything other than myself, the sire and source of all sentient beings. Do not say that any phenomenon, however it appears is other than my true condition which is that of the All-Creating Sovereign.

All (conventional) teachings distinguish cause and effect. An effect is desired as a result of practicing with a cause. Assigning the name "sentient being" to the cause and "enlightened being" to the effect, seekers hope to bring about the desired effect, the state of enlightenment. This I have never taught.

My essence transcends the duality of cause and effect. There is no duality of sentient beings and enlightened beings. Enlightenment is not an accomplishment brought about by sentient beings.

My state is the self-originating Wisdom of Pristine Awareness itself. Thus he spoke.

Here concludes Kunje Gyalpo.

Colophon

(The Indian pandit, Sri Simha Prabha, and the Tibetan translator Pagor Vairochana codified this text through translation and editing.)

* * * * *

Note: Jim Valby's translation and commentary on Kunje Gyalpo runs to five volumes and is currently the best single source for serious study of this great book. Kunje Gyalpo repays serious study because it covers every aspect of the pure, original Ati Yoga teachings of Garab Dorje.

All that exists in the animate
and inanimate universe,
all expressions and meanings,
are only the Infinite Consciousness.

The spaciousness of the nature
of Reality is Pristine, Pure Awareness,
beyond concepts and free of obscurity.

BOOK TEN:
The Cool Grove, Sitavana

If Garab Dorje was twenty years old when he became a hermit, he would at the end of thirty two years in solitary meditation have been fifty two years old. We know that he then spent three years collecting and writing down Ati Yoga Tantras, and that his move to The Cool Grove took place after this.

We can estimate that he was approaching his sixtieth year when he traveled south and settled down for good. We know that Manjushrimitra spent seventy-five years studying with Garab Dorje, which would make him at least a century and a quarter old when he transitioned into the rainbow body.

Sitavana seems to have been a spiritual magnet for the great yogis of Garab Dorje's day. We know that besides Manjushrimitra, Padmasambhava and Sri Simha spent time there and that even Sri Simha might have met Garab Dorje in person. Nagarjuna (150 – 250 AD) also spent long periods of time in spiritual practice at Sitavana.

The landscape of Sitavana has not changed greatly in the last fourteen hundred years. The holy ground is only reached after a rather steep climb up the rocky slopes of what is essentially a small, thoroughly eroded mountain. This mount is situated in and among other small mountains which are largely forested. The region as a whole has a wild and ancient feeling. There is the sense of some presence behind and beyond what is outwardly visible. The heat of the day is so intense that part of the afternoon is best spent in shade and rest. The blessed cool of the evening breezes encourages a return to life under the stars and moonlight. On a full moon night, the landscape is mysterious, magical. And the sense of invisible presence deepens.

The natural stone pillar which is the highest point of the Sitavana plateau is still there, complete with rock carvings of buddhas or boddhisattvas at its base. There is a large water reservoir, and several smaller water reservoirs not far away along with a few simple, traditional houses with thatched roofs suitable for meditators. The location is still an active cremation ground serving the nearby villages. And there is still a temple/stupa, perhaps the very same one where Garab Dorje would meditate.

Located as it is only thirty kilometers northwest of Bodh Gaya, the Sitavana cremation ground is not difficult to reach. As it is one of a small number of highly revered charnel grounds in India where respected spiritual masters lived and meditated in an unbroken tradition lasting for centuries, if not millenia, Sitavana draws many pilgrims throughout the year, not only Buddhist but also Hindu. Climbing the slopes of this small mountain/plateau is more challenging than the ride from Bodh Gaya to the village at its base.

Cremations take place from time to time on these grounds. The place retains its unusual feeling of being a spot where life and death move in and out of each other and the interplay of Heaven with Earth is constant. There is a sense that coming and going and other change occurs only on the surface appearances of this place, and that something unmoved and mysterious underlies everything and pervades everything.

It is this spot which Garab Dorje chose as his spiritual center, from which he gave out the foundational teachings of Ati Yoga. Sri Simha travelled all the way from China to assimilate the Wisdom of Ati Yoga radiating from this hilltop. He, Padmasambhava, and numerous other spiritual realizers have sat where the standing and sitting boddhisattvas are carved at the highest rocky outcrop. Many a time at this very location they would plunge into meditation and have direct experience of the Wisdom of Vajrasattva.

The body of water at the center of this hilltop plateau is the energetic focus for everything else. All the other elements including buildings, rocky promontories, vegetation and paths all gather in a circle around this body of water. This imparts a sense of nurture and peace to the place. There are more plants growing in and around the water than elsewhere on the rocky slopes that surround it.

However, apart from the peaceful look and feel of the water, there is also a sense of something energetic, wild and powerful in the air. If you are sensitive, it is possible to feel a certain spiritual or vital dynamism which imparts the feeling of "presence" to the place. It feels inwardly alive. This energy can deepen meditation if one chooses to harness it in this manner, in which case it conveys the power that is in stillness, and the stillness that is masterly power.

Some of the greatest spiritual masters of all time lived and meditated in this place, and among them was Garab Dorje. He chose to spend more years in this location than at any other in his long lifetime. The teachings of Garab Dorje infused and changed the lives of his disciples here, at Sitavana, the Cool Grove. Those spiritual victors who sought and found the supreme Wisdom travelled to Sitavana, lived here, and meditated in this very place. They may have entered the rainbow body at this location. And they would have studied and written out on palm leaves some of the earliest Semde teachings that have come down to us. In fact the charcoal dust rubbed into the scratched out letters would also have been made here from wood and local brush. The spoken language would at times have been Sanskrit. For the purpose of spiritual study, declamation of the tantras and memorization of their message, this would most likely have been the case, although the local seventh and eighth century dialect would also have been in play at other times.

All of this unfolded at various locations on and among the rocky slopes that surround the water of the central reservoir, and in the vicinity of the second, smaller water reservoir where a number of simple huts still stand and are currently in use.

The idea that the great spiritual beings who lived at Sitavana are no longer present is not true. Their Wisdom and their legacy are instantly present when remembered in a heartfelt way. Beyond that, the energy in the air conveys a feeling of presence too, something indefinable but out of the ordinary. Perhaps the point is not to explain that energy but to feel it, open to it, listen to it and attune. In Garab Dorje's Ati Yoga, awareness itself is the view, the teaching and the goal. Perhaps this mysterious energy is calling the busy mind to recognize its source in Presence and fall silent before the mystery.

Many things become possible when you visit Sitavana in person. If you bring devotional sincerity to Sitavana, you will go away feeling the mystery, perhaps also feeling the blessings.

Sitavana of the heart is never very far away, being the place where silence suffuses the mind, insight dawns and the light of awakening comes to the fore. The Wisdom of Garab Dorje is never distant when we bring the mind into the sanctuary of the heart and listen.

Notes

[1]In his doctoral thesis, Mihai Derbac makes the following comments about this tantra: "The 'Dra 'bag chen mo (Palmo 2004: 47) mentions that Mañjuśrīmitra wrote a text, rDo la gser zhun, after he attained a perfect understanding of the rDzogs chen teachings. This text is also known as Byang chub kyi sems sgom pa (Meditation on the Enlightened Mind), and a text with a similar title is ascribed to Mañjuśrīmitra in the lDan dkar ma (lHan dkar ma) catalogue (no. 610) (Lalou 1953: 354). According to Herrmann-Pfandt (2002), the catalogue is a list of translated texts made in 812 but "added to later," as it contains titles translated after 830 (135). The lDan dkar ma is the earliest surviving, first-hand datable source that cites a Sems sde text—one that most probably already existed in the eighth century. Some scholars consider Byang chub sems sgom pa (still extant) to be one of the "five earliest" texts (See Norbu and Lipman 1987: 6-11). However, text-critical preliminary research suggests that this is not the case, as the text is not a "root" text. The text is an exegetical work about the Victorious Ones (rgyal ba), described in third person, and their realization. It is expository in nature, its aim is to reaffirm what has already been said and proclaimed. The author points out that he has validated for himself the "excellent path" taught by the Victorious Ones (Norbu and Lipman 1987: 68)."

The Tantra of the Secret Wisdom of the Great Perfection

Book One

Pristine Consciousness, present in the mind instantly and non-dually, is the essential Reality of samsara and nirvana. All phenomena are nothing but this self-originating Wisdom which never departs from the essence of the mind.

We do not take up or contemplate the conceptualizations that arise from ignorance. Our perspective is that of Wisdom, which is like the sun arising in the spaciousness of the sky. There is no way to explain the utterly pure nature of the true condition. Pristine, flawless Presence has no object. Moreover, it is self-evident without any need of effortful concentration. In truth, there is nothing but the nature of Reality; it is all that exists.

The ultimate perspective is that of self- arising Wisdom, which is like the sun rising in the sky.

There is no (natural) way to evaluate the purity of the true condition. For pristine knowingness, there is no such thing as an object. We do not need to concentrate our attention to see this. The continuum of the true condition (of Reality) is all that exists.

Supreme Wisdom is unobstructed, unmistaken. Why? The lamp of Wisdom clears away the obstructions of ignorance primordially.

Great Wisdom nullifies samsara. The jnani sees this to be primordially true. All tendencies toward grasping, craving and (emotional) attachment are destroyed and rendered pure. The inspired victors who dwell in bliss know this.

In the spacious domain of bliss, all phenomena are one in Pristine Awareness (mind of awakening). This domain is all encompassing, like the sky.

All phenomena, including sentient beings came into being from the Bodhichitta. The enlightened state is to be found primordially in the continuum of the nature of Reality (ie: mind/consciousness). There is no way either to foster or to prevent this.

The mind may appear to itself in any way, but there is never a mental image of anything (that actually exists).

Wisdom is primordial enlightenment, the indivisible oneness of all appearances.

The various paths help to reveal Wisdom, which is the ground of being for all phenomena. The positive and the negative, the small and the large are all non-dual.

Samsara and Nirvana are non-dual in the light of self-sprung Wisdom. The mind's object of attention and mind itself are non-dual. Everything has always been enlightenment, primordially. Approaches such as active striving and intellectual discrimination are ineffectual.

The supreme Wisdom is utterly pristine. It is the matrix from which all phenomena appear. It is a boundless ultimacy, spontaneously realized. It is all things and no thing at all. It is spaciousness and bliss supreme. It is the magnificent purity of all three realms.

The domain of enlightenment in the mind is benevolent and expansive. It is the thigle (sphere) of the supreme view, the all-good. In truth, there is only this: the sky-like spaciousness of the true condition.

This is the end of the first book, which teaches the primordial nature of enlightenment.

Book Two

How is primordial Buddhahood to be understood? This secret great Wisdom is realized by relying on insight and the meditation which results in insight. We understand firstly in terms of conventional understandings, secondly in terms of insight-based understandings and thirdly in terms of ultimate understandings. We have our experience of things, and then also, there is the true condition of things. The ultimate Reality does not appear as a distinct thing, but it encompasses all phenomena, all appearances.

For those of true understanding, every phenomenon is the nature of Reality. This is their direct experience.

All manner of wonderful appearances arise from the birthless nature of mind itself (consciousness) without looking for them. All appearances are the essence manifest. Knowing Wisdom, we know the nature of all appearances. Absent Wisdom, all appears as samsara. But in Reality, there is only the play of the all-good.

The unborn Reality and the unlimited Wisdom cannot be separated. The birthless Reality is an experience of playfulness. This miraculous creation has a true nature. Wisdom and the nature of Reality are non-dual. All phenomena are encompassed within this experience.

The true nature is the hallmark of what is real. For this, there is no possibility of evaluation. Nor is there one who could perform this evaluation. Immeasurable and lacking one who could perform any measurement – these aspects (of Reality) are incontrovertible.

This is the second book of the Wisdom of Great Perfection; it lays out the secret meaning of Wisdom.

Book Three

Only after knowing one's own nature does the word "Buddha" come to exist. The yogi who knows the natural state, who has the eye of knowing, will belong to the family of the enlightened ones and will be born no more.

Knowing the world of appearances to be self-originating Wisdom, he uses this great Wisdom to transcend it all.

Knowing the inner and the outer to be of the nature of Reality (dharmadatu), he goes beyond it all into the ultimacy.

He knows great and small to be inseparably one. He knows the equality of the Dharmakaya (in direct experience). Knowing the non-duality of broad and narrow, his awareness flies in the spaciousness of the all-good. Coming to know the non-duality of good and evil, the wise one realizes the Wisdom of great bliss which can neither be blocked nor fostered.

Active striving and intellectual discrimination are both unnecessary. That which is self-sprung rises up from its own being. Coming to know the non-duality of bliss and pain, he goes beyond the enjoyment of great bliss.

There is vast merit in the direct knowledge of Bodhichitta (nature of mind). It could hardly be packed into the domain of the sky itself.

This is the end of the third book of the Secret Wisdom of Great Perfection, teaching the essential view and the greatness of knowledge (Jnana).

Book Four

In order to practice the meaning of this, what is to be done?

In a place of solitude, separate all connections to the inner and outer worlds. The body is the essence of bliss; its dharmas and the elements are the same.

Allow your mind to be in the natural state of your normal understanding. You need not ignore what can be seen and heard, just rest in the un-contrived suchness. Simply rest in the condition of not generating thoughts. Using your vigilance, sustain this absence of conceptual activity. The Wisdom beyond thoughts will come to the fore from this experience.

If your mind becomes busy, just pay attention to this. Be very vigilant about sustaining the absence of conceptual activity.

If the mind is no longer busy, attend to this condition of thought cessation intently and without distraction.

The time you spend at this depends on your own makeup, but the sessions need not be too long.

If you feel discontent, stand up and walk about for a while. Project yourself into the realm of the sky and bury this unhappiness in the nature of Reality.

When you are free of unhappiness, you will start to experience non-conceptual Wisdom. There will be no thoughts at this time. Notions and mental fabrications are naturally quieted when this Wisdom arises.

This is how nonconceptual Wisdom manifests. It takes no interest in the various (intellectual) perspectives of the mind. The unfabricated Reality is unmoving. (It can clearly be seen that) the outer and inner worlds are Dharmadatu (the nature of Reality). Wisdom beyond all fabrication is great clarity. This clarity is the abode of the Dharmakaya.

Whatever fabrications arise, coarse or subtle, see them as self-arising (appearances). It is like the suchness of the sky where clouds arise, condense and billow forth. The Wisdom which no longer fabricates concepts is indescribable.

The yogi who knows such things recognizes that external objects and the appearances which arise in the mind are equal. He is free from the coming and going of the inner breath. He leaps into the real meaning of un-contrived experience. Blissful Wisdom is inexpressible. Such a yogi will have little attachment or craving with regard to inner and outer appearances. He gradually dissolves the (emotional) poisons. Free of craving, he may act in any way, for he is equal to the pulls and pushes of desires.

The continuum of Reality, being the equality of all phenomena, has no joy or sorrow. Thus it is the highest bliss.

Whether it is miracles of the maras, teaching, transmission, receiving respect, being surrounded and praised by devotees, whatever auspicious or inauspicious concepts arise, they are merely aspects of the natural flow.

This is the Fourth Book of the Secret Wisdom of the Great Perfection, which comprises teachings for beginners.

Book Five

Obscuration of Dharmakaya happens because our minds get caught up in habit patterns of good and bad, arising from emotional defilements. Our minds repeatedly give attention to their objects and conceptualize them, bringing about samsara. The Dharmakaya, however, is our own true nature and does not change. The five Wisdoms are free from the grasping tendency of our conceptualizations. Knowing this, we are equal to the enlightened beings of all times.

Whether there is sleeping or sitting, standing or going, they are all Dharmadatu. Thus one understands Reality.

As to the six classes of sentient beings, it is possible to bring an end to their diverse levels. These differences are severed in the perceiver's mind by recognition of nonduality, by overcoming attachment, aversion, ignorance, pride and jealousy, and by applying the spiritual remedies. Even the hunger and thirst of the hungry ghosts is the true nature (consciousness). When appearances arise in the mind, who or what is burdening the mind with hunger and thirst?

Even the suffering of beings in hell is secret Wisdom. For the wise, there is no suffering, no hell. For the wise, hell is Dharmakaya.

Even those sentient beings who experience the obscurity and dullness of the animal realm are the light of self-aware Wisdom where there is no obscuration. It is manifestly clear, in the light of Wisdom, that obscurity is itself Wisdom.

In the light of secret Wisdom, misery and suffering cause joy and suffering.

Even the travails of the asuras caused by pugnacity and disputation are the self-originating

Dharmakaya is Wisdom. The essential, empty nature of suffering due to jealousy is self-evident in the Wisdom of equanimity.

It is said that the gods fall from their magnificence and suffer. But they only fall into the All Good, the Dharmakaya. Within the All-Good, there is no place to fall.

Even the emotional defilements arise in utter purity and are the play of Wisdom. Thus there is no suffering from emotional defilements. The five emotional poisons are essentially the highest Wisdom.

What the human mind takes as suffering is (in actuality) the enjoyment of great bliss. The six kinds of sentient beings are primordially the enlightened one.

This book teaches the Dharmakaya and how to end the different levels of the six classes of beings. It is taken from Book Five of the Tantra of the Great Wisdom of the Great Perfection.

Book Six

As regards the great wind of comprehension, one thing is evident: for the Great Perfection yogi whose Wisdom is pure, conceptual activity is Bodhichitta.

Whatever kinds of thoughts occur, their true character, in its purity, is nothing but self-arising Wisdom.

The yogi of understanding does not strive for attainment by suppressing or purifying the contents of the Dharmakaya. All forms of thought are self-evident Wisdom.

Dharmakaya is liberation. Every conceptual designation is self-manifesting Wisdom that appears spontaneously, by itself, and whose nature is Wisdom.

The great being who has knowledge of such things may look for signs of this Wisdom while continuing to be a living embodiment of Wisdom. This Wisdom is self-awareness. It is what it is, irrespective of what takes place.

Wisdom never becomes something other than itself. Therefore, even in the domain of symbols one continues to be pure. There is no need to renounce symbols.

The wind of conceptual activity is self-manifesting Wisdom. It is not something that you enter and exit, but rather it resembles the clouds in the sky that arise naturally.

Nirvana and samsara are both of the nature of self arising Wisdom. Everything is only THAT. There is no alteration from THAT to any other condition. Therefore, all that appears is the body of Wisdom.

The liberated who understand these matters do not enter and exit this Wisdom. In all times and places, they abide in the experience of the true condition, although in the beginning this understanding was not present.

The continuum of the nature of Reality (Dharmadatu) does not alter because of thoughts about seeking something. The samadhi known as "Wisdom Appearing in Space" is manifestly not something attainable by the activity of seeking.

All phenomena are clear in the mind. None of them dwell anywhere except in (this) space. All appearances, all seeming entities, are the Bodhicitta. (In all this), Wisdom is a constant, with no need to remember it.

A realized Wisdom-being is primordially perfect without acting or practising anything All material phenomena mentioned in all the scriptures abide without exception in the experience of Bodhichitta, inseparable from Wisdom.

All that appears abides in this domain. There is no phenomenon whatsoever to be taken as an object of meditation. People and things are the appearances of one's mind. None is an actual object. What we remember also is mental appearances. Dharmakaya, self-appearing Wisdom, is understood with no need to abandon conceptual activity. It is not different from or other than craving an object.

Impulses arise. The experience of Wisdom is to move in the space of the objectless mind. When this is not understood, there is obscuration.

This is the sixth book of the Secret Wisdom of the Great Perfection, teaching the great wind of samadhi arising in oneself.

Book Seven

The result of meditating on the Bodhichitta is that the Dharmakaya, Sambhogakaya and Nirmanakaya stand out (become apparent) even when they were not sought. The result of direct experience in meditation on the pristine Bodhichitta is, for those of acumen, the realization of Bodhichitta. In their ultimacy, the three bodies are simply called Dharmakaya.

The attainers, who reveal these matters to us, have the eye of knowledge fully opened and through this they have non-conceptual Wisdom, the diamond essence. From this they also come to possess the outer and inner mandalas. In this way, all of their vows (samaya) are preserved. Non-conceptual consciousness protects vows relating to morality. This is something lauded as the sacred objective of the practice of generosity in the three worlds.

The hostile forces are dismayed at this. Through these undertakings, the merit of the Bodhichitta is immeasurably great.

The people of this world, as known with the winds of conceptuality, are Buddhas. In truth, there is no entity apart from Vajrasattva. The yogi who knows that the wind of meditation never departs from consciousness, by that very knowledge, abides in Buddhahood. His body may appear to be that of a normal person, but his invisible attainment is equal to Vajrasattva. Even the gods, maras and the rest never transcend the truth of this instruction. Nothing whatsoever surpasses this instruction. Yogis of the highest attainment deploy this insight to cut through the very root of samsara. This done, they never revert to samsara. Supreme power is thereby perfected.

From the Tantra of the Secret Wisdom of Great Perfection, this is the seventh book, teaching the benefits of meditation.

Book Eight

Concerning the practice which is neither commenced or relinquished, we may refer to it as the authentic condition of the Bodhichitta. It is a form of practice without preferences or designation, beyond likes and dislikes. In this continuum (of the true condition), joy and suffering are non-dual. Here, anything that one could practice is an experience of great bliss.

Many practices take place in the domain of (conceptual) designations and symbols, but within this practice they are all without notions of self and other. In this practice, even bad behaviour is superlative. Ethical and unethical behaviour, in this practice, both flow from non-attachment. And yet in this practice, positive results come about.

One may in fact practice all manner of activities and methods (within this view) but it presents no problem and one's understanding is unclouded.

So-called difficulties and blessings, the chains of samsara and the freedoms of liberation may be taken up without craving or binding outcomes. The virtues and non-virtues may be practiced without placing reliance on virtue or altogether giving up non-virtue.

If there is a true understanding of equality, all things may be practiced without taking on anything (such as limitations).

Anything touched by the Monarch of Medicine becomes medicine. In Great Perfection, emotional defilements, unforgivable sins and the five forms of wrong action (killing, stealing, etc.) are all flawless and harmless.

On this path, any kind of practice can be taken up without grasping or rejecting anything. The teaching is to cultivate freedom which resolves into spaciousness.

You may not understand what has been explained here, in which case it is meaningless chatter. If you attempt to practice this without truly knowing what has been indicated, the emotional poisons will land you in a world of torment. Best always to practice in accord with your actual level of experience (and insight).

This is the eighth book of the Tantra of the Secret Wisdom of the Great Perfection concerning the practice which is neither taken up nor set aside.

Book Nine

The result which is neither commenced nor concluded is practice for accomplishment of the essence, which is the Dharmakaya. Its nature is beyond elaboration. This is the way that unmoving Wisdom comes to the fore. This is the approach of nonduality. Here I point to the Dharmakaya which, because it cannot be grasped, is unlike any ordinary dharma.

Dharmakaya is realized effortlessly and naturally without any need for seeking. The continuum of one's true nature is a constant and there is no need to seek for it. Primordially, all has been undivided and pristine. Results come with no need for going after them.

Realization is a singularity, free from any leanings in any direction and beyond notions such as center and periphery. It is beyond causes and conditions. It is a Reality that emerges and expands in primordial space. It pervades all things and is known by encounter with the supreme Wisdom of self-awareness. The Bodhichitta is immaterial. It is free from elaboration. It is the unfabricated suchness of Reality itself; it is awareness abiding in suchness.

The Dharmakaya Buddha is also non-dual and beyond separation. In this indivisible state, there is no transmigration through the three times. The immutable body transcends birth and death and abides from the beginningless beginning in the Absolute. Thus the Buddha need not be sought in any other abode.

This is the Bodhichitta that the worldly domains in all directions acknowledge, so there is no need to seek it elsewhere.

This is the Ninth Book from the Tantra of the Secret Wisdom of the Great Perfection concerning the Dharmakaya as the result.

Book Ten

The result of practice is something neither commenced nor discontinued and it is the way to attainment of the essence. The Dharmakaya, self-arising, is the essence. Its authentic nature is ineffable. In this way, unmoved Wisdom arises. This is the supreme, non-dual approach. The Dharmakaya of which I speak here is in no way like the ordinary phenomena (of our conventional experience). Without (any need for) active seeking or striving for a result, this is spontaneously realized.

The true condition is always a constant beyond any need to seek it out. All dharmas (phenomena) are primordially pure. The immanent Reality is there, you do not need to hunt for it.

Beyond description, beyond our notions and partiality, this experience is uncompounded. It transcends past, present and future or notions like "middle" and "extremes". It is not oneness simply because experts have declared it so. Because the true nature of duality is oneness, the liberated yogi who has relied on the approach outlined here does not enter the Region of downfalls.

When examined, past, present and future and the primordially pure timeless continuum are not found to be unequal. The clarity of awareness is un-directed, like the light of a butter lamp. The nature of Reality, changeless and unmoved, has no center and no extreme. It is like the sky, changeless in its clarity and non-dual. This non-dual spaciousness is beyond polarities. The essential nature of phenomena is thus said (by the wise) to be pure.

Consider how the self-arising radiance of the Dharmakaya is to be attained. It is in the moment of insight that you have the result. There is nothing augmented, nothing obstructed in terms of cause and effect. There are some who fixate on the conditions (that appear) in this life and in the intermediate life. They will never be so fortunate as to become realizers.

The ultimate realization in this life and in the intermediate state is Dharmakaya. Consider how this is accomplished: the greatest of yogis liberate the body from the web of conceptual thought.

The Yogi first gains access to the cause(s) of the five elements. He closes the gateways of the subtle body. Then, the clarity of the Dharmakaya, which is the bardo, arises. On the strength of his understanding, the yogi integrates the five elements. In short order, he becomes the Victorious One, empowered by the Wisdom of Awareness. There is no need to practice the five paths or gradually work through the (bodhisattva) ten levels.

Dharmakaya is perfection, all-encompassing. The Secret Wisdom reveals its realization. The cause is also the result. Inner and outer goals are all attained through the Dharmakaya.

Knowing this, if a yogi nevertheless takes up practice with inner things and outer things in mind, the goal is missed. He may not recognize this result, but he will (nevertheless) have future rebirths in the three realms of the cosmic gods. He will not be born in inauspicious conditions. Because he holds to Reality, he will have holy friends and associates.

Your mind comprehends the prophecy enunciated here: in your future birth you will directly embody Vajrasattva himself.

This concludes the tenth book of the Tantra of the Secret Wisdom of the Great Perfection, concerning the method of attaining the result.

Book Eleven

However the Dharmakaya may give rise to appearances, there is no Reality except for the Bodhichitta. When there is enjoyment of non-dual Reality, and when there is enjoyment of Wisdom, its adornment, there is no requirement to relinquish desire-based practices. They are the playfulness of the Dharmakaya appearing in you and this is known as "the Body of Perfect Enjoyment." It comes to the Bodhisattvas of the ten levels and it is also the sport and play of their Wisdom.

Great compassion manifests in an all-encompassing manner and brings a downpour of sacred teachings to sentient beings. The nectar of the Dharma brings bliss to all beings. The non-dual Bodhichitta is all-encompassing, all-inclusive. The disciplines of spiritual seekers are shaped by compassion and the play of illusion is (thereby) put to shame.

The manifestation of the Supreme Reality arises in the mind and that which is known as "Compassionate Mind's Manifestation-Body" is secretly revealed.

In Vajrasattva's Ultimate Body, the Secret Wisdom Body, birth and life in all their inner and outer forms are perfected. Every sound, every language, high, middle and low are clarified as Vajrasattva's Secret Wisdom. All intellectual comprehension, basic or elaborate, is nothing but the consciousness of Secret Wisdom.

Body, speech and mind are a continuously turning wheel. Beyond this and apart from this there is no other secret action and practice. There is nothing at all to be achieved from any other source apart from Secret Wisdom, despite any possible appearances to the contrary.

This is the eleventh book, concerning conclusive action from the Tantra of the Secret Wisdom of the Great Perfection.

Book Twelve

The actuality of Nirvana and Samsara are primordially non-dual. Teachings of a dual nature come into being because appearances are so overwhelmingly dual. This being the prevailing situation, teachings reflect these conditions. This teaching, in its purity, states that Samsara and Nirvana are not different. Whatever the origin of non-dual Wisdom, it is the only Reality that exists.

The Buddha-Consciousness and the minds of sentient beings are in essence Dharmakaya and therefore one. In this unity, compassion and karma come together. This eliminates any possibility of there being problems, even though beings see things in different ways. Those who are wise see everything in terms of the Body of Wisdom. Those who lack understanding experience samsara. This is the full explanation of the two ways of seeing things.

Ignorance is the cause of samsara. Karma and the five emotional poisons are the circumstances. This brings in the rest of the elements in the chain of interdependent arising. Samsara originates from causes and conditions. No problem and no unreasonableness is to be found in this.

Samsara derives from ignorance. But ignorance arises from the Bodhichitta.

The identity of Vajrasattva (the Sambhogakaya Buddha) is Bodhichitta, which is also the identity of all things. In any place that the unmanifest becomes manifest, there will also be the obscuration of misunderstanding. For those of right understanding, omniscience is an actuality. Dual realities (so called) are authenticated by the use of reason.

All things abide within self-arising Wisdom. Everything is, in essence, one with the experience of self-arising Wisdom, free from any problems arising from uncertainty.

Anything whatsoever can arise from nothing at all. Is there anything that could possibly be permanent in all of this?

Wisdom arises in stages. These teachings are not defiled by any sort of problem.

Bodhichitta is the view. Conceptualizations are Bodhichitta. In the enlightened consciousness of the Victorious Ones there are no conceptual delusions; indeed, the mind's fabrications do not and never have existed. This does not hinge on purity, however things may appear.

All appearances arising in the play of Secret Wisdom are in actuality spontaneously realized Wisdom. There is no aspect of these teachings that falls into the extreme of purity.

Thus spoke Vajrasattva, and his auditors rejoiced in delight.

From the Tantra of the Secret Wisdom of the Great Perfection, this twelfth book clears doubts concerning the view.

Book Thirteen

Secret Wisdom makes clear that the continuum of Reality is beyond extremes such as meditating and not meditating.

Non-meditation cannot possibly be a thing. (If you think that it is) then you will be drawn into rejection of meditation and approval for non-meditation. Once the mind has busied itself with its classifications, there is really no problem as regards meditation, however appearances may arise.

In such cases, the meditation has been directed into some kind of conceptual grasping. But in actuality there is nothing, no topic, upon which to meditate. Let the mind roam in the spaciousness beyond the conventional meanings of sounds, the space of the realities of non-meditation. The supreme domain of right understanding comes into play naturally and is realized by an inspired connection to the primordial wind.

Once you clearly recognize that there is no location for the practice of meditation, the downside and the upside will become clear, as will the sky-like spaciousness of the realm of suchness. Realization comes only through conscious meditation on this.

A time will come when you will be able to rest in a natural knowledge of these things. But even then, like any man, you will not be without your stomach. This teaching is far beyond any difficulties relating to non-meditation.

This, the thirteenth book, clears away difficulties regarding meditation, and is taken from the Tantra of the Secret Wisdom of the Great Perfection.

Book Fourteen

If you understand that bliss and desire are one within the Bodhichitta, all your practices are Wisdom. Moreover, cause and outcome are nondual within this view.

If you clearly understand that all practices rooted in desire, information, and striving are the Bodhichitta, there is no assuming or renouncing at all. Thus, one does not fall into inferior forms of practice.

With regard to the five unforgiveable sins (patricide, matricide, killing an arhat, injuring a buddha, creating schism in the sangha), for the yogi of the Great Perfection, they are all the Bodhichitta. There is no place for falls in the Bodhichitta. It is similar to excising the root of a banana tree. Large groups of mature human beings and other sentient beings are (inherently) perfect and (must be allowed to) practice all things. There is a need for stupas, chapels, ritual recitation and invocations to have to have a place of equanimity in the minds of these beings.

For those who have come to a right understanding of awareness, even inauspicious birthplaces are domains of bliss. When you have right understanding, you may take up any form of practice and not encounter a downfall. If you lack the Wisdom of Self Awareness, even the domain of the Victors will appear to be inauspicious.

What is indicated here is by no means an ultimate view. Those who have no experience of the equanimity of the Dharmakaya are not required to take up all manner of practices, but they should avoid evil and develop their merit.

This is the fourteenth book of the Tantra of the Secret Wisdom of the Great Perfection which clears away difficulties in practice.

Book Fifteen

The essence of Secret Wisdom is the Dharmakaya, free from all extremes and free from embellishment. Yet somehow the dharmakaya contains in perfect purity the opposites and the fabrications. Although without form, the Dharmakaya brings all forms to perfection. How is it that the Dharmakaya, which is free from ornamentation, give rise to such extremes of elaboration? To see this is to see with total clarity the emptiness of the true nature of Wisdom.

The Dharma Body and the Form Body are manifest from the force and efficacy of disciples' prayers, and the purposes of self and others are thereby perfected. The benefits conferred by blessings are supreme. We are of the view that the three bodies are a singular experience, undifferentiated.

All sentient beings abide within the continuum of Reality and as a result right understanding may be attained in three ways (discipline, knowledge and samadhi).

At the moment of insight, the essential role of the all-encompassing Dharmakaya becomes clear. The greatness of the Dharmakaya places it beyond attainment by any external means. Here, there is no cause and effect. The single taste of (so-called) cause and (so-called) effect presides overall. Even enlightened beings of the bardo are only this, and in no way different from this.

Those who have been empowered by the pure, perfected state of enlightenment first free themselves from conceptual fabrication. From this comes right understanding, unsought.

The Reality of Secret Wisdom abides in the natural unity of the Dharmakaya. But inauspicious causes and conditions can obscure this so that the beneficial implications are not apparent, like a butter lamp inside a vessel. I am identical to the intuitive insight which opens this secret.

In the overarching Reality there is no difference between the present condition and the bardo. The Dharmakaya yields all attainments of the present and the future.

Ideas about causes and results constitute an inferior view. The intermediate view is that realization belongs only to the Vidyaharas (Wisdom holders). These two lines of thinking arrange things along the lines of gradual attainment. In the superior view, however, there is no idea of difference whatsoever.

However things may appear, the playfulness of the Dharmakaya causes unsought manifestations such as the three bodies to arise. In this there is no craving or clinging. This is how samsaric manifestations come into play. This is the play of impartial Wisdom. It brings all things to realization. All appearances are seen to be the body of Secret Wisdom. Fame is its speech, remembrance and thought its mind. Nothing exists except for the body, speech and mind of enlightenment.

This fifteenth chapter of the Tantra of the Secret Wisdom of the Great perfection clarifies doubts concerning the result.

Book Sixteen

Secret Wisdom is like a mass of mountains, of vast benefit, beyond all else. Foremost among the sages, the King of Secret Wisdom is a lamp for the world. We prostate with reverence to this lamp of the world.

We prostrate with reverence to the teacher of the utterly pristine meaning, he who expresses the teachings that are held in the highest esteem across the entire world, whose Wisdom-body expresses these teachings of pure meaning with ultimate clarity, the lion among those who propagate the teaching.

We reverence the consciousness which abides in equanimity in all phenomena, consciousness which is like an ocean of inconceivable, highest truth, fully and perfectly making clear all that is peace and not peace.

We revere and praise the preceptor who embodies this Wisdom, in whom the blessings are perfected without dilution. He is the ultimate lamp that clears away the obscurity of ignorance. It is he who is the full and prodigious treasury of teachings.

We revere and extol the one who dispenses the suffering of living beings. His lion-like utterances promote this declaration of peace. He defeats all opposition from those of extreme views. He levels the prison of this world with his powerful instruments of Wisdom.

This is Book Sixteen from the Tantra of the Secret Wisdom of the Great perfection where all who hear this teaching take delight and praise the Sovereign of Secret Wisdom.

Book Seventeen

This sovereign of all Tantras which I, the King of Secret Wisdom have proclaimed is the mirror of all Dharmas. All teachings stem from this. It is the supreme path that defines the stages surpassed by those who move in bliss beyond the three times. This is the ultimate path which dispels ignorance. It is the King of Tantras, the highest transmission, the root of the teachings which are utterly reliable.

If those who assemble to receive these teachings are full of ill will, of retrograde desires, adhering to the lower yanas, verbose, destructive, avaricious, abiding in defiled emotions, disrespectful of the teacher, speaking with skill to control others, hoarding their words, stealing sacred teachings, failing to keep their vows, spiteful of the holy ones, and self-vaunting, - to such as these this Tantra must never be proclaimed. If this tantra is shared with the unworthy, the consciousness of the Victorious Ones of all times will shudder.

Those who instruct the unqualified will be sequestered from the presence of Secret Wisdom. They will anger the Noble Ones. The body-mind connection of such teachers will be sundered. Dakinis, Dharma guardians and protectors will lay out such a one's body as if for a feast. They will render this the final moment in such a one's life. That very instant the vajra hell teaching will manifest and the descent of such evil will be unsupportable.

I pass this to you, great yogi, for those who are qualified to receive these teachings, who honour the master, who are strong in faith, ardent in application, acute in knowledge, who revere the Mahayana, and hold loving kindness toward their brothers and sisters, who have the gentleness of great compassion, who give joy to the guru by body, speech and mind. They take delight in being unattached to anything, and their good karma and supreme fortune makes it possible for them to be recipients of these teachings.

This great sovereign of Tantras is meant only for one or two devotees. If it is given out even among three, there will be a downfall into hell. Hold this as a treasure for those few whose view is rooted in the fullness of certitude. It is not meant for those of diverse opinions and notions.

This seventeenth and final chapter teaches the first transmission of these instructions to a gathering of Brahmins. It is from the Tantra of the Secret Wisdom of the Great Perfection.

Colophon

The Indian Garab Dorje gave the first copy of this Tantra written on golden parchment with melted vaidurya to the Brahmin Samvara in the upper region of Sukhavati. ... The Indian sage Sri Singha Prabata and the Tibetan translator Acharya Vairochana together translated and edited this work.

Those who have been empowered
by the pure, perfected state of
enlightenment first free themselves
from conceptual fabrication.

From this comes right
understanding, unsought.

The Ocean and the Wave

A Story of Spiritual Awakening

Roger Calverley

It was not the meditation cave with the boxes of ancient sutras written on palm leaves, or the discovery of a relic of the Buddha, or the miracles, or the mystical interventions and higher guidance, but the encounter with a wise but humble Mahayana Buddhist monk which made those five years in Southeast Asia so special.

In a direct heart-to-heart transmission, only rarely granted to spiritual seekers from the West, Lama Atal actualized the mystical realizations of the spiritual masters in direct, living experience. His fresh powerful and direct transmission of the awakened state adds a unique chapter to the East-West spiritual convergence.

ISBN: 978-1-6086-9237-8
$10.95 pb, 112 pages, Item# 990936

Available at bookstores and natural food stores nationwide or order your copy directly by sending $10.95 plus $2.50 shipping/handling ($.75 s/h for each additional copy ordered at the same time) to:

Lotus Press, PO Box 325, Twin Lakes, WI 53181 USA | Toll Free Order Line: 800.824.6396 | Office Phone: 262.889.8561 | Office Fax: 262.889.8591 email: lotuspress@lotuspress.com | Web Site: www.LotusPress.com

Lotus Press is the publisher of a wide range of books in the field of alternative health, including Ayurveda, Chinese medicine, herbology, aromatherapy, Reiki and energetic healing modalities. Request our free book catalog.